WORKING IN INDUSTRIAL LOS ANGELES
PHOTOGRAPHS BY MARTIN H. KRIEGER

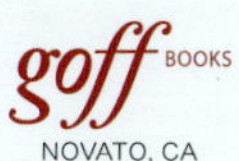

goff BOOKS

NOVATO, CA

EDITED BY JONAH GREENSTEIN

WITH AN ESSAY BY GREG HISE

Martin H. Krieger began photographing the streetscapes of industrial districts in the early 2000s.
Every once in a while, proprietors invited him in to photograph their workshops and the people
who worked there. Soon, he was systematically walking along industrial streets, making thousands
of pictures, showing the choreography of work. The images in this book were made at more
than 225 sites in Los Angeles, one of the major industrial cities in the United States. They are
presented in the order in which they were taken.

– Jonah Greenstein

CONTENTS

PREFACE

I am a voyeur.

When I am walking or driving in Los Angeles, where I teach, I keep asking, What's going on here, in this place at this site? Being a professor of city planning, my curiosity seems appropriate, although most academic studies depend on archives, interviews, statistical information, and remote sensing. When I notice a high frequency of the same phenomenon, say storefront houses of worship, eventually my awareness is awakened and I wonder, What's going on here, and why? Initially, I do not go out and look for these phenomena. But their insistence and ubiquity kick me in the pants.

Almost nothing is without a history and sociology, worked out by my colleagues in the universities. And for administrative reasons, corporations and governments gather information that may put my curiosity in context. I am not the first to be interested in what is going on around himself, and monetizing these phenomena (say, taxes or sales) is a powerful motivator.

The phenomena are ubiquitous and frequent, although most of the time we are trained to ignore what is in front of our noses—we have work to do. I find that whatever it is I am discovering, let us call it an "identity," is presented to me in manifold examples or profiles. Each such profile is distinctive, but shared features impress upon me that I am seeing something rather more general, that "identity." After years of driving to work on the same street, it finally occurred to me that there were many storefront churches on the way. And sure enough, those churches were often Pentecostal. Early in the twentieth century, Los Angeles was a source for the revival of such experiential religiosity.

There was a time when Los Angeles was taken to be quite far from the centers of manufacturing, and the costs of transport (even by rail) encouraged local production of automobiles and tires. Eventually, that distance was conquered by interstate highways and trucking, and so there was less need for the Ford Model A plant near downtown Los Angeles, or the General Motors plant in the San Fernando Valley, or the Goodyear tire manufacturing facility just south of the Huntington tract I discuss below. Such infrastructure came to be used for warehousing, mass-retailing in shopping centers, and for smaller manufacturing enterprises. The small stores around trolley stops, frequented by transit commuters on the way to and from work, were less viable as the automobile became dominant, and so those stores located at the intersections of main streets and trolley lines were available at lower rents for other uses, such as a small house of worship.

Los Angeles is the major industrial center in the United States. For the past decades, Greg Hise has been writing historically on the relationship of industry to housing and urban development in Los Angeles. In the first decade of this century, I photographically documented major Los Angeles institutions, including its storefront houses of worship, its electrical distributing system, and its industrial streetscapes. All of this work has been intimately informed by historical and social-science understanding of cities, Los Angeles, and industrialization.

Comparatively little is known or documented about Los Angeles' industrial enterprise and its structure. There are the better-known documentary traditions in cities like New York, Chicago, Paris, and London. But few cities have invoked the power of images as insistently as Los Angeles. That relationship may be illustrated most readily by reference to place promotion and the creation of a regional identity through the marketing of Southern California's climate, landscape, and agricultural abundance. But what sold the region in the 1880s (richly detailed portraits of fruit and vegetables) was quite different from Chamber of Commerce advertising in the 1920s (oblique aerials of manufacturing and production) or more recent promotions of social and cultural diversity and architecture (both high-style and low-brow). Photography and processes of city building have developed in a reciprocal manner over time.

I began to photograph industrial Los Angeles when I encountered the Union Pacific Avenue industrial complex (located in the area of East Los Angeles bounded by the 101 and the 710 freeways) while photographing some storefront houses of worship that I had tracked down. (I had been photographing the facades of hundreds of storefront churches in Los Angeles.) It was hard to miss the grain elevators. I mentioned my discovery to my historian colleague Professor Greg Hise, who then showed me his recent article on industrial Los Angeles. I was launched.

I then received a small grant from the John Randolph Haynes and Dora Haynes Foundation to photograph industrial streetscapes. Every once in a while, I would shoot a few photographs of the insides of these firms through an open bay, or if I happened to be invited in. People were curious about what I was doing in their neighborhood. I discovered that if I asked to photograph inside small- to medium-sized firms, I would get a "Yes" perhaps one-third to one-fifth of the time. We then received a more substantial grant from Haynes to do intensive photographing of industrial Los Angeles factories, warehouses, and other such sites. I have photographed at perhaps 225+ such sites.

In addition, with the guidance of Professor Dominick Miretti, a long-time member of Local 63 (Marine Clerks) of the fabled International Longshoremen's and Warehousemen's Union (ILWU), I photographed extensively at the Ports of Los Angeles and Long Beach. Also, I flew six helicopter trips (with traffic reporter Chuck Street) to see the lay of the industrial land and how it was intermixed with all sorts of other uses. And with the support of its administration, I photographed people at work (avoiding patients, as HIPPA rules required), at the iconic Los Angeles County-USC Hospital just before a transition to a new hospital building nearby. Many a regular television medical drama would begin with an image of that massive building.

My focus was people at work, at their worksites, and also when they were on breaks or on the way to work. Using Reference USA and Dun's Million Dollar service, I was able to get further information on most of the firms I photographed, but not all.

I spent a lot of time in an industrial area south of Slauson and north of Florence, between Central and Avalon, readily recognized from the air. Almost surely, it was

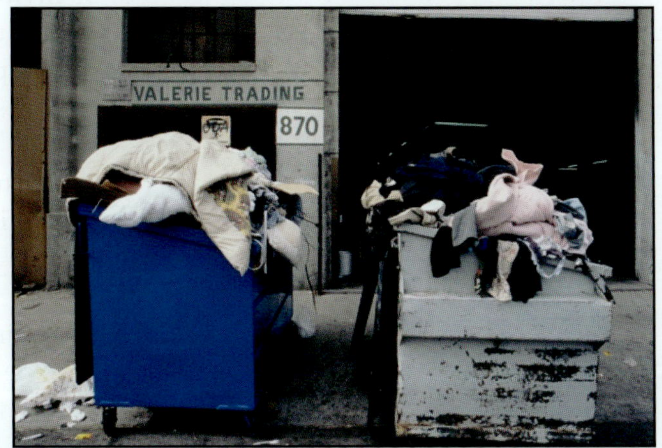

developed by Huntington interests in the 1920s. More generally, it is straightforward to discover industrial districts from the satellite imagery supplied by Google. The extensive grey roofs are the sign.

It may be useful to give a concrete example of the fieldwork (Friday, September 12, 2003, 8:30-10:30am). I had been trying to photograph the actual production processes of industrial Los Angeles, and not only the streetscape. I decided to drive down Central Avenue to that Huntington tract industrial district. I had already systematically photographed all the buildings and streets in this district. And I had earlier photographed a furniture factory and a plastics molding factory.

The manager of a used-clothing sorting enterprise welcomed me in. Charities collect clothing, they take the best clothes for their thrift shops, and sell the rest (98%), by the 1,000-pound bale, to these enterprises. Clothing is then sorted, different customers get different quality and kinds of clothing: white T-shirts become wiping cloths for paint stores; Japanese college students go through specific piles of clothing for specific sorts of garments, according to faxes they received from Japan the previous evening. The proverbial T-shirt ends up in Central America or Africa, although Central and South America usually demand higher quality clothing. The best used clothing comes from places with too few thrift

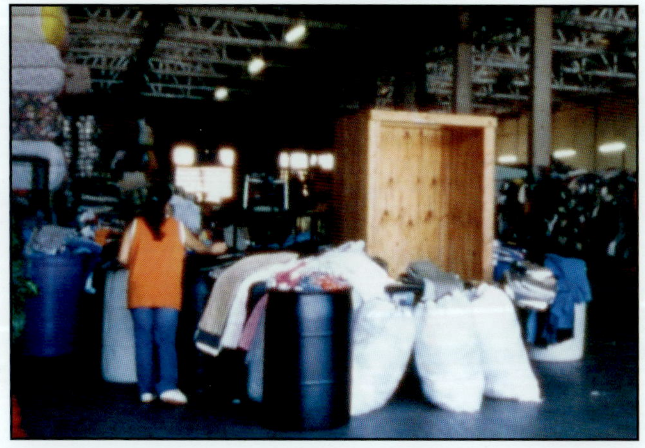

shops and the right sort of givers, so this company's used clothing comes from Detroit and Grand Rapids charities. The business is a low margin enterprise (say, buying at 2c a pound and selling at 3c). All the usual issues of the minimum wage, workers compensation, etc., come to the fore.

I photographed the worksite where sorting, folding, and packing take place. I also recorded the acoustic ambience of this place and of the surrounding areas. What is valuable here and what is distinctive is its concreteness and specificity, the flesh and mortar, so to speak.

Much of what we call visual documentation is often of those less powerful, less well off, less protected by status and bureaucracy. In looking over my archive, I realize that almost all the work pictured requires no more than a secondary education and perhaps trade school. In part, these were the places I had access to. They were not corporate bureaucracies. Working-class people, a fraction of whom actually made good wages, were at the mercy of the minimum, filling jobs that they had filled for much of the time since the beginning of the twentieth century. They are working for a living. Their children and grandchildren might go to college and not follow in their footsteps. I'm not sure who will do the same sort of work in twenty-five years.

To colleagues, I say that I have been doing social-science-informed photographic documentation of Los Angeles. By "social-science-informed" I mean that I have

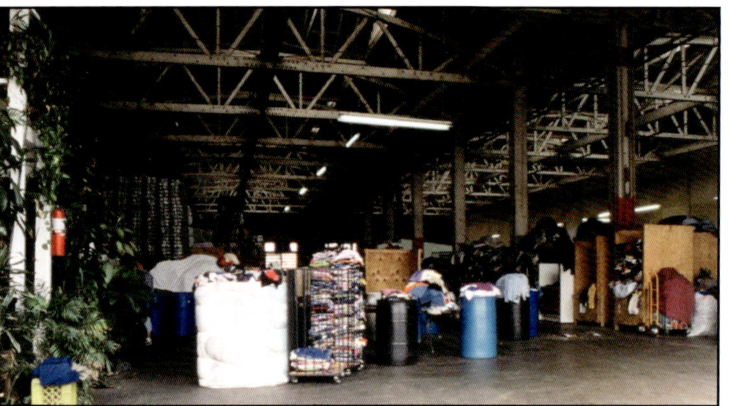

tried to be systematic and I have chosen my subjects for their implications for the larger structure of the City as understood in the scholarly literature. Storefront houses of worship (650+), Los Angeles City Department of Water and Power electrical distribution stations and related sites (150), and the industrial streetscapes (maybe 125+ blocks and streets, perhaps 5,000+ images) are such topics, and my photographing has been all over the City and to some extent the County as well. Along the way I have in addition extensively photographed at the Ports of Los Angeles and Long Beach, the Los Angeles County Hospital just as it was about to close, and made five short videos of particular firms. And I made six helicopter trips to see the lay of the industrial land (intermixed with all sorts of other uses).

There have been similar efforts over the years, whether they be documentary photography of social conditions, the Mass Observation movement in Britain in the 1930s and '40s, or the work of Mark Klett in landscape documentation.

My reflections on this work are in my book, *Urban Tomographies* (2011). In writing about what I called the vernacular sacred, those storefront houses of worship, I discussed such informal religiosity, Pentecostalism, and the intimate connection with Los Angeles' history. The work on the industrial streetscape connects with an account of the urban economy as a diversified, mixed specialty and export economy, with niche markets, networks of factories supplying each other, and a highly adaptable industrial sector (what is sometimes called "flexible specialization"). These conceptions have been drawn from Hise's historical work and the social-science literature.

My goal has been to produce photographs that are of high quality, in their detail and definition, and in the choice of perspective and composition. Good technique leads to photographs that are information dense—especially if those photographs are part of a systematically produced and organized corpus. I have not aimed to produce photographs that would be conventionally thought to be fine-art photographs. (However, I have learned much from fine art photographers [for example, Lee Friedlander] and from photojournalists, about ways one might do this sort of documentation.) I have tried to avoid irony and celebration. I want to show what's there, what's ordinary, what is repeated again and again, ubiquitously, in its variety and particularity. And what you see (or hear) is deeply rooted in larger societal and economic processes. I want to make the city visible and hearable to those who live in it.

I should note that Charles Marville, photographing Paris's transformation (or evisceration) under Baron Haussmann and Napoleon III in the mid-nineteenth century (~1870), used glass plates 10 ½ x 14 ½ inches and a tripod, and the wet plate collodion process he employed was effectively grainless whatever its intrinsic definition—and surely the lens was not so well corrected as a modern optic. But if you have a hundred times the area of a 35mm negative, as Marville did, there is lots of room for information. In any case, when I was photographing the churches I did use the medium-format (2 ¼" square) Hasselblad—someone, sometime might want detail that I had otherwise ignored. By the way, for the *Encyclopédie*, a century earlier, Diderot went out and interviewed workers and observed their actual work. The engravings for the *Encyclopédie* are inspiring, and are available in a Dover Books reprint.

Almost all the photographs were taken with 35mm transparency film using a wide-angle 19mm lens on a Leica R8 single-lens reflex camera, or a 21mm lens on a Contax G2 rangefinder camera—mostly Kodachrome 200 shot at 500, and when that was no longer possible, Fuji Provia F400, often pushed to 800. (The outdoor streetscapes were often shot with Kodachrome 64, but the problem would then be, what if I were invited inside?) I did do some industrial photographing with a Hasselblad SWC/M, wide-angle medium-format camera, and then sometimes with color negative film.

Zeiss referred to the f/4.5 lens on the Hasselblad SWC/M as suitable for documentation, and given the medium-format of the SWC/M (5.6 x 5.6 cm.) there was a lot of information in the image. Given the impromptu nature of my visits to industrial sites, and my desire not to disturb people at work too much, the 35mm camera with a faster lens was less obtrusive and more convenient. However, given the higher speed film I needed indoors

(I did not use a flash), the camera-film system was not up to "documentation." Of course, there was lots of detail in the 35mm image (2.4 x 3.6 cm.), but nothing compared to what was achievable with a larger negative.

The transparency film is usually mounted slides (but not for the medium-format work). When I was photographing streetscapes I did not mount the images, but left them in strips so the adjacencies were apparent. (One then has to be sure that one is photographing in the right direction–the direction of the film's motion, so that adjacent images on a strip continue each other.)

Again, my purpose in photographing is to show the world as it is, the photograph being detailed enough and of sufficient definition, that if you got curious you could enlarge the image and might discern what was written on a desk or on the wall. Again, I want to show what's there, what's ordinary, what is repeated, again and again, ubiquitously, in its variety and particularity. And what you see (or hear) is deeply rooted in larger societal and economic processes.

There is, however, another form of documentation provided by a photograph–that of the ambiance and experience of a place and time, and here the 35mm camera is more than adequate. The idea is to create images that engage the viewer, ask the viewer to look more closely, to imagine what it is like to be there, doing that work, working for a living in industrial Los Angeles. To get lost in an image, to allow your imagination free reign, to be free of the demands of the caption and the detail provided by the conventional scholarship, may well allow for a veridical experience vital for understanding a world that

is quite nearby, literally down the street, but practically taboo for most residents of a big city like Los Angeles. Yes, your uncle or mother might work manufacturing furniture or sewing garments, but in general most residents are in fact quite unattached to the industrial life right around them.

There is much more photodocumentation work to be done on industrial Los Angeles, exploring areas I have not documented as well as revisiting some that I have, photographing inside these industrial places, showing both the manufacturing processes and the worksites. There are particular industries that call out for further work: fashion and furniture, for example. There will be surprises, such as the "rag trade" I described earlier. There is as well the Alameda Corridor, currently of great interest to policymakers and transportation scholars.

As for the choice of sites, I have aimed for a range and variety of locales throughout Los Angeles, focusing on older and smaller-sized areas, often adjacent to residential areas. (Hise has shown how important is the interaction of the residential and industrial areas.) Still, lots of territory remains unexplored.

Along the way, I photographed interesting commercial strips for selected streets, since retail is an industry. But the main reason, my motive, was when we were doing work on Boyle Heights as an ethnic neighborhood, and I noted the wonderful strips on City Terrace Drive. Subsequently, I did some inside photographs of ethnic stores, showing their wares (as displayed) and customers. This was done under the rubric of Vernacular Visual Merchandising.

Aural documentation. I did some accurate and calibrated aural documentation of the sound environment of these various sites. So far, much of the work on sound documentation of urban life is allied with music or with art (performance, environmental). There is much to be learned from these endeavors (e.g., CDs of the sounds of New York buildings' heating and air conditioning systems, or their elevators; Tokyo at "the turn of the millennium"). But, again, my imperatives and goals will be somewhat different. I think it is important to experiment with combining sound and visual documentation, less as in a museum and more in an attempt to start asking new questions about Los Angeles.

In Professor Hise's essay on industrial Los Angeles, you will find economic and historical context, as well as social and political motives. But for me, in making these photographs, in going out and knocking on doors, saying, "I am a professor of city planning at USC and would like to photograph people at work in your factory (what I sometimes called the choreography of work) for our archive," the greatest reward was going out and getting inside.

The archive of images produced in my fieldwork is extensive. Many of the images are available in the USC Digital Library, at calisphere.org. Some of my diverse work on Los Angeles and New York City may be found at sites.google.com/view/urban-tomographies.

I was fortunate to enlist Mr. Jonah Greenstein, a filmmaker, to select and color-correct the images. His efforts and my earlier ones were supported through grants from the John Randolph Haynes and Dora Haynes Foundation. Professor Dominick Miretti of Local 63 of the ILWU was my guide at the Ports, Mr. Frank Toscano was my guide at the former County Hospital, Mr. Chuck Street allowed me to fly along with him in his traffic reporting work, and Professor Greg Hise guided me about industrial history and geography.

I am a voyeur.

Martin H. Krieger
Fall 2022

"NATURE'S WORKSHOP": INDUSTRIALIZATION AND METROPOLITAN EXPANSION IN SOUTHERN CALIFORNIA

BY GREG HISE

Revised from:

G. Hise, "'Nature's workshop' industry and urban expansion in Southern California, 1900-1950," *Journal of Historical Geography* 27, 1 (2001) 74-92.

Scholars and pundits have defined Los Angeles as a prototype for the twentieth-century metropolis. Their accounts focus primarily, often exclusively, on residential development and rely on stock theses for interpretation. Despite its centrality for a metropolitan economy that has led California for a century and that today leads the United States in manufacturing employment, analysts have underappreciated production and overvalued consumption. Little is known about why and how firms, investors, business and trade associations, and civic officials created space for industry. An historical investigation reveals that manufacturers' choice of location has been a key determinant of urban form and that industrial, commercial, and residential development have been coordinated and concomitant. These complementary enterprises recast the region during the first half of the twentieth century. There were three types of industrial zones in Los Angeles during this period: the Eastside Industrial District, a mixed-use, home-market district adjacent to the Central Business District; an industry predominant, mass-production, branch-plant zone in East Los Angeles, Vernon and Torrance; and oil, film, and aviation satellites on the metropolitan periphery.

In 1949, a journalist visiting Los Angeles on assignment for *Fortune* magazine drove a four-mile, west-to-east transect along 190th Street. Beginning in Redondo Beach, the writer passed through Torrance, the city of Los Angeles, Carson, and unincorporated county land observing what she or he described as a "truck farm landscape with acres of new factories." (Fig. 1) An image of factories sprouting in farmland confirmed readers' conceptions of Los Angeles as a place of agricultural abundance and the great boom city of the twentieth century. These tropes of southern California provided a counterpoint for this reporter's understated assessment of the city: "The most remarkable thing is that in the Los Angeles of 1949, [190th street] is utterly unremarkable. In and around Los Angeles, in the space of a very few years, there has grown up one of the great industrial complexes in the world." Continuing north into Vernon this visitor found "absurd Moorish factories of the 1920s around the corner from narrow, dark streets where the high walls and catwalks seem to have been transplanted from New England," a juxtaposition that seemed even more fascinating given the proximity to "some of the most exciting industrial architecture in the United States in the Santa Fe railroad's carefully zoned Central Manufacturing District."[1]

In their account of industry and urban expansion the reporter sought to capture first-hand the magnitude and nature of change in southern California during World War II.[2] The topic is novel: it cuts against the grain of popular depictions of postwar Los Angeles as the "biggest darn collection of suburbs in the world." Read thematically, the *Fortune* essay underscores the pervasiveness of stock suburban narratives. Accepted accounts of suburbanization, especially those devoted to the post-World War II era, feature a number of protagonists and a variety of sites. They employ four narrative conventions: the settings depicted represent a new landscape order; once outside the "city," specific location is secondary; the vast array of individual development projects that constitute a particular suburb are staged and completed without the benefit of coordination or deliberate planning; and the resultant physical and social patterns display a greater degree of homogeneity relative to past trends.[3]

Consider the *Fortune* excerpt with these conventions in mind. The essayist's intent is to interest readers in the newness of industrial Los Angeles. The current crop of factories, completed "in the space of a very few years," are presented as absent discernible logic that would explain why facilities were located in particular locations; expansion does not appear to have limit or boundary. What the author discerned, in essence, was industrial sprawl; over time and across space this sameness or repetition becomes "utterly unremarkable." In the final analysis, industries are undifferentiated, perhaps interchangeable; plants might be located in a number of sites throughout the metropolitan region.[4]

The novelty in the *Fortune* report is the object of investigation. The analysis is generic, the plot is known, the explanation is formulaic. Is it appropriate? I think not. The dispersion of industry and associated land uses has a history that can be traced to the mid-nineteenth-century. Mixed-use districts were the norm across North American cities, not the new landscape order that mid-twentieth-century analysts imagined.[5] Historical analysis of industrial geography in Los Angeles requires a reworking of each of the conventions associated with the standard suburban narrative. The decades leading up to the World War II defense emergency are a benchmark for this examination of shifts in industrial sectors, production techniques, and the creation of new districts.

In Los Angeles, as elsewhere, industrialists working in concert with subdividers, financiers, realtors, design professionals, and other city builders helped shape patterns of urban expansion. The Los Angeles Area Chamber of Commerce (LAACC or the Chamber) and other boosters touted Los Angeles as "Nature's Workshop, [the city] where nature helps industry most."[6] This conceit of a benign climate and sunshine as free externalities obscures the fact planning, both comprehensive and incremental, created the conditions necessary for eventual industrial expansion. In Los Angeles, industrial, commercial, civic, and residential development were coordinated, concomitant, and complementary. Previous interpretations of this expansion treat industries as homogeneous, yet they are distinguished by type and by the particular requirements of firms within a specific sector. These variations have implications for locational choices and prior or subsequent transformations in the urban landscape. The critical variables include land availability and acquisition; access to transportation, water, and power; proximity to ancillary firms and services; and securing and maintaining a workforce.

Investigating industrial Los Angeles has led to revision of a higher order. Prior accounts of manufacturing in the United States and Canada chronicle a sequence of industrial regimes, each with its associated spatial and social orders. They present a march of progress toward a penultimate state. Put simply, in Los Angeles, the nature, timing, and rapidity of industrial development compressed putatively discrete epochs such that standard theories have value only if these are elastic enough to describe and explain states presented as successive yet were coincident in Los Angeles and elsewhere.

Industry and a comprehensive dispersion of urban functions

Through the auspices of its Industrial Department (initiated in 1918), the LAACC promoted industry's reputed advantages in southern California. They courted investors and financiers touting a benign climate; low-cost and abundant hydroelectric power and petroleum-derived fuels; labor costs below the national average; a bungalow-dwelling labor force; and the open shop.[7] They had success enticing corporations such as Ford Motor Company, General Motors, and Willys-Overland to select Los Angeles for satellite production facilities or branch plants. Promoters anticipated a secondary benefit. Branch plants, they reasoned, would create the impetus for investment in resource extraction, basic in-

dustries, and ancillary production.[8]

Branch plant expansion, as well as the growth of proprietary firms, did not result in a generic industrial Los Angeles.[9] Firms set up shop, hired workers, and manufactured products for a local market and then increasingly for export. It is important to ascertain how these processes unfolded. The timing of development and the urban patterns that resulted raise questions regarding location, taxes and municipal ordinances, labor requirements, and intra-metropolitan competition. Growth, or not, depended on temporally contingent variables: the value of land, the availability and cost of financing, infrastructure, zoning, and the choices of workers and their families. To cite one example, developers and industrial realtors capitalized on variance in tax structures among municipal jurisdictions as fundamental variation that made property in one location more attractive than the parcels available in another. At City Industrial Tract, which straddled a city-county divide in East Los Angeles, the Walter Leimert Co. advertised a tax advantage industrialists would gain in the county. Leimert's location decision translated into a saving of $1.26 per $100 of valuation. Just as critical, "Industry located in the county is freer from governmental restrictions." Leimert capitalized on municipal tax and infrastructure often and creatively. He located the housing component of this workplace-dwelling development package on the city side of the jurisdictional divide and trumpeted the advantages location afforded lot buyers in advertisements for City Terrace.[10] Leimert and his contemporaries knew that tracts designated industrial on land use maps were not equivalent. William French made this point in a 1926 study of manufacturers' decisions regarding location. He surveyed available land and its value in seventeen municipalities in Los Angeles County and

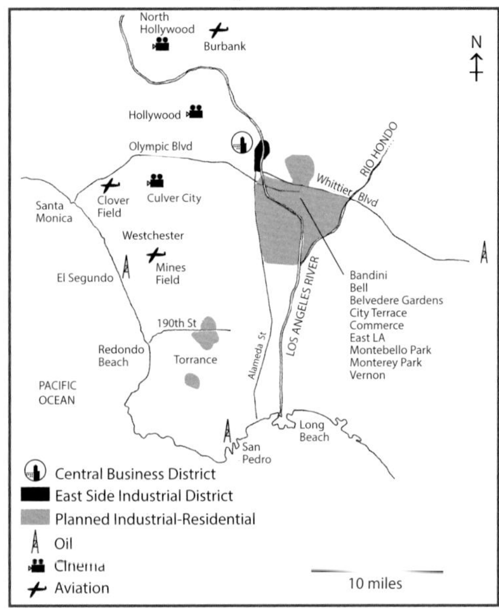

Figure 1. Industrial Districts in Metropolitan Los Angeles

documented "unimproved sites being offered as low as $400 per acre and improved land in outlying districts being sold for as high as $35,000. Some of the land in Los Angeles is valued as high as $60,000 to $100,000 per acre. The range of prices does not represent the range in industrial values of the sites offered, because some of the cheaper sites are better situated than others held at higher prices."[11]

Some analysts surmised the extent of land zoned for industry exceeded what manufacturers required. Economic consultants Eberle & Riggleman shared that assessment in "The Industrial Land Situation in Los Angeles," an August 1925 report. They urged manufacturers to be attentive to infrastructure and articulated a concern regarding "indiscriminate dispersion" that would mitigate "cohesion and interdependence of industrial facilities." These consultants valued regional co-operation.

They argued against the internecine competition that had characterized industrial development to that point and suggested municipalities specialize in a "particular type of industry in which they are most interested and for which their geographical situation may be best adapted," for example furniture manufacturing in Inglewood and heavy metals and machinery in Torrance. If industrialists heeded these recommendations, competition could be reduced and a more effective operating area established for each sector.[12]

It is evident the actors creating industrial Los Angeles recognized that all manufacturing was not equivalent. In its prospectus for City Industrial Tract, the Leimert Co. highlighted restrictions they had written into the property deeds. These regulations were not intended to protect residents living in City Terrace. Rather, they were a case of private sector zoning intended to protect those who purchased industrial property from the intrusion of "obnoxious or detrimental types of manufacturing" including chemicals, fertilizers, and insecticides; stockyards and rendering; and excavation of clay for brick, tile, or terracotta.[13]

Industrialists knew distinction among sectors informed the geography of manufacturing. A comprehensive assessment would account for the concomitant development of residential and commercial districts, and the location of services and institutions. In Los Angeles, these developments were concomitant. This was not happenstance. City-builders understood their enterprises recast the city during the first half of the twentieth century. There were three interrelated types of industrial zones in Los Angeles during the first half of the twentieth century, two were emergent, but each was vibrant and expanding (see Fig. 1).[14]

The East Side Industrial District

> As recently as ten years ago [that is c.1895] a booster discussing the future of Los Angeles would never claim that it was ever likely to become an important manufacturing center. Today, in the main city thoroughfares he beholds the business bustle of New York, along the old river bed a small Pittsburgh of factories and workshops, away toward the west and south a sweep of parklike lands covered with the homes that have made Los Angeles world famous.[15]

This is a surprising characterization of turn-of-the-twentieth-century Los Angeles, a city promoters, residents, and visitors heralded unceasingly as an intentional antipode to centers of industry of the east and Midwest. Los Angeles elites acknowledged that their city lacked the bustle of commerce and manufacturing mandatory for claiming a high rank in the urban hierarchy. Angelenos knew the "small Pittsburgh" of factories and workshops along the river by another name, the East Side Industrial District, a zone of mixed-uses that afforded access to main and spur lines of the national railroads. A constellation of heterogeneous structures housed diverse manufacturing and its service concerns: foundries, boilerworks, patternmakers' shops, iron works, stores, restaurants, saloons, and residences that ranged from single-family dwellings to apartments, hotels, and furnished rooms.[16] A majority of manufacturers in the East Side district produced for a local market and Angelenos owned a high percent of firms. The Los Angeles Soap Company, representative of a mid- to large-size operation with deep roots in the district, originated in the 1860s when John A. Forthmann moved his soap business to a greenfield site adjacent to the San Pedro, Los Angeles, and Salt Lake railway. Over time, the product line expanded to 75 brands, output increased, and Forthmann incorporated. In 1898, he secured a parcel on East First Street and contracted for the construction of a glycerin recovery plant with business offices on the second floor. The company repeatedly acquired neighboring parcels and conducted an on-going building campaign that culminated in plant and yards occupying 20 acres, a workforce of 500 employees, and bar, laundry, and toilet soap shipped "east to the Mississippi River with trade out of Los Angeles harbor to Hawaii, the Orient, and the Gulf of Mexico."[17] The district also has been a center for apparel, furniture, and food processing, as well as a prime location for jobbers, wholesalers, and associated warehouses. One mile south of Los Angeles Soap, on a 27-acre parcel, the Union Terminal Company developed a two-million-square-foot produce center. This facility, sited at the "western edge of the industrial section and the eastern edge of the retail section," provided switching and private rail tracks for immediate access to Pacific Electric freight cars with a connection to the Southern Pacific depot at Stephenson Street between Third and Fourth streets. The first phase of construction, begun in 1917, included three six-story buildings with 2,000,000 square feet of leasable warehouse space, 1,000,000 cubic feet of cold storage, and a set of two-story market structures forming an open-air yard for wholesale trade. The development company patterned this project, the largest of its kind west of Chicago, after the Bush Terminal Company's facility in New York and a similar project completed by the Piedmont Lines in Charlotte, North Carolina.[18]

Los Angeles Soap and the Wholesale Terminal were representative of the larger firms and facilities in the East Side District. The soap company developed its site and plant in an accretive fashion; the Union Terminal Company controlled a significant parcel and planned for and then constructed an assemblage of up-to-date warehouses and offices. The majority of firms in this district occupied small lots and produced irrigation machinery, chemicals and pharmaceuticals, machine parts and ornamental ironwork, paint, furniture, and bakery confections, and other household goods. Reformer Bromley Oxnam noted in 1925 that the area around the Macy Street School "is gradually being changed into industrial sites. The land in this section is held by more than 120 owners, most holding one to six lots."[19]

When William French surveyed property holdings and land value for his 1926 study, he found that with the exception of two or three parcels, property zoned for industry was either built to capacity or valued at a price prohibitive for manufacturing. He concluded that "This tendency has forced some industries to move from the district in order to expand."[20] Although French and other observers noted the perceived shortcomings that might restrict industrial development in the East Side District, this did not reflect a consensus; investors and firms continued to locate there. In 1919, the California Commission of Immigration and Housing (CCIH) reported that just over 33 percent of manufactories in the city were located in this district. The East Side remained a desirable location and a robust and expanding mixed-use zone throughout the 1920s and into the postwar years. A classified advertisement from 1926 in the *Los Angeles Times* offered a parcel on Alameda Street for long- or short- term lease. The lessor presented the land as "industrial acreage...suitable for graders' or contractors' headquarters, livestock market, dairy, poultry, factory, lumber yard, race track or amusement arena." During the WWII defense emergency when the demand for floorspace exceeded supply, aircraft firms that had dispersed out from the Eastside and recentralized in specialized districts around outlying airfields, returned some of their operations to loft buildings they had vacated. More recently, these structures have been repurposed as "incubator sites for immigrant entrepreneurs."[21]

Industrialists took into account multiple factors when deciding whether to remain in the East Side district or to relocate to City Industrial Tract, the Union Pacific's Metropolitan Warehouse district, Vernon and the Central Manufacturing District (CMD), Torrance, Culver City, and additional locations. Preeminent among these were zoning and employees' determination to improve shop-floor conditions and secure greater authority in their negotiations with management.

Los Angeles residents approved zoning in response to the noise, filth, and hazards associated with brickmaking, animal slaughtering, petroleum refining, and other noxious industries.[22] The city council crafted and approved ordinances that designated where manufacturers could locate within city boundaries beginning with regulations restricting certain industrial uses in a residential area in 1904. This was followed by statutes, passed in 1908 and 1909, that parsed the city into two residential and seven industrial zones. The next year, an ordinance designated as residential all city land not falling within the industrial districts. Other incorporated communities followed suit and assigned land for industrial development. Designed to protect single-family housing, these codes promoted dispersed industrial clusters that encouraged manufacturers and developers to plan for working-class housing and services in proximity to employment.[23] This restrictive legislation benefitted the industrialists. Following passage, their interests were pre-eminent across swaths of the city where other uses were deigned non-conforming.

In 1928, the LAACC's Manufacturing and Industries Committee reported to the directors regarding an "ideal plan worked out by the Trackage Committee" under the direction of County Regional Planning Engineer W. J. Fox. Fox was an LAACC member, a committee chair, and a public official; who better than he, his colleagues must have determined, to coordinate the activities of landowners in a given locality for the purpose of "obtaining trackage connections, especially where the tendency was to subdivide such property into residential lots." The plan, and the Chamber's support, underscore the ways industrialists capitalized on planning initiatives. In this case, they helped craft the planning agenda through cooperation and coordination with one of the county's senior planning officials. The Chamber's position on the zoning issue was expressed tersely during a 1922 board meeting. When a director asked if the Chamber had gone on record "in favor or against the policy of zoning," a colleague replied: "It is a child of the Chamber. We started it."[24]

Relations between labor and management had complex effects on industrial location decisions. Metal-workers had the most impact. During the first decade of the century, these workers walked off the job en masse on three occasions (1902, 1903, 1910) in order to secure a nine-hour workday, overtime pay, and fixed hourly wages. These firms had concentrated in the East Side district, the majority north of the plaza. Fred L. Baker and John Llewellyn, proprietors of Baker Iron Works and Llewellyn Iron Works, organized their management cohort in a Founders' and Employers' Association (FEA). This group's board of directors included representatives from the region's 25 largest concerns; collectively these employers led a militantly anti-union crusade. Baker and Llewellyn repeatedly hired non-union workers to replace strikers. Following the 1903 walkout, Baker demanded that workers sign an affidavit of non-membership in any union. Both men lent their support to the 1910 employers' initiative to criminalize picketing, a response to a strike that drew 1,500 metalworkers off the job and threatened production at all FEA member plants. Llewellyn and Baker Iron Works, as well as two of the firms' project sites, were targeted in the explosions that racked Los Angeles that year. The primary evidence does not link definitively a decade of labor activism and the dynamiting of the *Los Angeles Times* and Llewellyn Iron Works causally with the decision of firms like Llewellyn to establish satellite facilities outside the East Side District. Still, Llewellyn's decision to locate in Jared Sidney Torrance's eponymic "model industrial city" cannot be explained entirely by the purported advantages of a greenfield site with "protective zoning for industrial use," "non-speculative ownership in large tracts," and low land costs.[25]

Planned suburban industrial districts: Torrance, East Los Angeles, Vernon

> It will be our own fault if we do not direct
> our city into proper channels of growth.
> This means that industries must be scat-
> tered throughout the whole metropolitan
> district. It must be decentralized. Such
> decentralization will make for better living
> conditions and better citizenship, as well as
> for cheaper overhead costs.[26]

On one hand Torrance represented a second industrial landscape: greenfield sites engineered with up-to-date infrastructure and services, intended for firms whose mass production relied on the beltline and other technologies to manufacture metal fittings, refinery equipment, tires and tubes, and automobiles for a regional market and increasingly for export throughout the Pacific. In other aspects Torrance was atypical: a single corporation, Dominguez Land, owned the 2,800 sites; developer Jared Torrance engaged prominent designers F. L. Olmsted Jr. and Irving Gill to oversee the drafting and implementation of a master plan for a comprehensive satellite community; and Dominguez Land sold and leased parcels encumbered with "reservations, conditions, covenants, charges and agreements." Race restrictions confined "any person other than of the white or Caucasian Race" to the "foreign quarters." The timing, relative to incendiary explosions and the mayoral bid of socialist lawyer Job Harriman, was not incidental. Industrial development was piecemeal until 1916 when Dominguez Land donated a 125-acre parcel to the Pacific Electric Railway for its construction and repair yard, a standard gambit in the internecine politics of urban growth.[27]

City builders viewed industrialization and land use in a manner akin to Jared Torrance. They believed manufacturing ought to be segregated geographically by function, be distributed by sector, and be proximate to residences, services, and community institutions. A majority favored boundaries segregating the "races." All industry did not disperse and recentralize in new districts, all outlying districts planned and zoned industrial did not become sites for production, and consensus regarding the optimal location for local firms or companies either relocating to the region or setting up branch facilities was subject to revision. A number of suburban industrial districts were planned, serviced, and marketed during the 1920s but remained sparsely developed up to the defense emergency.

During a meeting in January 1922, members of the Chamber of Commerce engaged in a rancorous debate regarding the relative merits of "opening up" a section of San Pedro Street adjacent to the central business district (CBD) for industry, a move, they duly noted, guaranteed to antagonize voters on Boyle Heights. At first glance the topic concerned where Westinghouse ought to site its initial plant in Los Angeles. The board favored a parcel at the corner of Ninth and San Pedro streets. At another order of magnitude, were the Chamber to adopt the proposal, San Pedro St. would be transformed into a "wholesale district." As Chamber president Weaver noted, "all those who do not believe in it as a wholesale section and who do not want [the construction of additional] grade crossings will be in opposition." Those who opposed argued for a Vernon location where there is "plenty of vacant ground served by three railroads only 20 minutes from 7th [Street] and Broadway." At this inflammatory session, the latter made unsavory comparisons to New York, Pittsburgh, and St Louis. President Weaver argued that he was all for "giving Los Angeles the advantages those cities have." Though united in principle–growth equals progress–these antagonists drew distinctions among different types of industry, the exact needs of particular firms, the appropriate location for various manufacturing activities and, most critical-

ly, the optimal pattern of land uses in Los Angeles. The ideal intra-metropolitan geography of industry, as the majority defined it, had warehouses and jobbers serving downtown commercial and retail with production segregated to outlying districts such as Vernon, the Union Pacific's Metropolitan Warehouse and Industrial District, or the Southern Pacific's tracts in present day Commerce. This reflected patterns of land ownership by board members but it also reflected concerns about property values in the CBD and the depth of anxiety during the 1920s regarding transportation and congestion in that part of the city.[28]

Residents also perceived the city dichotomously. In 1924, a contributor to the *Times* stated boldly that in order to understand Los Angeles it was necessary to motor south through the manufacturing districts. "The rest of the city, from the winsome foothills to the glittering beaches, when viewed alone does not convey an adequate idea of the true situation. Along with all that it has been in the past, this city is now an industrial entity." A drive from the eastside southward would bring into view a "stage for the newest and biggest act in the great Los Angeles drama." Here the air "is filled with industrial haze and queer smells, huge trucks trundle along paved thoroughfares. [This] is the new city; it is not amusements or tourists, it is industrial production."[29] (Note the concurrence with *Fortune*'s report a quarter century later.)

The Chamber expended its prowess and power to set growth in the city and region on a firm industrial foundation. Pleas for weaning the metropolitan economy from the "tourist crop" and attendant real estate speculation and orienting it toward industry were voiced with great urgency during the 1920s. A *Times* editorial from 1923, "Balanced Progress," declared that the region "stands at the dawn of a golden tomorrow." Though the city "glittered" with promise and opportunity, the future was "fraught with great problems." Why? Because population growth routinely "staggered all power of anticipation."[30] The author identified infrastructure improvements: water and power; an expanded harbor; solutions for traffic congestion; and police protection, schools, and parks as pressing needs. To advance, the city required "men with a large enough vision, prophetic instinct, and practical unselfishness to make these dreams come true." Enterprisers had to reach "further into the back country. To get coal and iron and wool and cotton to feed the industries which will grow; we will be compelled to add great areas of tributary country."[31]

In response, the Chamber's Industrial Department pursued industrialists who might invest in southern California. Reference to one sector, rubber and tire production, reveals the scale and rapidity of change. In 1919, when Goodyear decided to build a Southland plant, only a few independent firms were in production and these manufactured less than one percent of the national output. A decade later, after Firestone, Goodrich, and U.S. Rubber, the nation's number two, three, and four producers, had followed suit, the region's share had grown to six percent (which translated into 35,000 tires and 40,000 tubes a day). By then employment had increased from a few hundred workers to more than 5,000 (almost seven percent of the industry total) and annual output reached a value of $56 million. Los Angeles' location and transit infrastructure were critical factors in terms of raw materials and sales for finished goods. Goodyear and Firestone's subsidiaries supplied the intermountain and Pacific states including Alaska and Hawaii.[32]

The Chamber members' exchange and the *Times'* call for territorial expansion underscore the significance of local initiative for the creation of industrial Los Angeles. As Goodyear and Firestone executives divided the continent into what economist Frank Kidner labelled "branch plant empires," Los Angeles entrepreneurs and civic elites imagined the creation of a "back country" empire.[33] This signified the emergence of Los Angeles as the epicenter of a metropolitan region whose entrepreneurs and financiers would exercise influence over dependent territories. It represented enhanced material and symbolic connections in national and international systems of trade and culture as well as an extension of local authority. Like their counterparts in Chicago and New York, Los Angeles entrepreneurs sought to control the hinterlands in two ways: as a center for procuring and processing resources and as a center for shaping preferences for consumer goods.[34]

Distinctions between east and west sides of the city, between metropolitan Los Angeles and other urban centers, and between southern California and other nations were more complex than these dichotomies suggest. In 1925, a Chicago-based engineering firm, Kelker, De Leuw & Co., presented a report to the Los Angeles city council and the county board of supervisors with recommendations for a comprehensive rapid transit plan. This study revealed that contrary to accepted narratives regarding mass transit, residential dispersion, and sprawl, a significant share of workers employed in the East Side Industrial District lived within walking distance to work, and between one-fifth and one-third of all workers employed in the East Side and Vernon districts lived less than two miles from their place of employment. This is equivalent to the standard measure urbanists accept as a metric for the pre-industrial walking city. If the compass is extended to a circle of three miles it captures over one-third of the workers in North Main, one-half of those employed in Vernon, and three-fifths of those employed in the East Side.[35]

Mixed-use development was the norm for a wedge-shaped segment of the county beginning at the Los Angeles River south of Whittier Boulevard and extending eastward to Montebello and then south along the Rio Hondo to Gage Avenue. This zone encompasses segments of Boyle Heights, East Los Angeles, Commerce, Vernon, and Bell; during the 1920s, it was the site of intensive development. Within these boundaries W. H. Daum and realtors with expertise in industrial property leased or sold land to B. F. Goodrich, Samson Tire and Rubber, Union Iron Works, Truscon Steel, Okeefe and Merritt, Illinois Glass, and Angelus Furniture. Daum began his career as an agent for the Atchison, Topeka, and Santa Fe Railroad's industrial division. In 1913, he opened his Los Angeles firm and over the next four decades helped set the pattern for industrial dispersion in the region. Holding companies he managed oversaw property in the East Side Industrial District while he simultaneously developed sections of Vernon and property along Slauson Avenue. In some cases, Daum leased land to firms such as the Pacific Coast Planning Company that relocated from parcels he controlled in the East Side District.[36]

Daum and his associates were not simply responding to market opportunity. These land developers created locational advantage. Elements such as the rail lines were in place, the land was sparsely developed, and it sold at attractive prices. But much had to be done. Property entrepreneurs like Daum established institutions such as the Eastside Organization and Ninth Street Club to promote collective endeavors. These organizations agitated for street improvements and river-spanning viaducts to "utilize the unsurpassed natural advantages [of the Eastside]; the facilities of location and uninterrupted territory, the trend of development, and the power of numbers...to remove all barriers–natural, unnatural, and prejudicial–to its fullest and most permanent development."[37]

Concomitant with this industrial program firms such as the Janss Investment Company, J. B. Ransom Corporation, and Carlin G. Smith were promoting Belvedere Gardens, Samson Park, Bandini, Montebello Park, and Eastmont. Smith noted that Eastmont, his first subdivision on the eastside, was "neighbor to a mighty payroll...facing a destined city of factories. The amazing development of the great East Side–teeming with its expanses of moderate-priced homes–has become almost over-night one of the most startling features of the city's growth." The Janss Company, known for Westwood, Holmby Hills, and other restricted residential projects on the city's west side, had been developing Belvedere Heights and later Belvedere Gardens since 1905. The latter tract, immediately east of Los Angeles' municipal limits, was intended for "workingmen with limited capital." Advertisements presented Los Angeles as a city awash with humanity "overflowing to the east." The projected exodus to a "new suburb" would bring workers to a district cheek-by-jowl with "big industrial development." By 1922, the firm concentrated on parcels adjacent to the Hostetter Tract, site of Sears-Roebucks' regional distribution center, and added its voice to calls for street widenings to provide for the anticipated 25,000 new residents "who will make their homes in Belvedere Gardens owing to the great industrial program inaugurated for this section."[38]

During the 1920s, nation-spanning firms including Swift & Company, Goodyear, Phelps-Dodge, U.S. Steel, Willys-Overland, and Liquid Carbonic established branch plants in Los Angeles. Swift & Company joined local firms such as Deshell Laboratory, Reo Motor, and Sperry Soap in a 300-acre development planned, constructed, and managed by Chicagoans John Spoor, A. G. Leonard, and Halsey Poronto of the syndicate responsible for that city's Central Manufacturing District. These entrepreneurs purchased a section of the Arcadia Bandini estate, rancho land that had been held in trust and leased for cattle grazing and farming. Beginning in 1922, the Los Angeles Central Manufacturing District (CMD) recast the site for modern industry with single-story, open-span, fireproof buildings, top of the line services and amenities, and low taxes. Apropos their Chicago venture, the first phase of development centered on a 100-acre livestock market and the construction of a central administration building, a terminal warehouse, and a manufacturers' building with leasable production and storage space for small operators. They subdivided the remaining acreage into 125 parcels with switch track connections for sale or lease to manufacturers. The syndicate offered prospective lessees and buyers financing and construction assistance; infrastructure improvements including parkways, landscaping, and ornamental street lighting; and access to the Los Angeles Junction Railway, a beltline with direct connection to all trunk lines entering the city.[39]

The incorporated municipality Vernon annexed the CMD in 1925. In 1929 the Chicago syndicate sold out to the Atchison, Topeka & Santa Fe Railroad which purchased the remaining 2,000 acres in the Bandini estate and extended track and industry west into the remainder of Vernon and east into Commerce. Workers resided in Maywood, Huntington Park, and Bell; the latter, "an island of homes in a sea of industry," was an unincorporated community of 9,000 with direct bus service to the CMD.[40] Promotional materials and publicity photographs for Maywood, the eastside residential tracts, and Torrance's model community depict houses under construction on vacant land. Like other frontiers, this crabgrass frontier required an imagined and, in some cases, actual removal of people. Advertisements for the small, working-class cottages intended to replace self-built or "makeshift" quarters made it clear that industrialists and land developers imagined the new eastside "miracle city" as an Anglo-only enclave. In Vernon, industrial development benefitted from the removal of "shacks" and of a "Mexican village." The impetus for this renewal can be traced to an outbreak of bubonic and pneumonic plague. The City Department of Public Health and County Health Department initiated a quarantine replete with searches of house-courts occupied by Mexican nationals and Mexican-Americans. Quarantine and clearance were justified as public health.[41]

By 1930, comprehensive development linking workplace with residence had become an acknowledged type. Thomas Coombs, an engineer with the Los Angeles City Planning Commission, stated simply: "The work shops of the city, the industrial and manufacturing districts, should be selected with great care. [These ought to be] far enough from the residential section...but not so located as to make traveling between the two a disadvantage. These areas should be large [with] a small part reserved for a local business center. Before it is possible to intelligently subdivide a city, all these subjects should be given careful consideration and be well planned."[42]

Creating a metropolitan economy: oil, cinema, and aviation

In almost every municipal and geographic division of Los Angeles, as well as in outlying satellite centers, small industrial districts occur. Hundreds of manufacturing establishments of diverse kinds are widely scattered over the metropolitan district. ...Even such noteworthy residential suburbs as Hollywood, Beverly Hills, Santa Monica, Pasadena, and Long Beach have their industrial tracts. Airplane manufacturing is rapidly giving a new industrial importance to the Inglewood-Santa Monica district.[43]

In 1922 the Los Angeles County Board of Supervisors sponsored a conference devoted to regional planning. A diagram published in the proceedings depicted Hollywood, Pasadena, Inglewood, and Laguna with their spheres of influence encircling the CBD of Los Angeles. These engineers, civic officials, and design professionals found the "whole district crystallizing around natural centers and subcenters...each with its own individual character and identity." They saw a network, linked by transit, functioning as a region.[44] Had participants at the Pasadena conference extended their map to encompass firms and plants in oil, film, and aviation the diagrams would have coincided. Firms in these sectors established industrial districts at the metropolitan periphery during the 1910s and 1920s. There local and national firms produced primarily for export. Petroleum extraction and refining, motion picture production, and aviation engaged relatively large numbers of craft-based workers employed either directly or indirectly in component manufacture and assembly. These firms, in turn, served as generators for the development of residential districts with a compliment of commerce and institutions. "Suburban indus-

trial clusters" developed adjacent to oil fields and refiner-
ies. Pipelines linked clusters into a network. Standard Oil
and other petroleum concerns engaged in city-building.
Proximate to production in Brea or San Pedro, small-
er-scale entrepreneurs subdivided land and built housing
in residential districts such as La Habra and Long Beach.
In Vernon, an oil refinery site, zoning and land use regulations restricted residential development but oil workers
and their families chose to reside immediately adjacent
in Huntington Park and Maywood. Before 1917, four
suburban industrial clusters, Whittier-Fullerton, San
Pedro-Long Beach, El Segundo-Manhattan Beach, and
Vernon-Huntington Park formed a metropolitan industrial district.[45]

The movie colony established an initial locus in
Hollywood. A 1915 directory of manufacturers records
firms in Long Beach, Santa Monica, Mount Washington,
and multiple districts in between. Thomas Ince established a studio in Harry Culver's new community on the
former Rancho Ballona eight miles west of city hall in
1915. Within five years, Goldwyn Pictures, the Henry
Lehrman Studios, Sanborn Laboratories, and the Maurice
Tourneur Film Company had joined the Ince studio in
Culver City making it the "greatest producer of pictures
in the world" after Hollywood.[46] The Ince firm meta-
morphosed into Metro-Goldwyn-Mayer and in 1927, a
promotional pamphlet welcomed Cecil B. DeMille, Hal
B. Roach, and the United Artists studios; they had established "plants" in Culver City. The brochure attributed
the 71 percent home ownership rate to employment in
the studios "where great forces of men and women are

maintained. As studio development is increased and as
the industry becomes more stable, the trend of workers,
including professionals, toward the community increas-
es."[47] Similar development in the North Hollywood area
began in 1915 when Carl Laemmle converted a former
chicken ranch on county land into Universal City. This
practice continued into the 1920s when Warner Brothers
moved from a site along Hollywood's Sunset Boulevard
to an outlying location in Burbank.

The model accounts for aircraft and parts, a sector critical for understanding industry and urban expansion in Los Angeles. The origins of southern California's
aviation (later aerospace) sector can be traced to small,
undercapitalized companies that rented space for offices
and plants in warehouses and loft buildings in the East
Side Industrial District before acquiring more suitable
sites along the then urban fringe. Glenn L. Martin, who
directed mechanics assembling biplanes in a former
Methodist church and then in a cannery in Santa Ana,
founded the first Los Angeles firm to manufacture aircraft. In 1912 Martin relocated into a brick loft building
with a first-floor storefront, a former bedding and uphol-
stery shop, at 943 South Los Angeles.[48]

Donald Douglas, an engineer and Martin
vice-president, formed the Douglas-Davis Company in
1920, when he rented the backroom of a barber shop at
8817 Pico Boulevard south of Beverly Hills. Former Martin employees crafted components for a transcontinental
plane in a second-floor loft space at Koll Planning Mill,
a woodworking shop ten miles away on Colyton Street,
near Alameda and Fourth Streets. Finished parts were

lowered down an elevator shaft and trucked for final assembly at the Goodyear Blimp hanger in south Los Angeles. After securing a contract for three experimental torpedo planes, Douglas, with financial support from Harry Chandler, incorporated as The Douglas Company in July 1921. The following year 42 employees relocated to a movie studio on Wilshire Boulevard in Santa Monica, chosen for its adjacent field; it proved inadequate for test flights and completed aircraft were towed to Clover Field. Between 1922 and 1928, Douglas produced 375 units, and by the latter year, the company moved its entire operations to Clover Field, which the City of Santa Monica had purchased two years earlier.

Municipal ownership assured continuity of operation, the requisite zoning, and eminent domain for expansion. Concomitantly the firm opened a subsidiary adjacent to Mines Field, an airstrip the city of Los Angeles had recently leased for a municipal airport. When the city purchased the property in 1937, the district had become a nucleus for prime airframe contractors, subassembliers, and parts and component manufacturers.[49]

During World War II, homebuilders, anticipating an influx of defense workers drawn by these employment centers, selected sites in close proximity for community projects. Adjacent to Mines Field, four developers converted a five square-mile parcel, owned by Security Bank, into a district for 10,000 residents. A map accompanying advertisements for Westchester in the Los Angeles Herald-Express plotted prime contractors and 11 ancillary manufactories. The copy underscored the district's proximity to a "wide variety of employment." Broadsides enticed potential buyers who could "Live within walking distance to scores of production plants."[50]

Conclusion

> The industrialization of [Los Angeles] was not unwelcome; in fact, it was to a considerable extent deliberately planned and cultivated.[51]

Accepted theses of suburban development do not account for Westchester, Culver City, Torrance, Belvedere Gardens, and like developments. These projects were not intended as suburbs, if the term invokes bedroom communities populated by middle- and upper-income households. Just as significant, precedents of mixed-use districts can be traced back at least a century. Huntington Park, East Los Angeles, and similar zones were planned and, more often than not, attracted a range of residents in terms of occupation, income, and status, though race and ethnic exclusion continued.

During the 1920s and continuing to the post-WWII era, Los Angeles had a vibrant mixed-use warehouse, production, and residential district between Alameda Street and the Los Angeles River organized principally for home-market production while Chicago-based entrepreneurs developed a district engineered to the latest standards for mass-production firms in Vernon. At the same time, Harry Culver worked with Thomas Ince and other fledgling studio executives to create a film industry satellite along Ballona Creek, midway between the region's central business district (in down-town Los Angeles) and the beach cities. Attention to the particularities of place and circumstance challenges the tidy chronology of ascension, transformation, and succession.

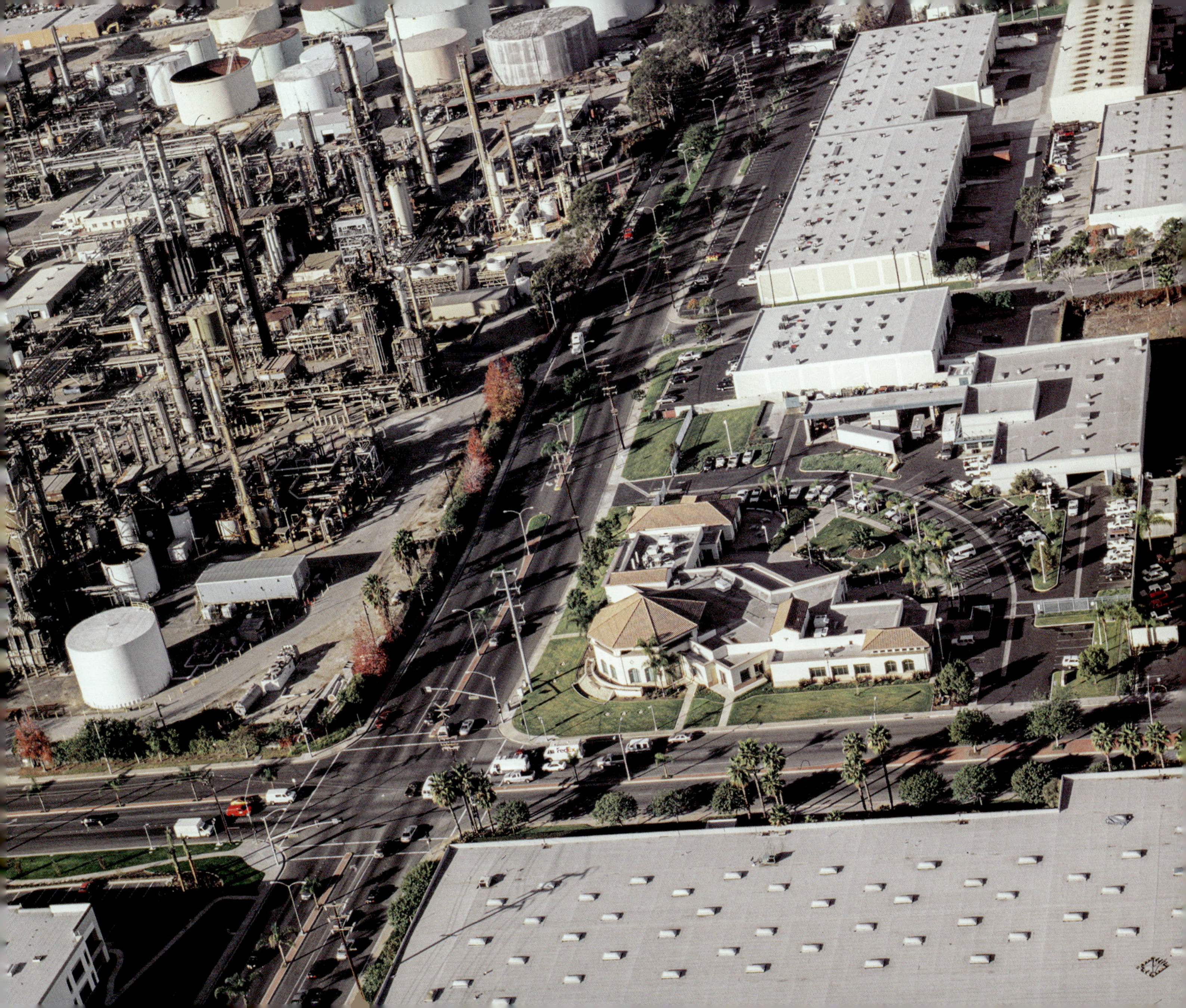

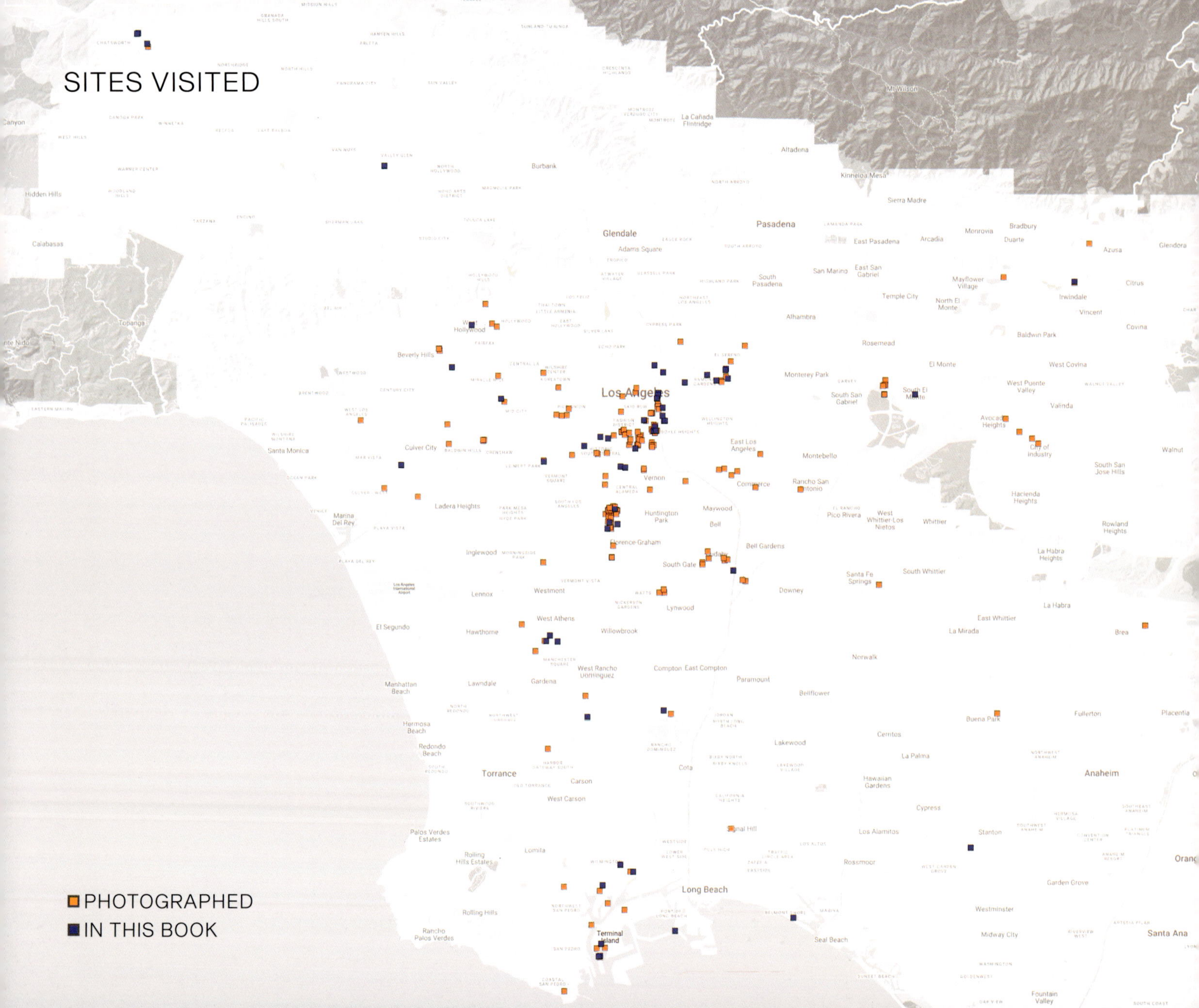

SITES VISITED
PHOTOGRAPHED
IN THIS BOOK

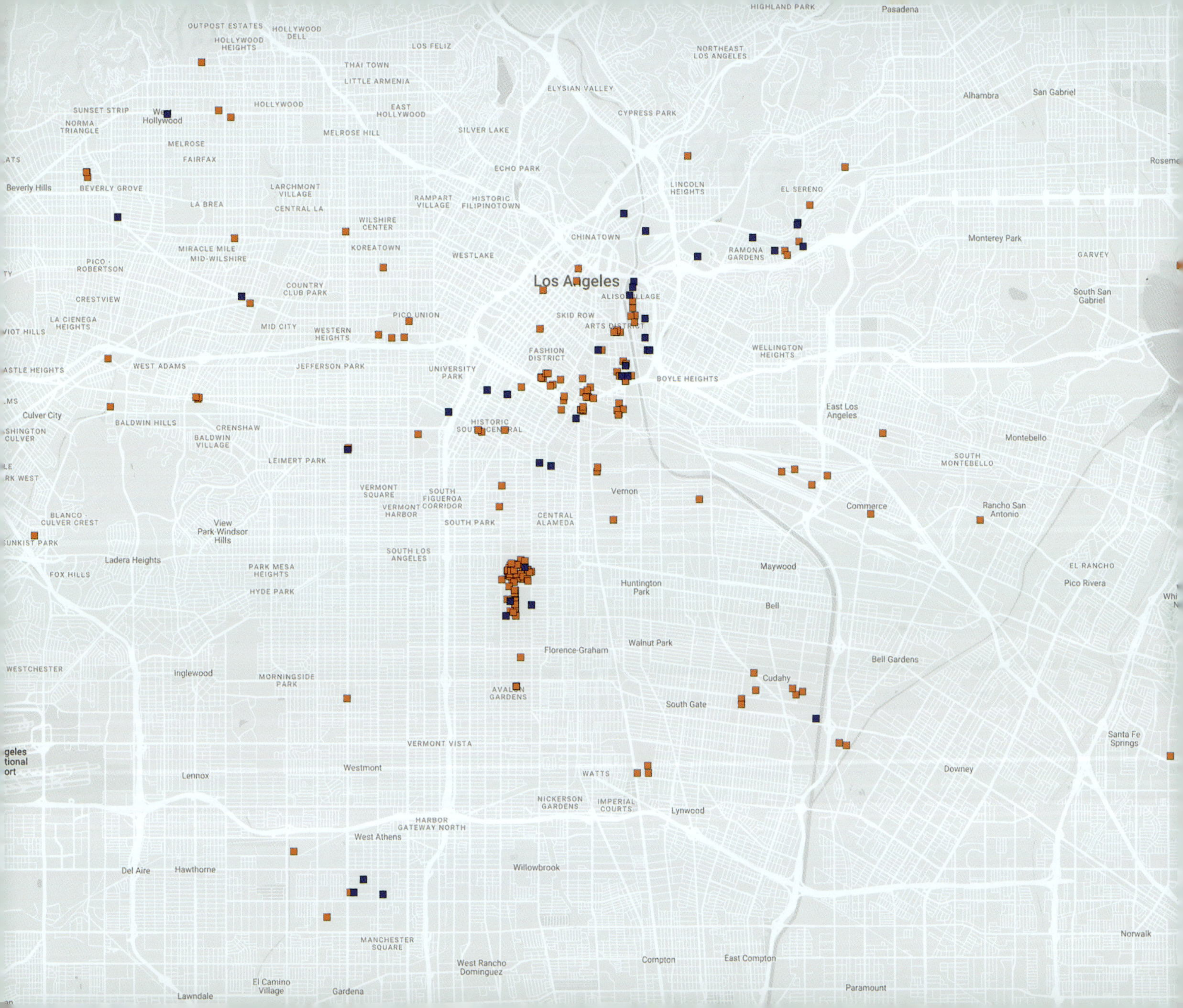

HIGHLAND PARK
Pasadena
OUTPOST ESTATES
HOLLYWOOD DELL
HOLLYWOOD HEIGHTS
HOLLYWOOD
LOS FELIZ
NORTHEAST LOS ANGELES
Alhambra
San Gabriel
THAI TOWN
LITTLE ARMENIA
ELYSIAN VALLEY
SUNSET STRIP
West Hollywood
EAST HOLLYWOOD
CYPRESS PARK
NORMA TRIANGLE
MELROSE
SILVER LAKE
Roseme
MELROSE HILL
FAIRFAX
ECHO PARK
LINCOLN HEIGHTS
EL SERENO
ATS
BEVERLY GROVE
LARCHMONT VILLAGE
WILSHIRE CENTER
Monterey Park
Beverly Hills
LA BREA
CENTRAL LA
CHINATOWN
RAMONA GARDENS
TY
MIRACLE MILE
MID-WILSHIRE
KOREATOWN
RAMPART VILLAGE
HISTORIC FILIPINOTOWN
GARVEY
PICO-ROBERTSON
WESTLAKE
Los Angeles
CRESTVIEW
COUNTRY CLUB PARK
ALISO VILLAGE
South San Gabriel
LA CIENEGA HEIGHTS
MID CITY
PICO UNION
SKID ROW
ARTS DISTRICT
WELLINGTON HEIGHTS
VIOT HILLS
WESTERN HEIGHTS
FASHION DISTRICT
BOYLE HEIGHTS
MS
WEST ADAMS
JEFFERSON PARK
UNIVERSITY PARK
East Los Angeles
Culver City
BALDWIN HILLS
Montebello
SHINGTON CULVER
CRENSHAW
BALDWIN VILLAGE
HISTORIC SOUTH CENTRAL
SOUTH MONTEBELLO
LE
LEIMERT PARK
RK WEST
VERMONT SQUARE
SOUTH FIGUEROA
Vernon
Commerce
Rancho San Antonio
BLANCO-CULVER CREST
VERMONT CORRIDOR
VERMONT HARBOR
CENTRAL ALAMEDA
SUNKIST PARK
View Park-Windsor Hills
SOUTH PARK
EL RANCHO
Ladera Heights
PARK MESA HEIGHTS
SOUTH LOS ANGELES
Maywood
Pico Rivera
FOX HILLS
HYDE PARK
Huntington Park
Bell
Whi N
Florence-Graham
Walnut Park
WESTCHESTER
Inglewood
MORNINGSIDE PARK
Bell Gardens
Cudahy
Bell Gardens
AVALON GARDENS
South Gate
Santa Fe Springs
geles tional ort
Lennox
VERMONT VISTA
Downey
Westmont
WATTS
NICKERSON GARDENS
IMPERIAL COURTS
Lynwood
HARBOR GATEWAY NORTH
West Athens
Del Aire
Hawthorne
Willowbrook
MANCHESTER SQUARE
Norwalk
West Rancho Dominguez
Compton
East Compton
Paramount
Lawndale
El Camino Village
Gardena

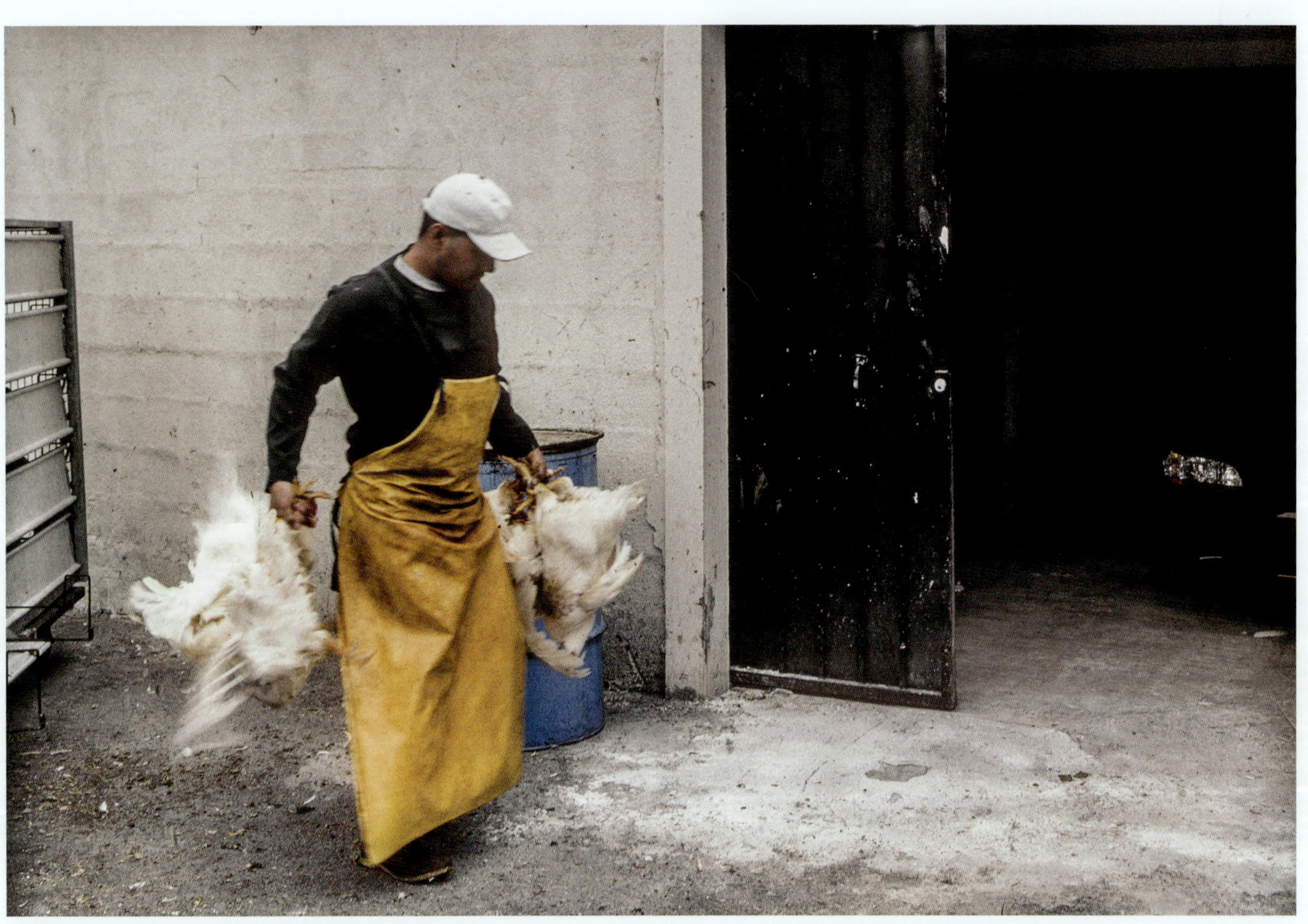

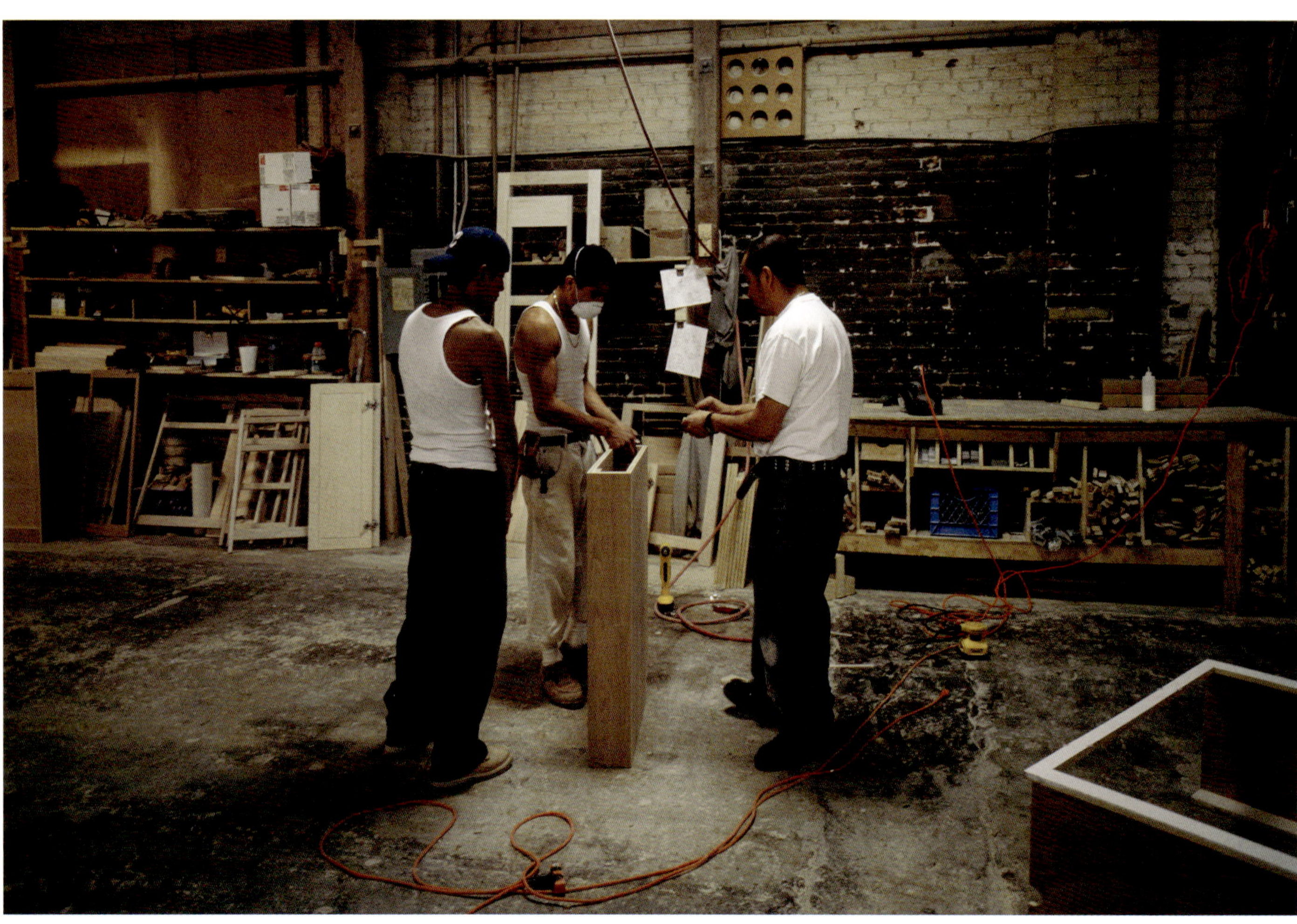

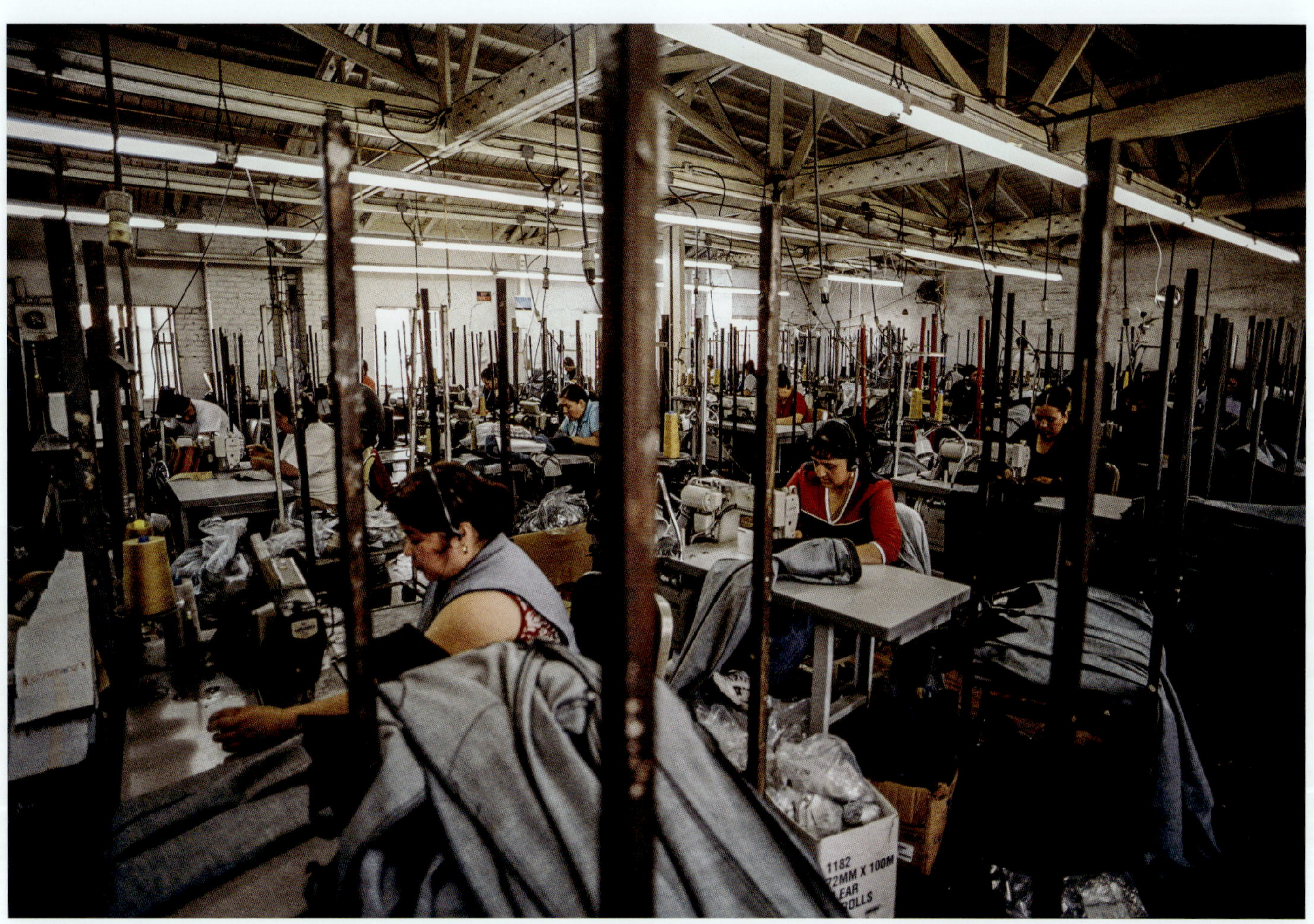

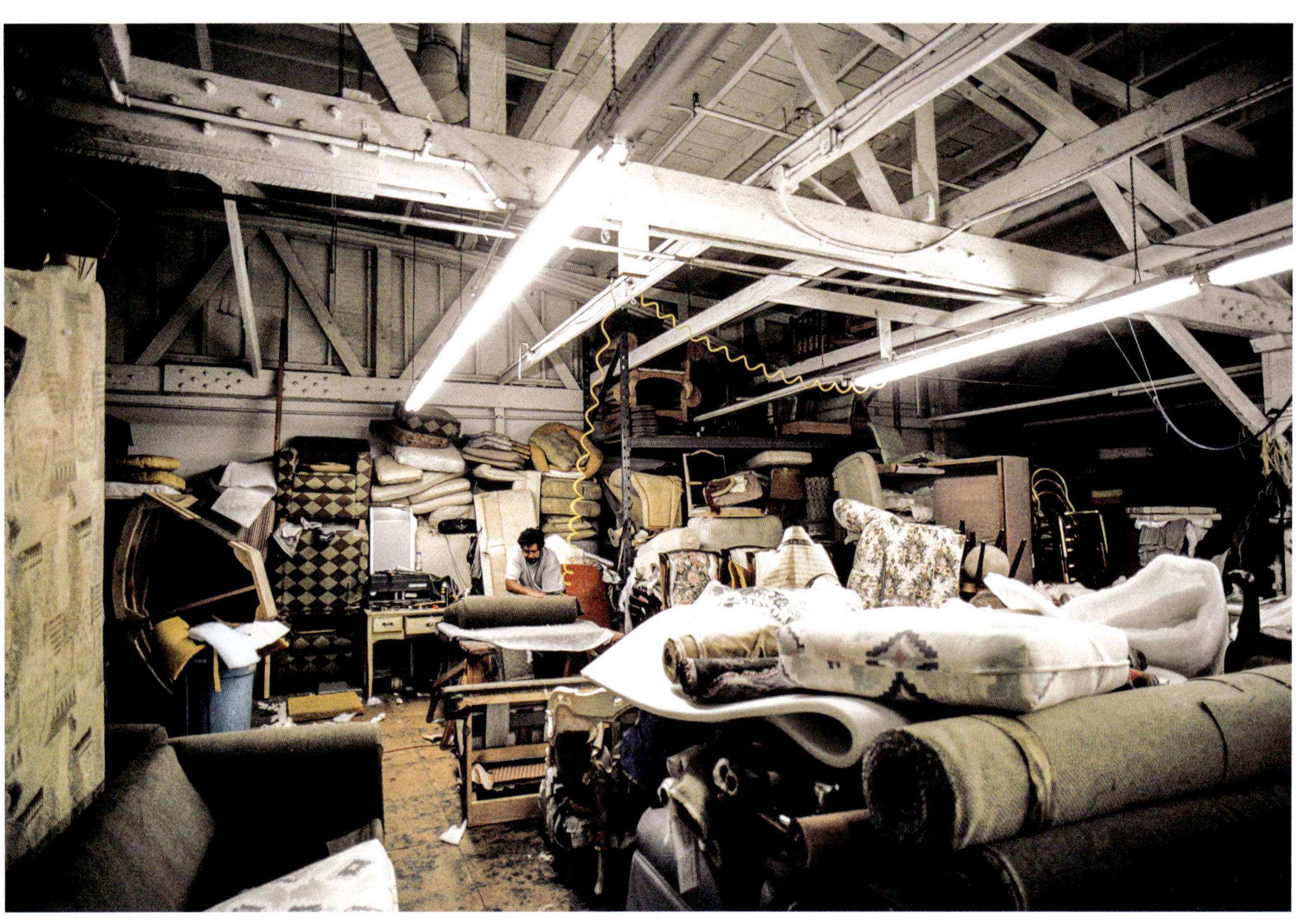

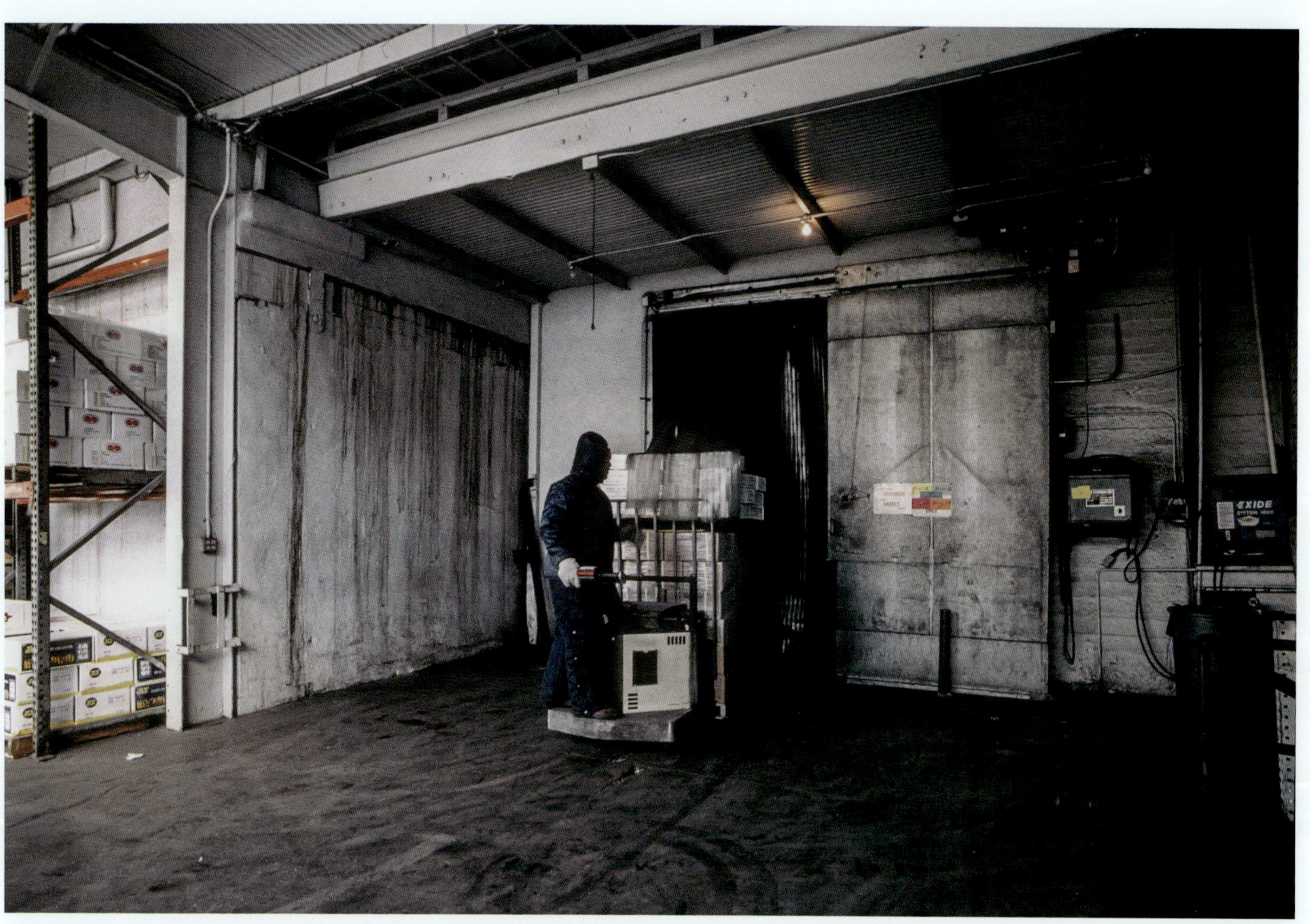

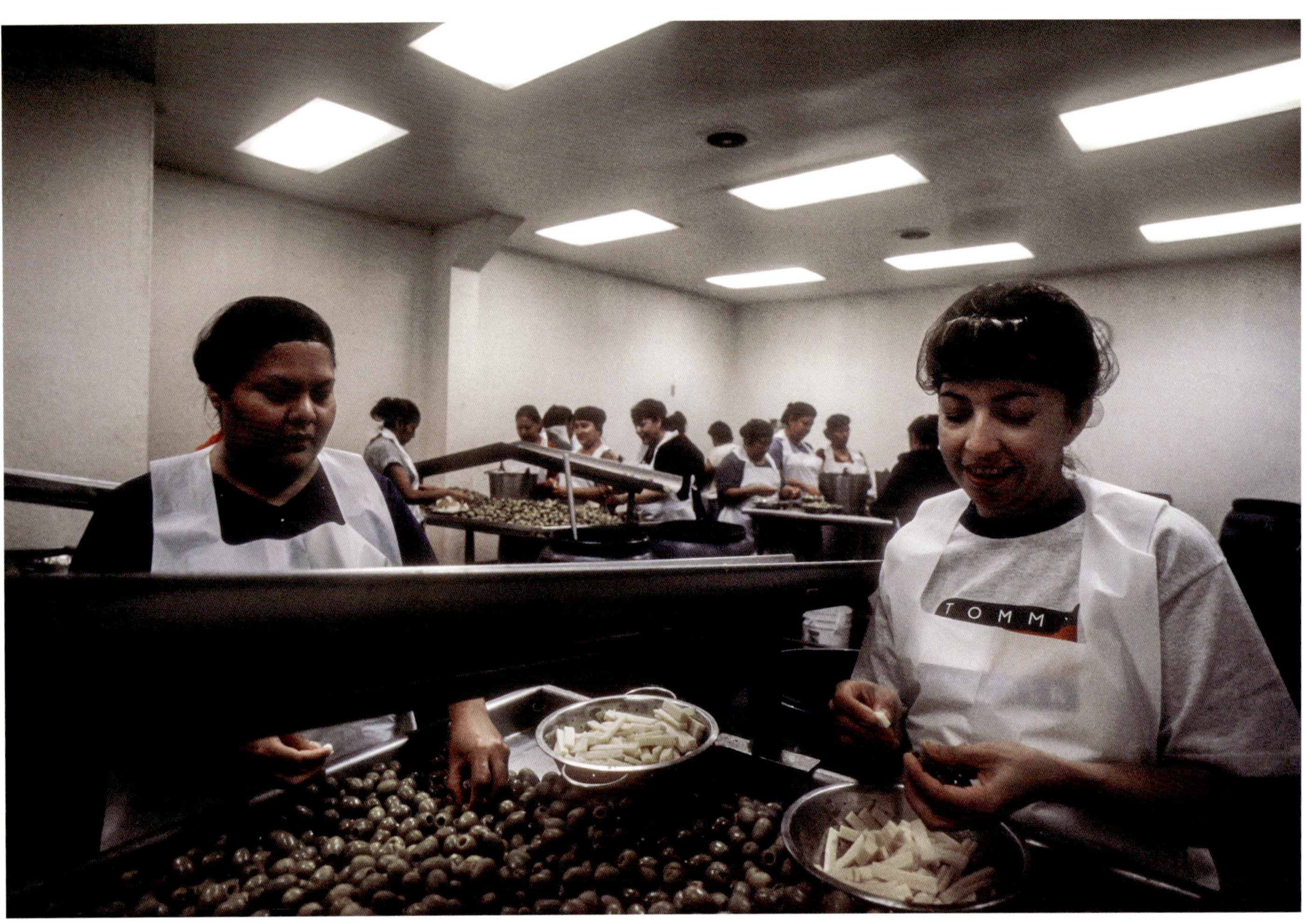

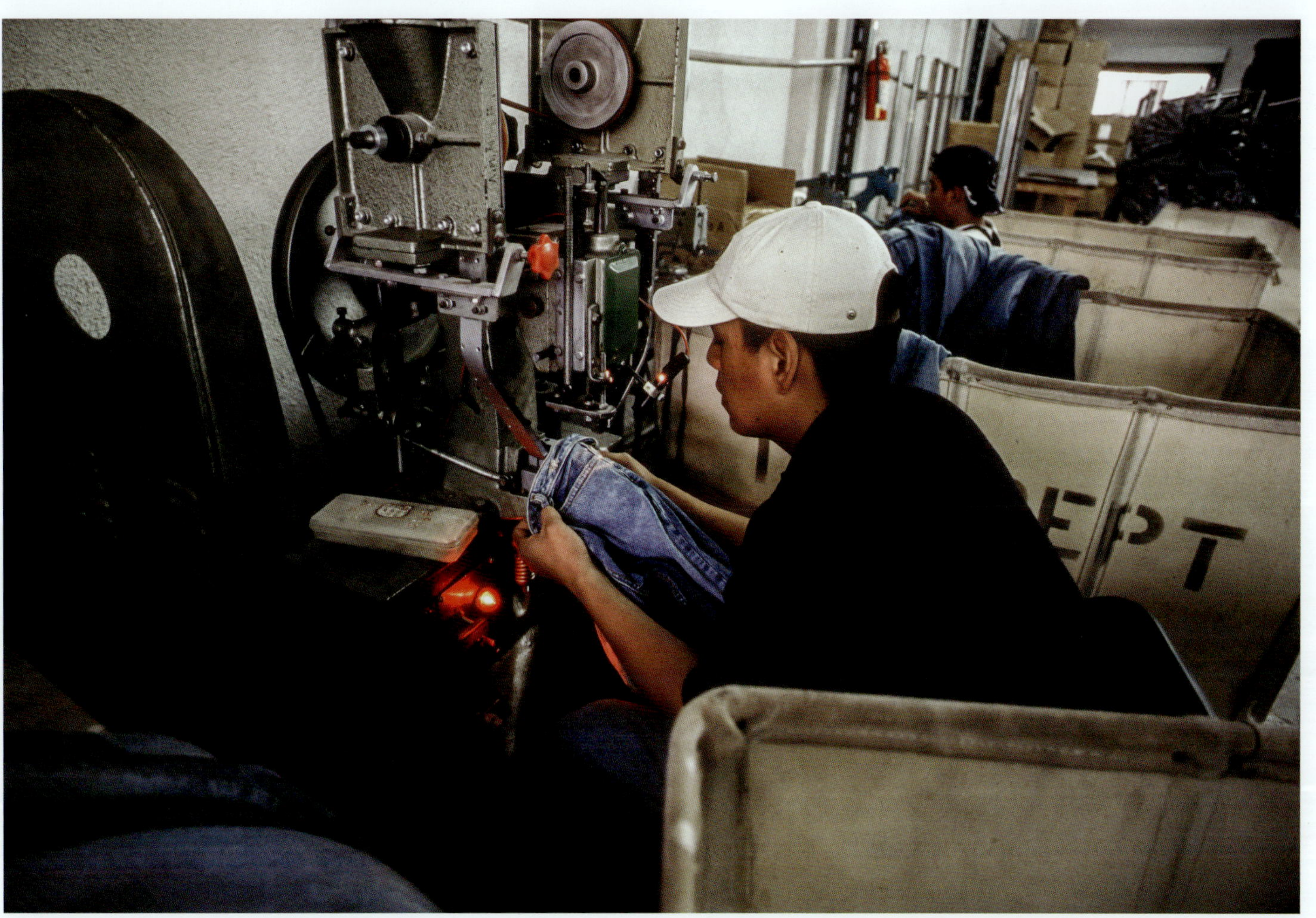

EPT

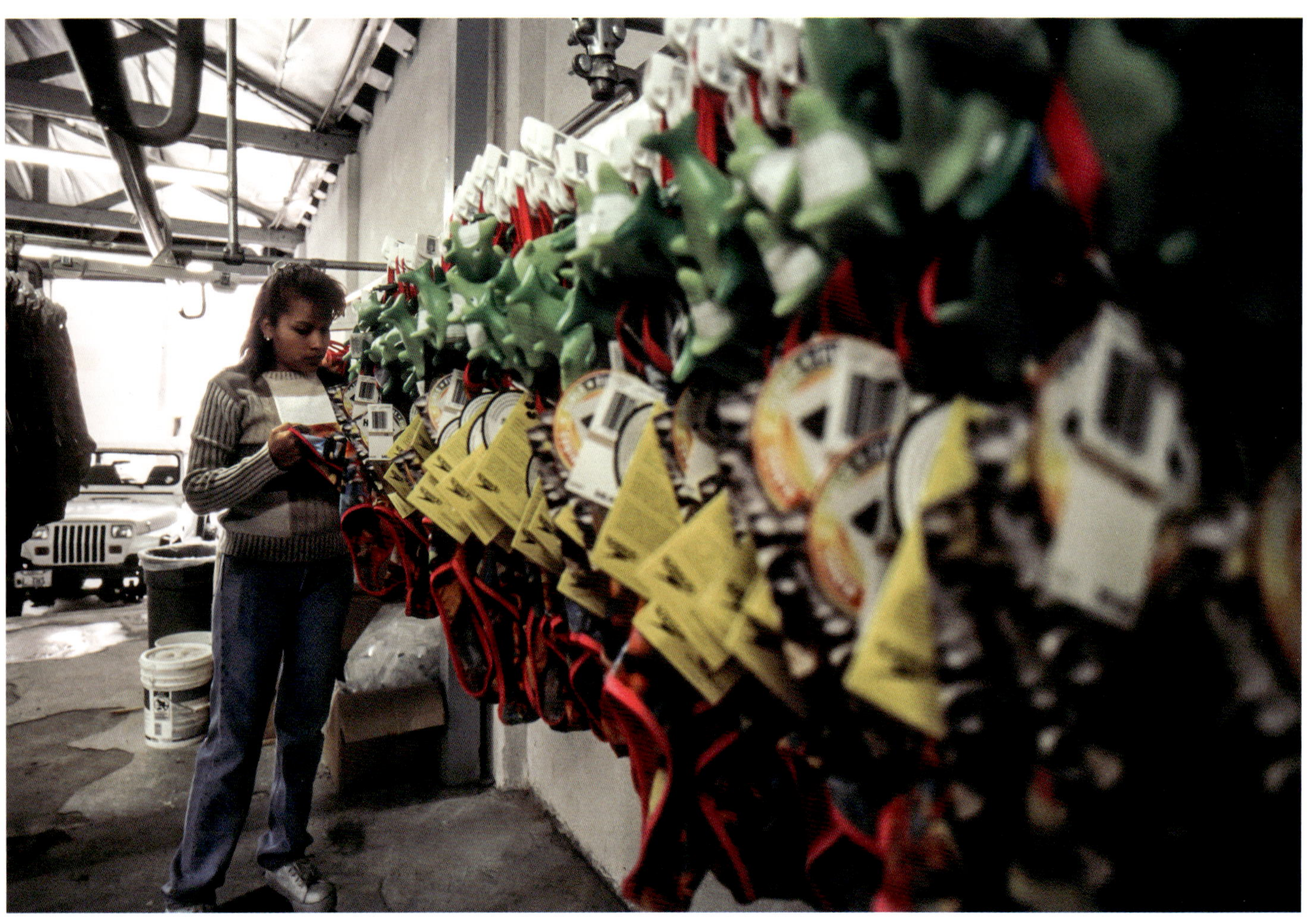

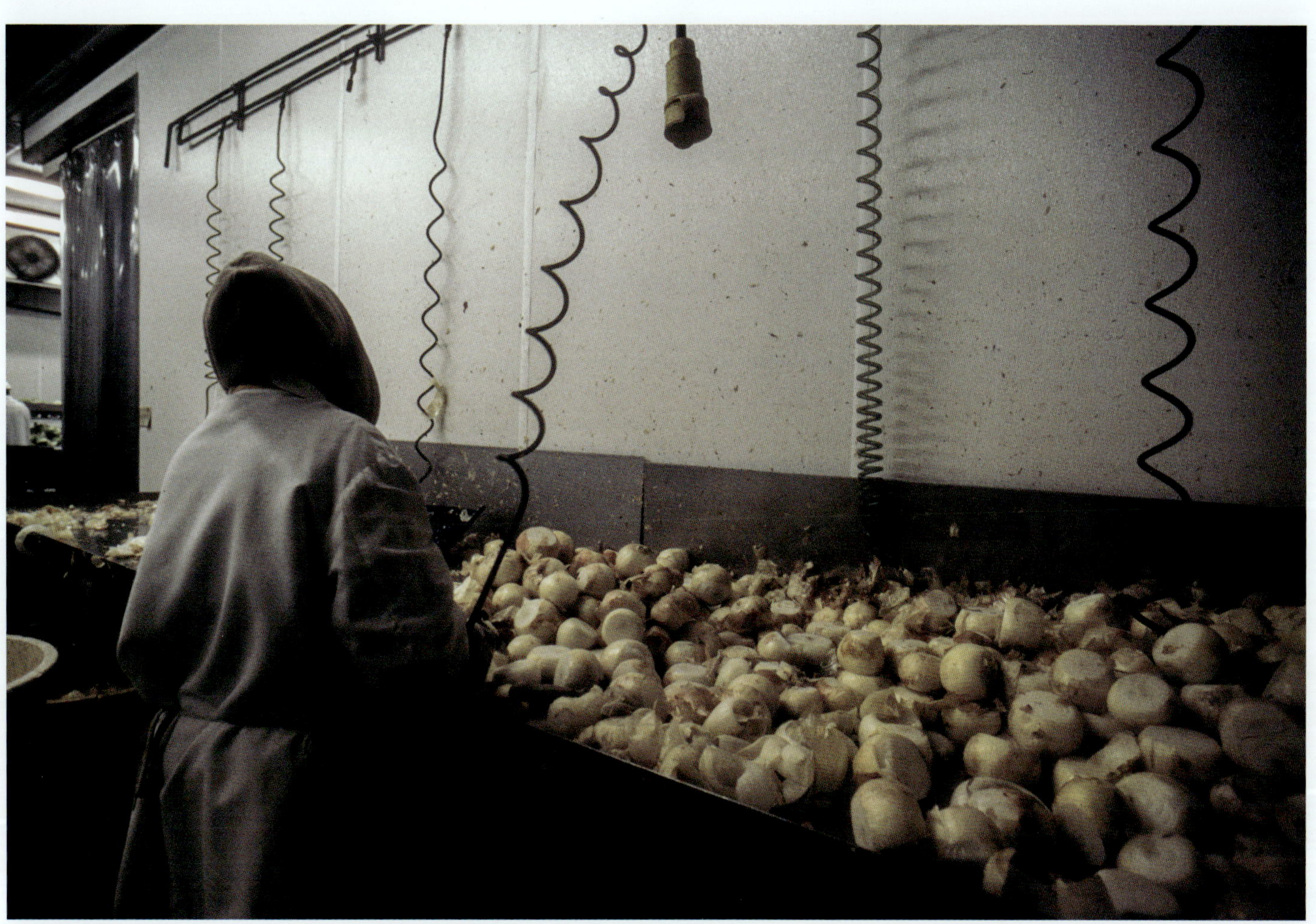

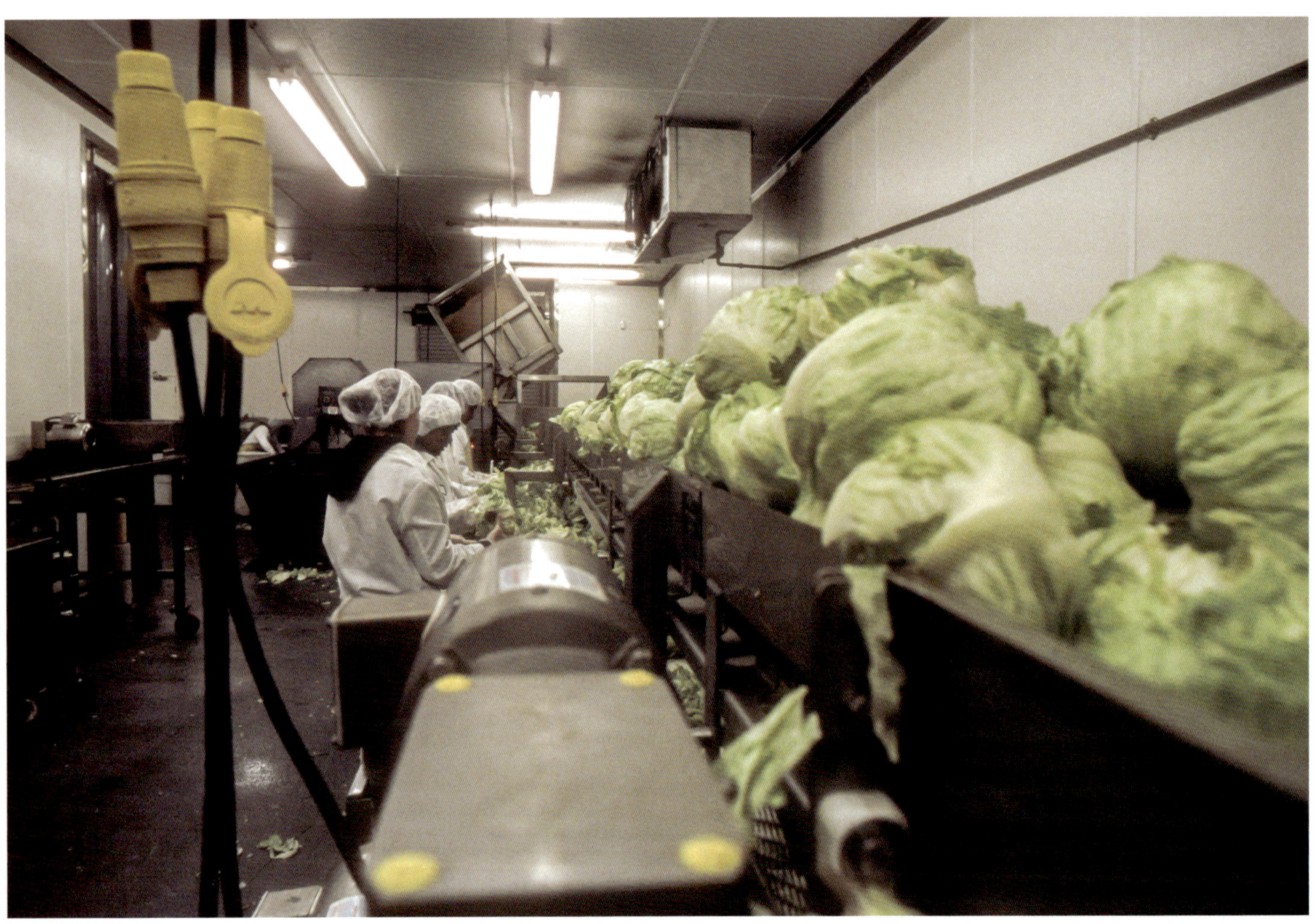

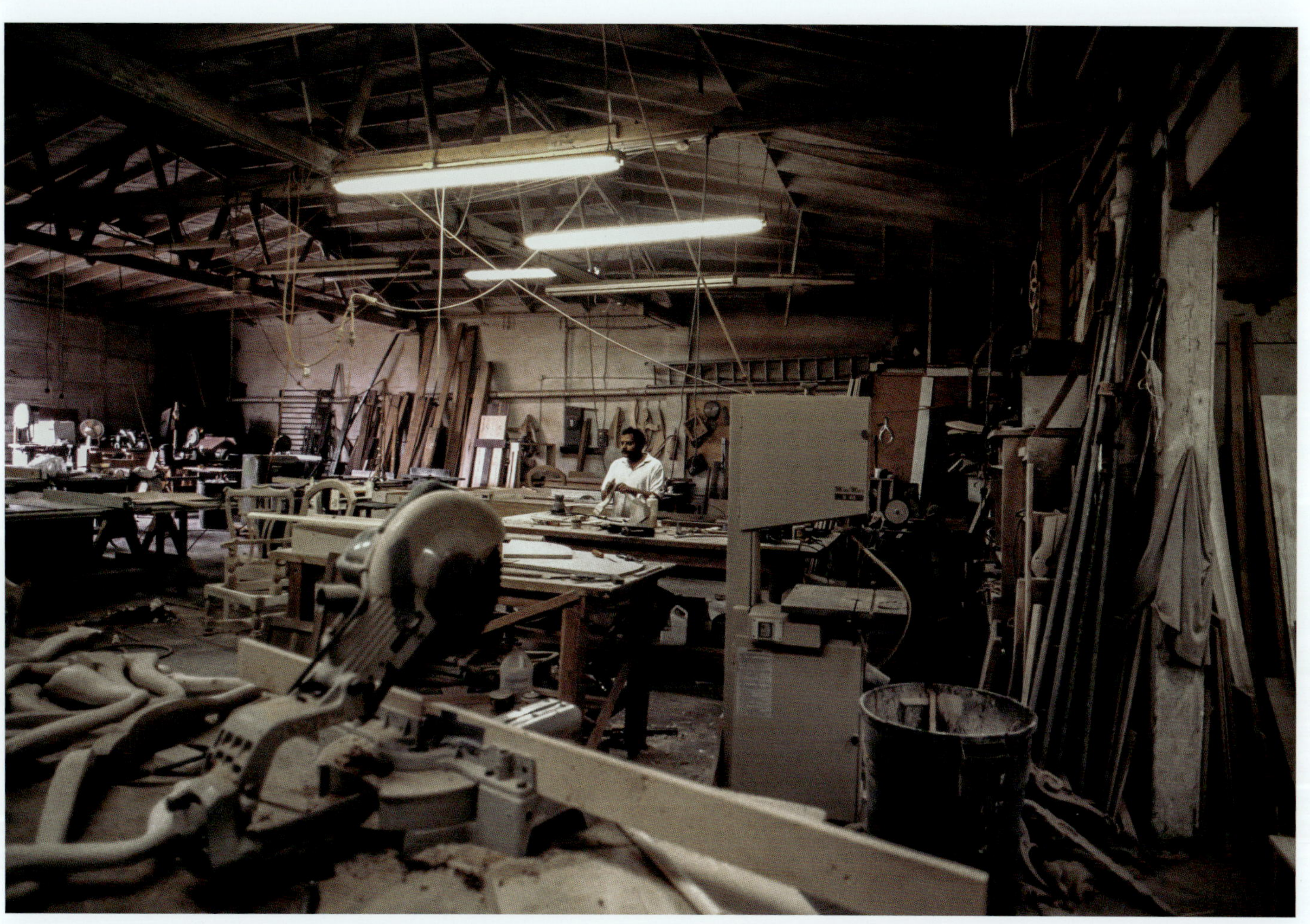

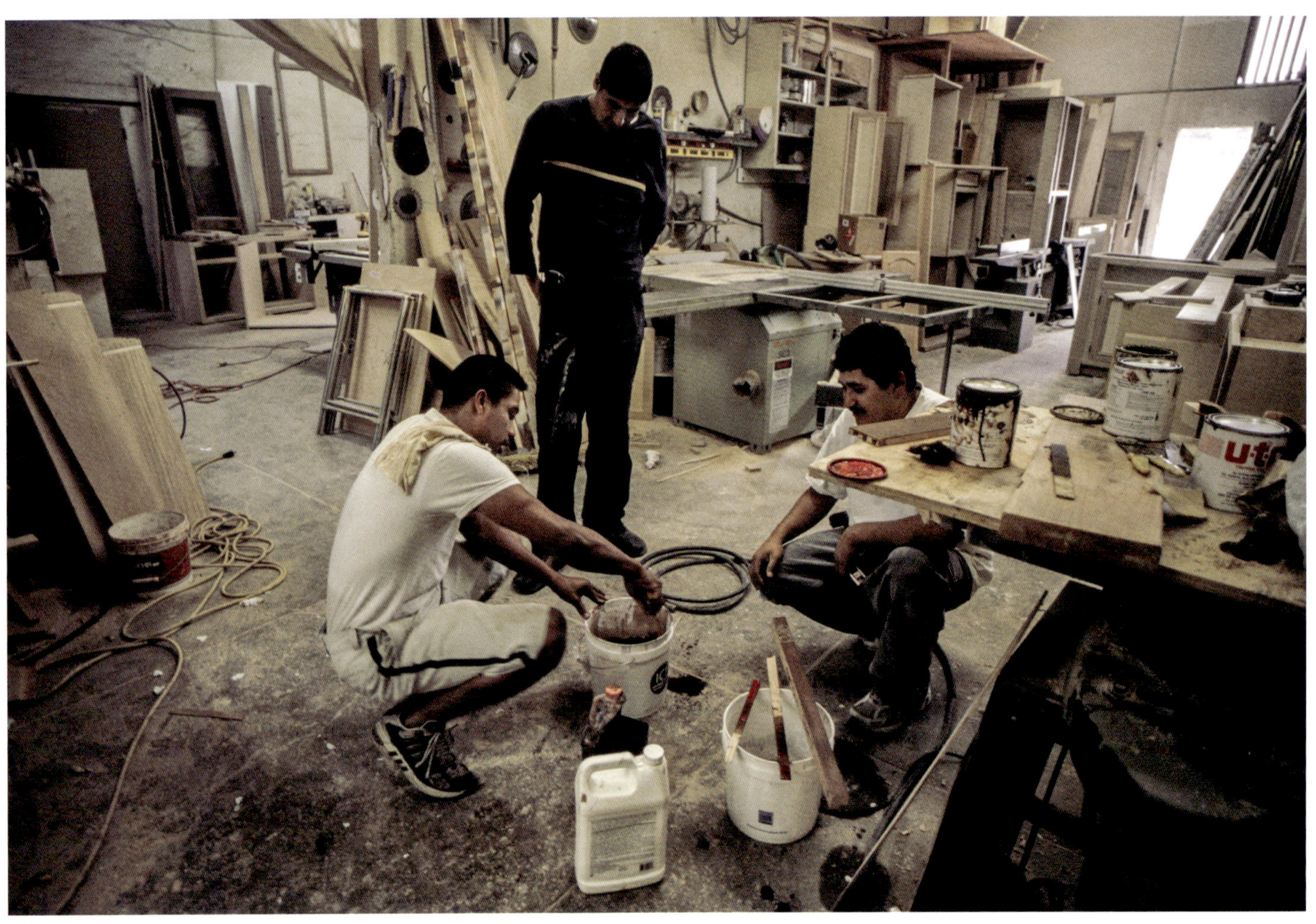

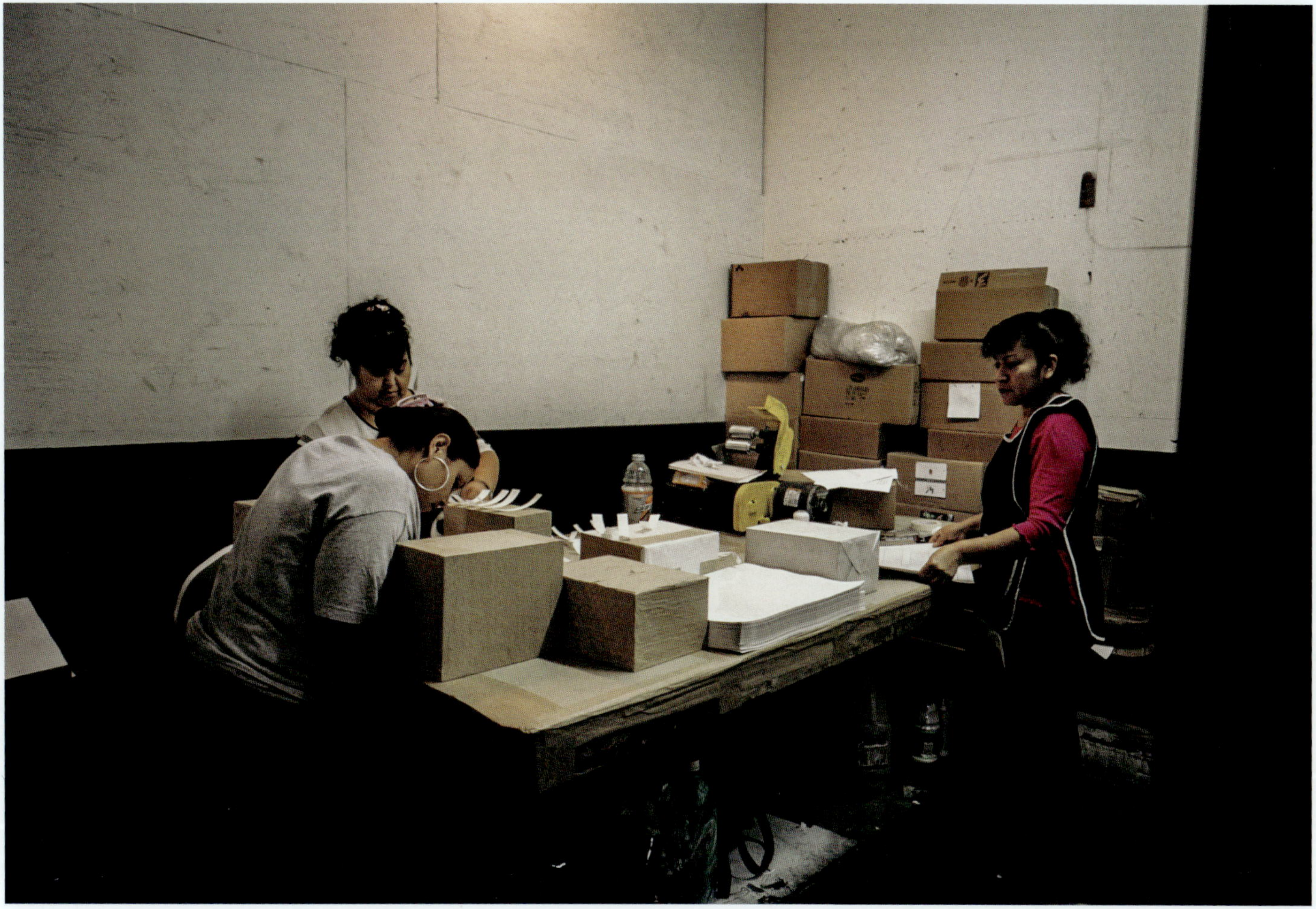

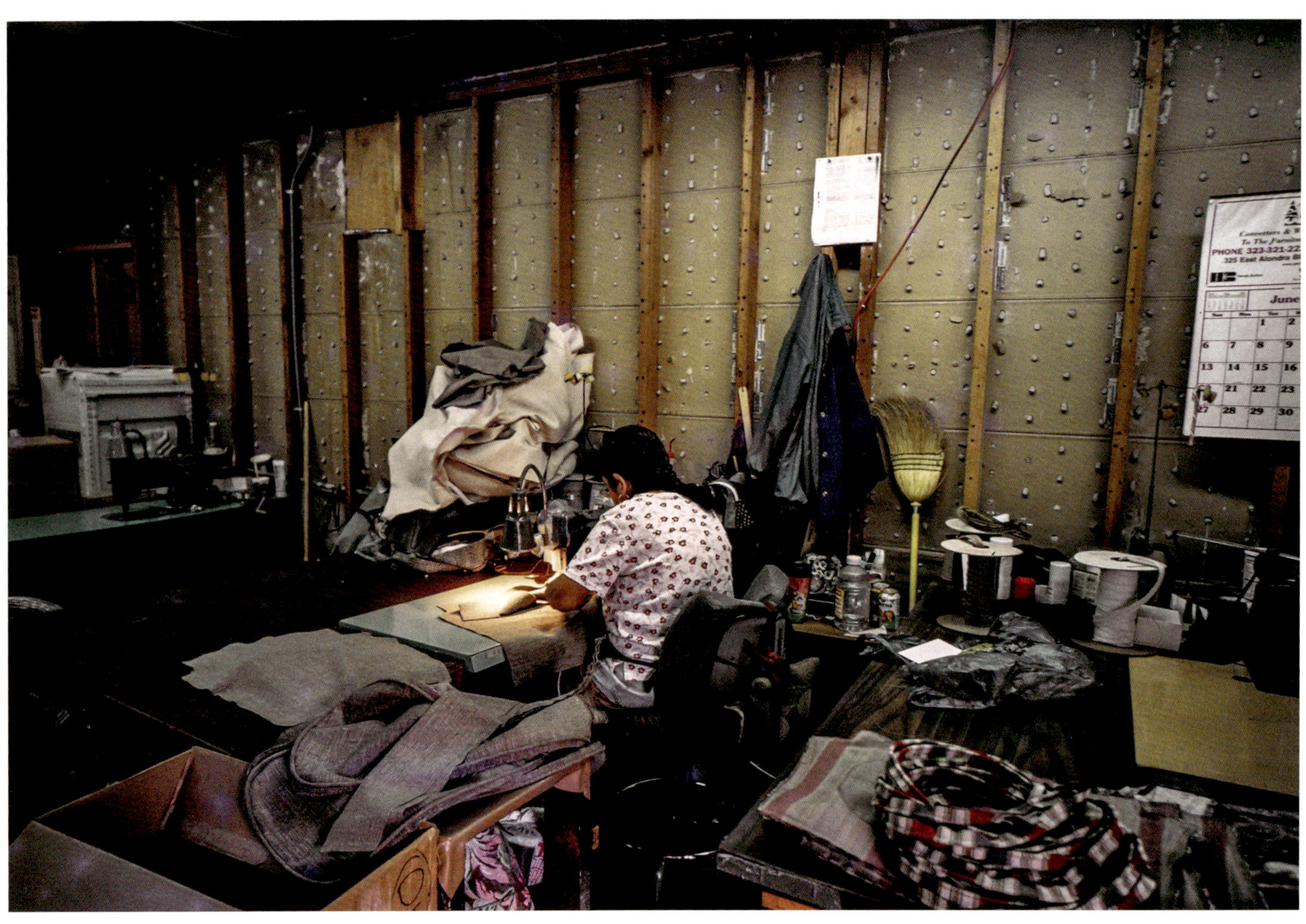

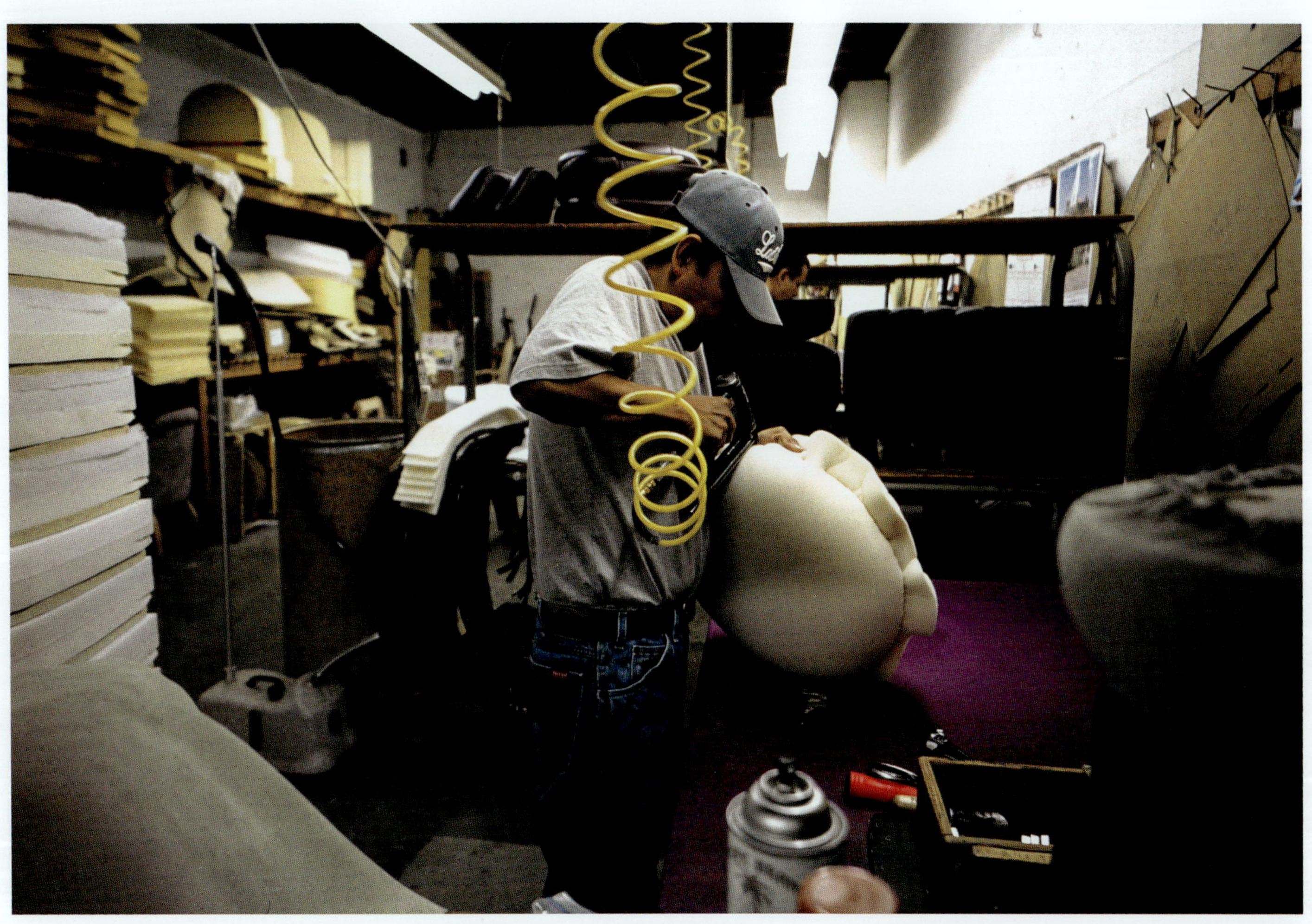

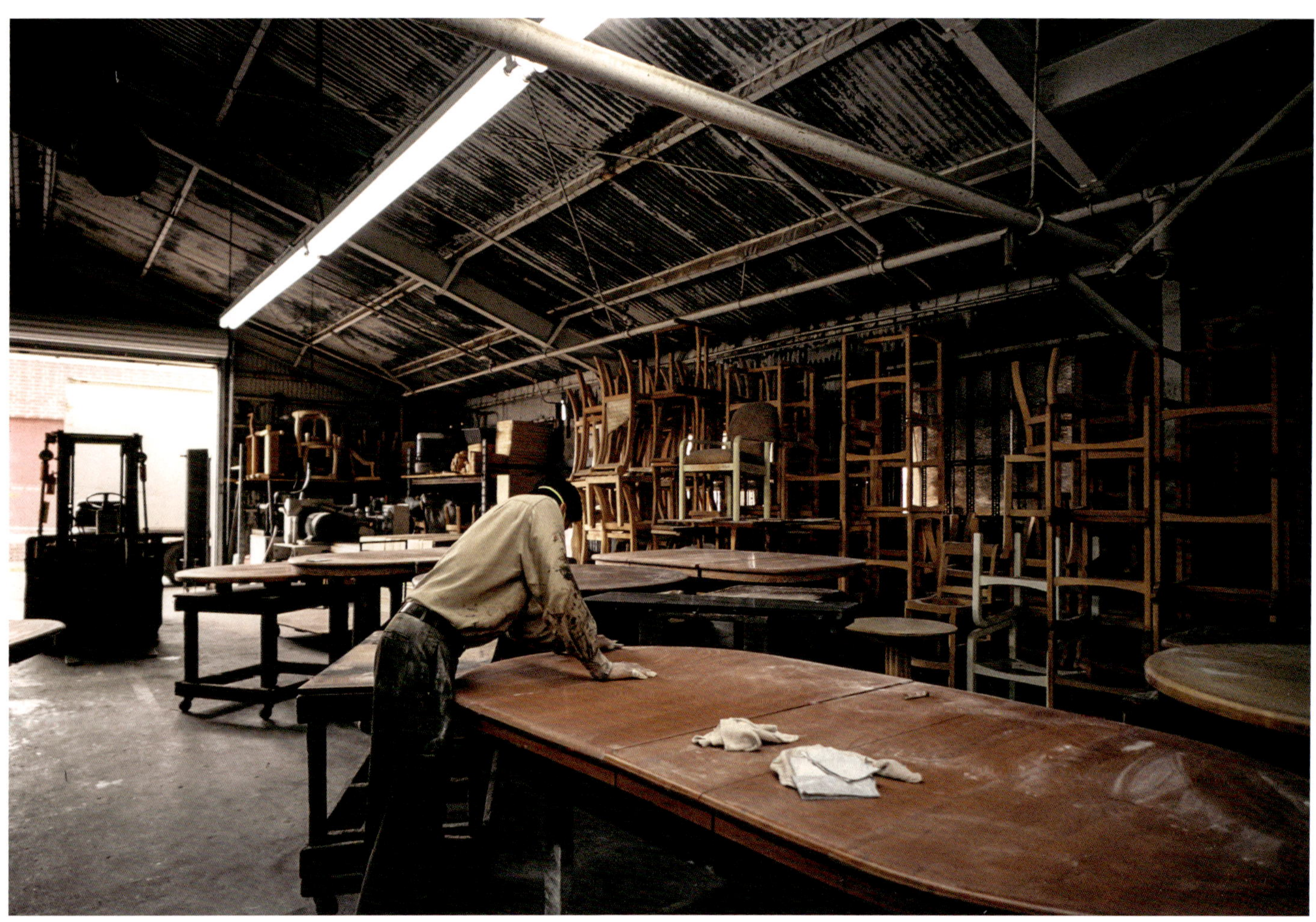

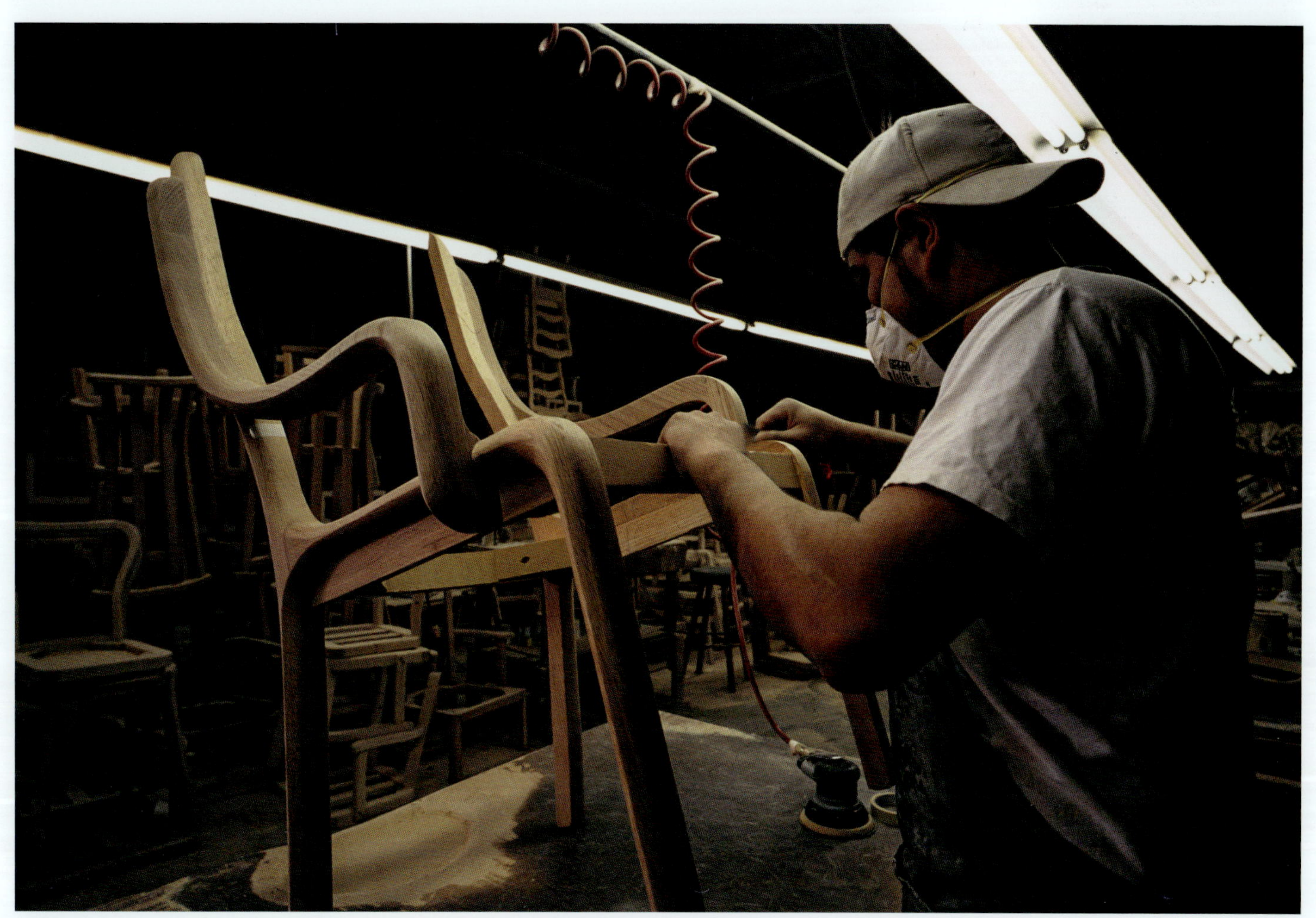

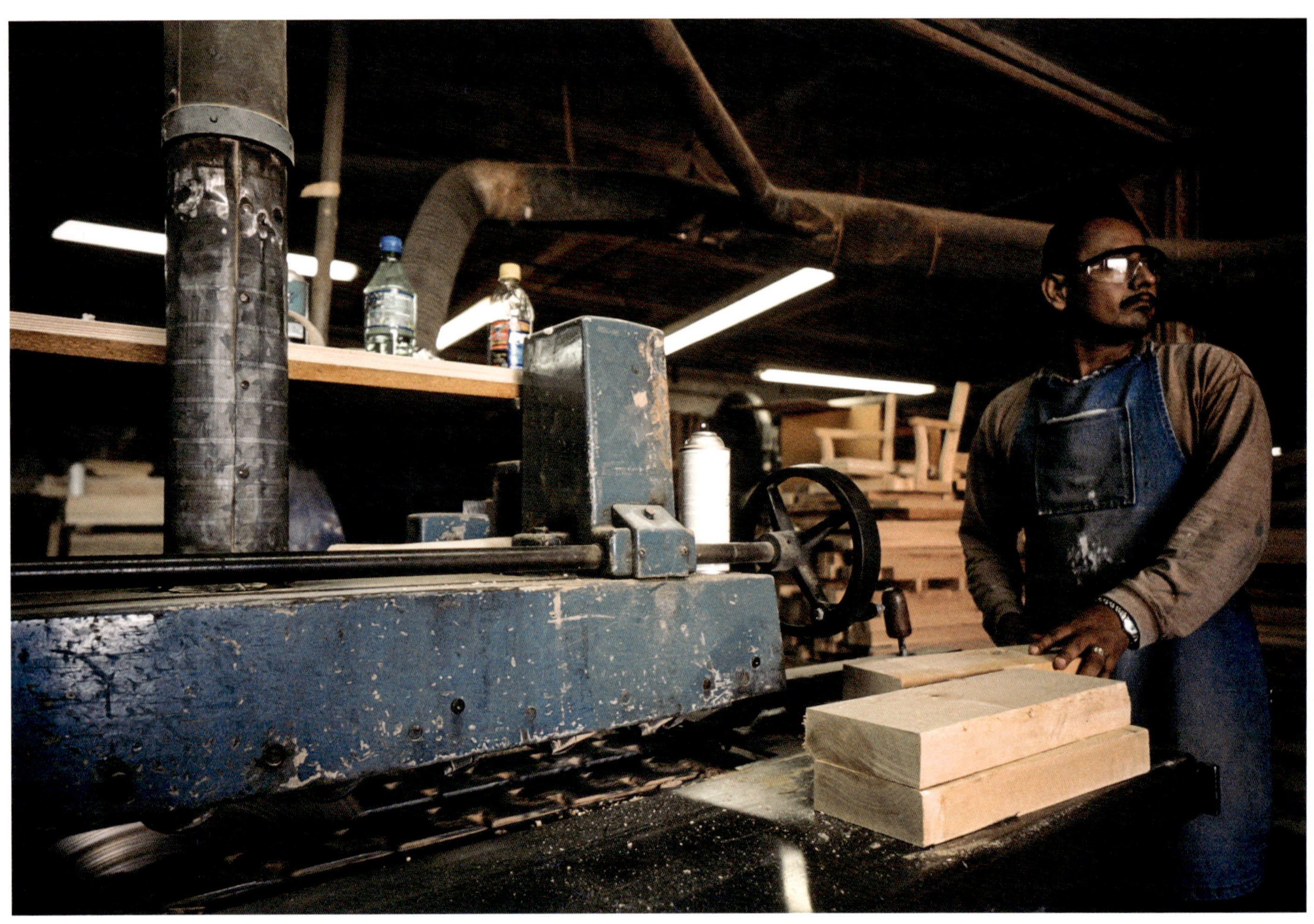

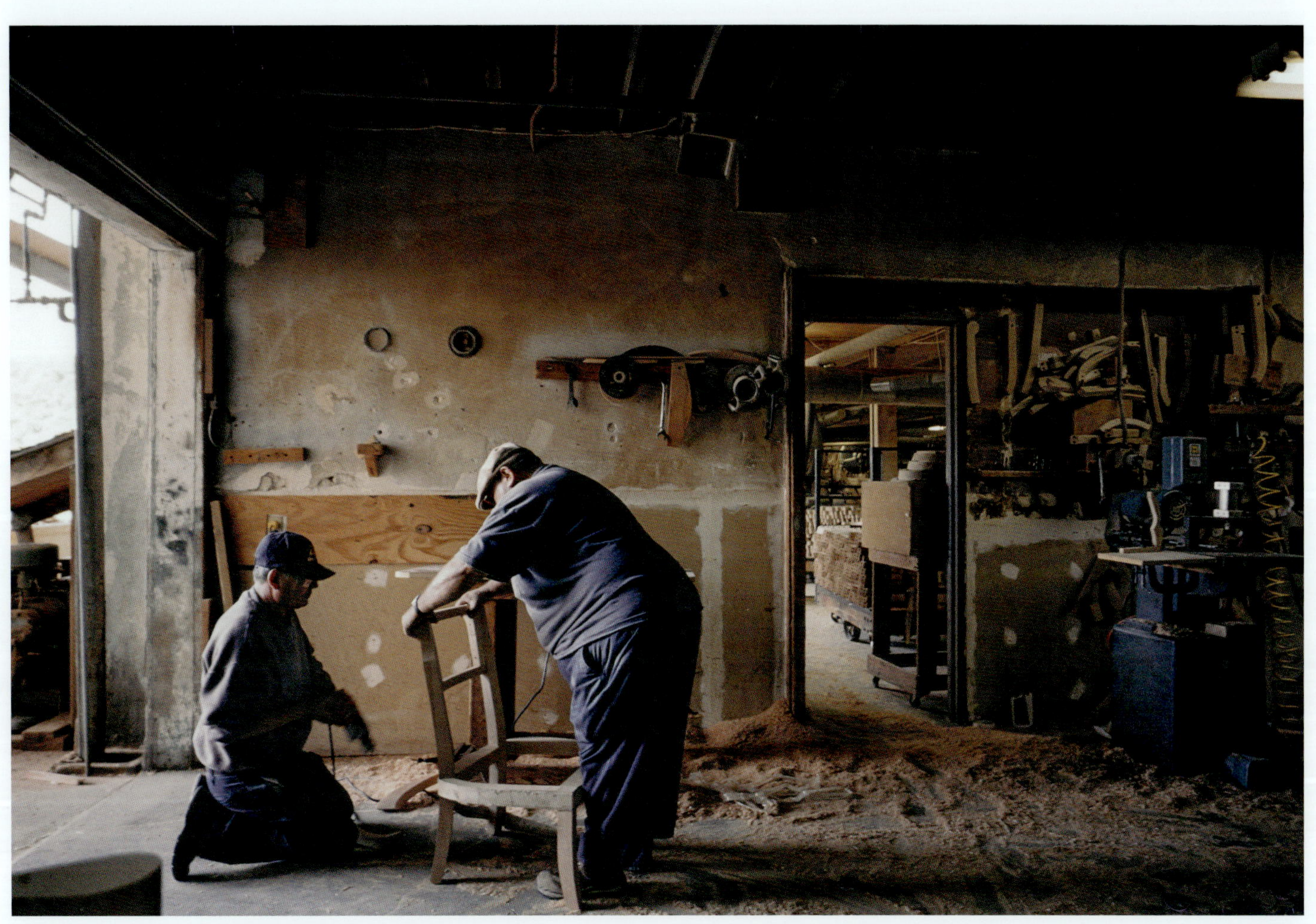

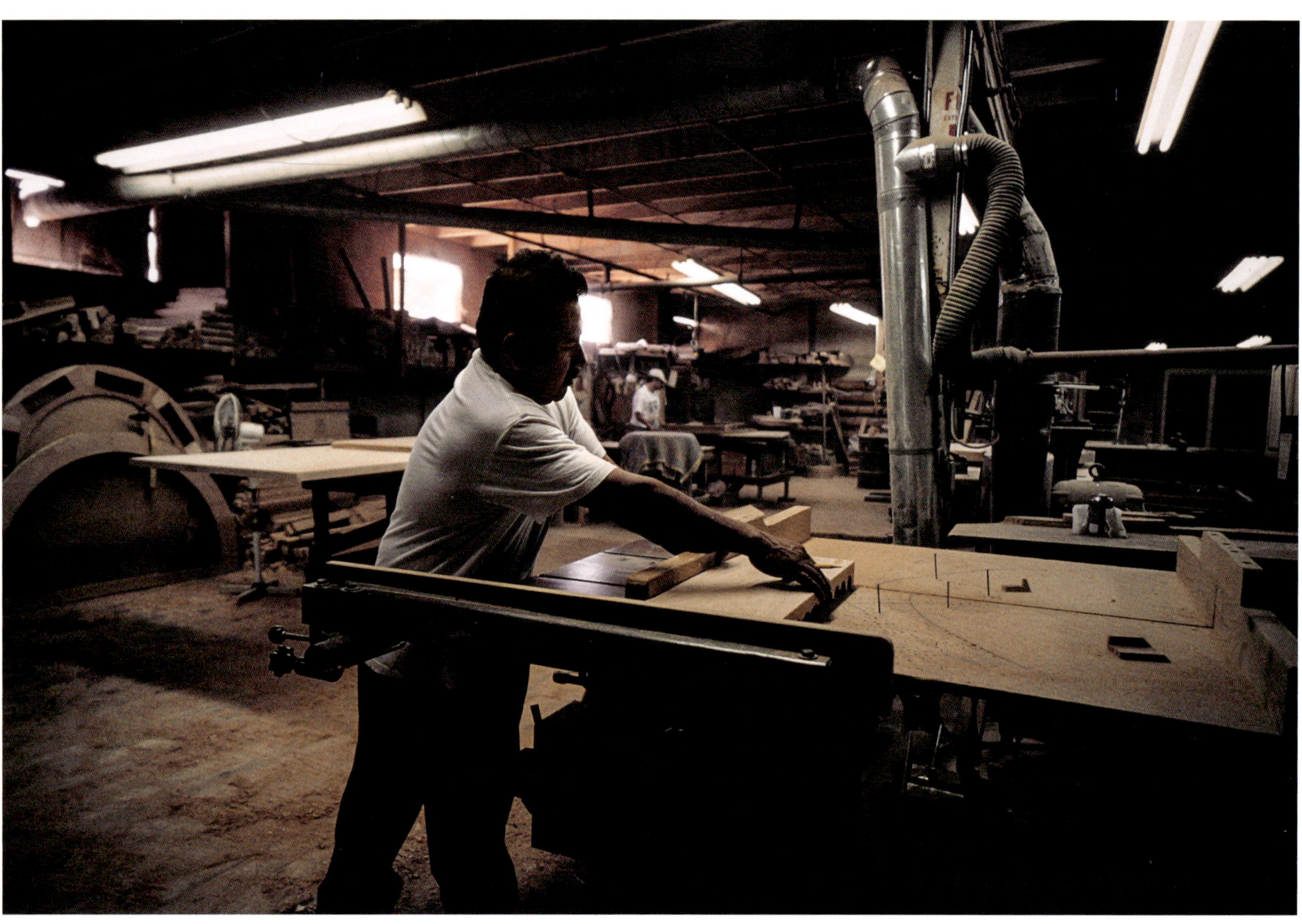

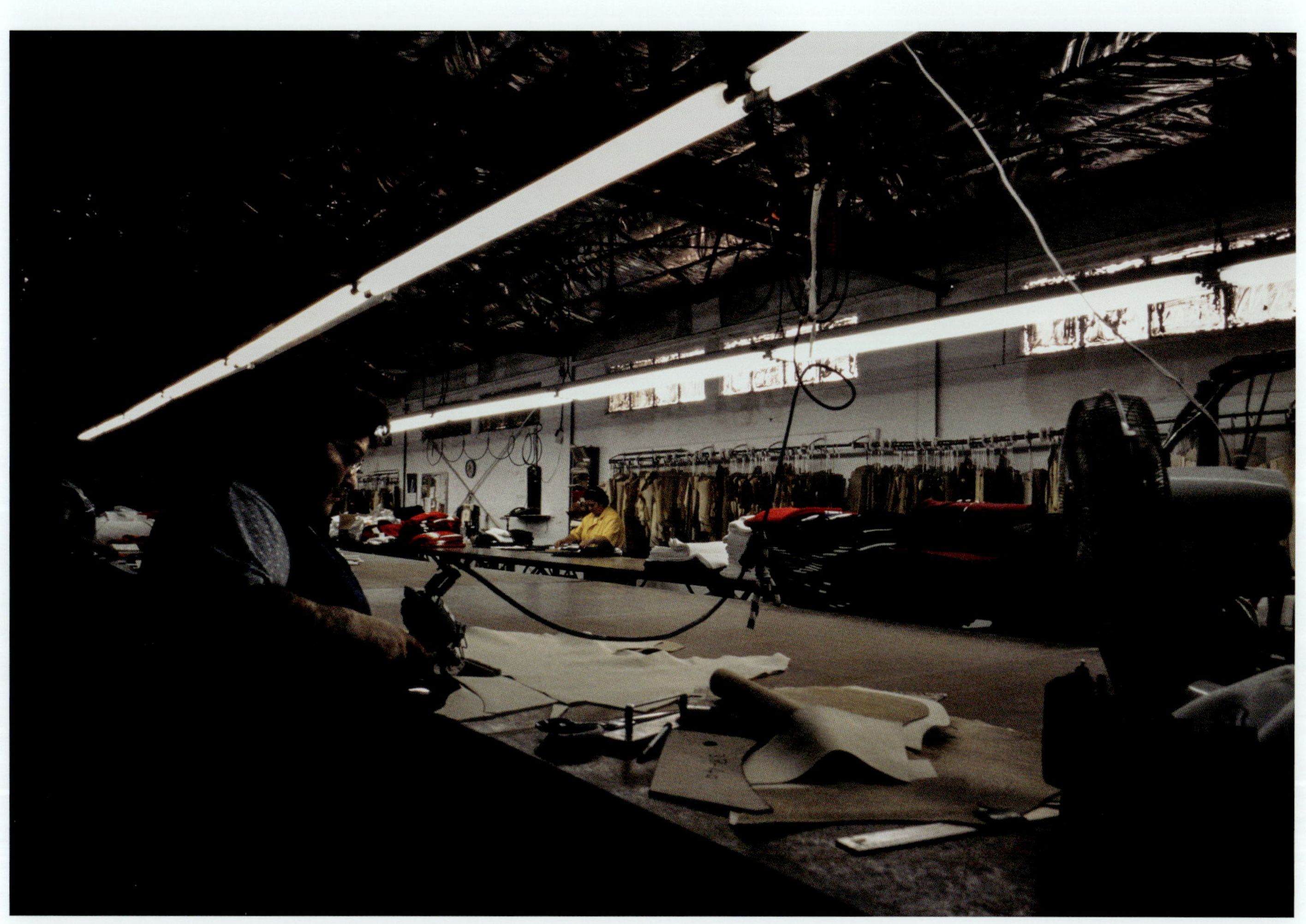

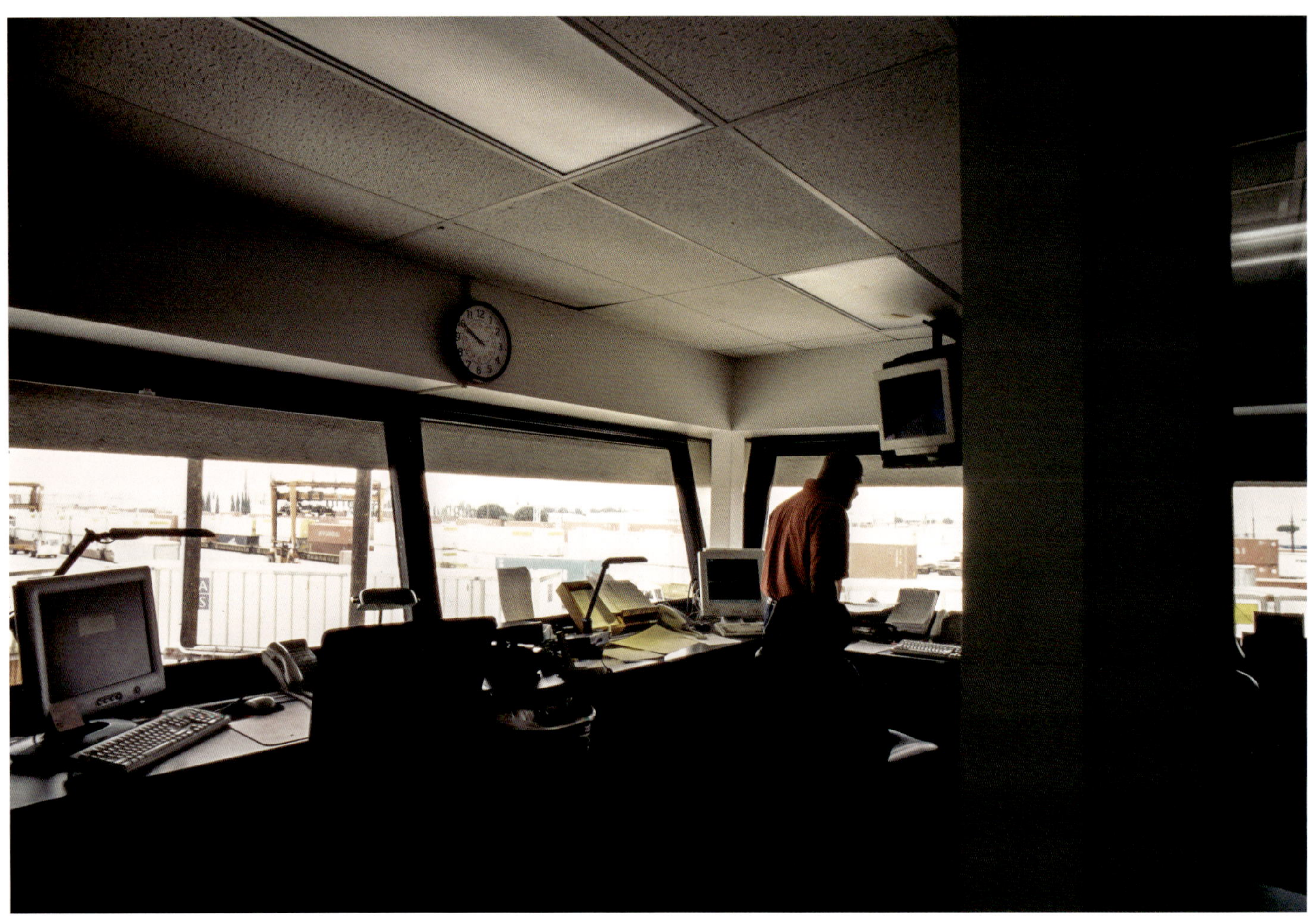

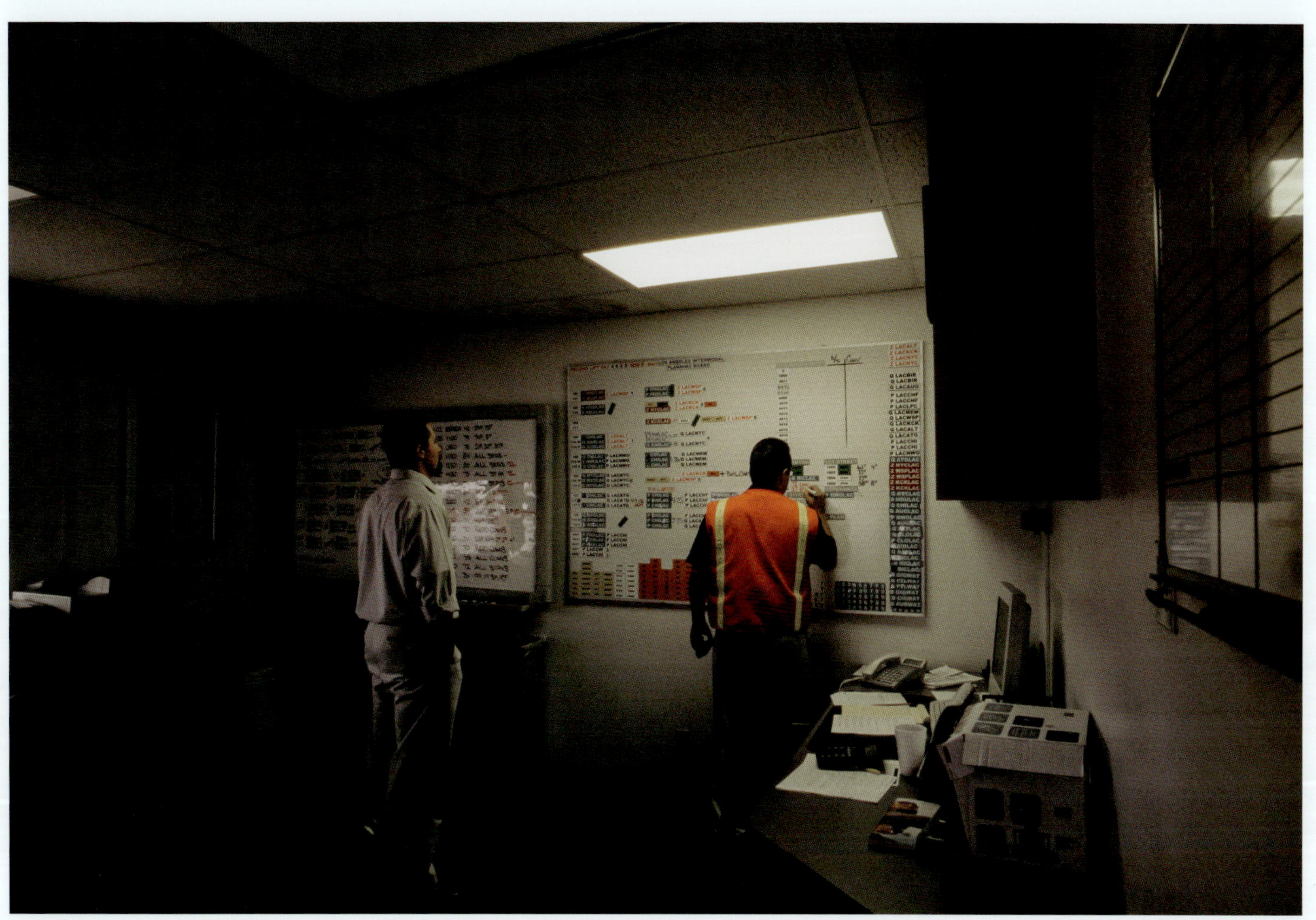

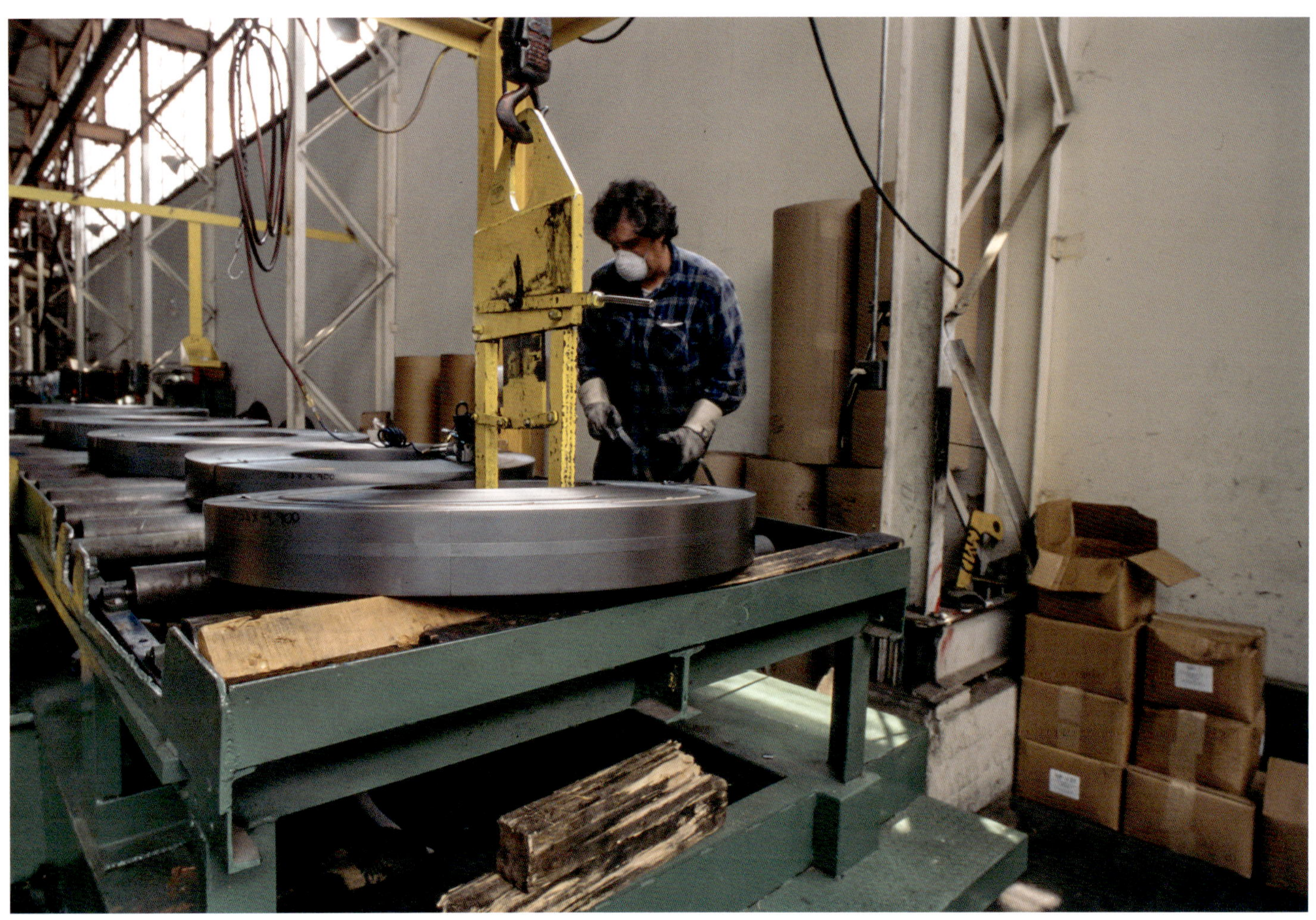

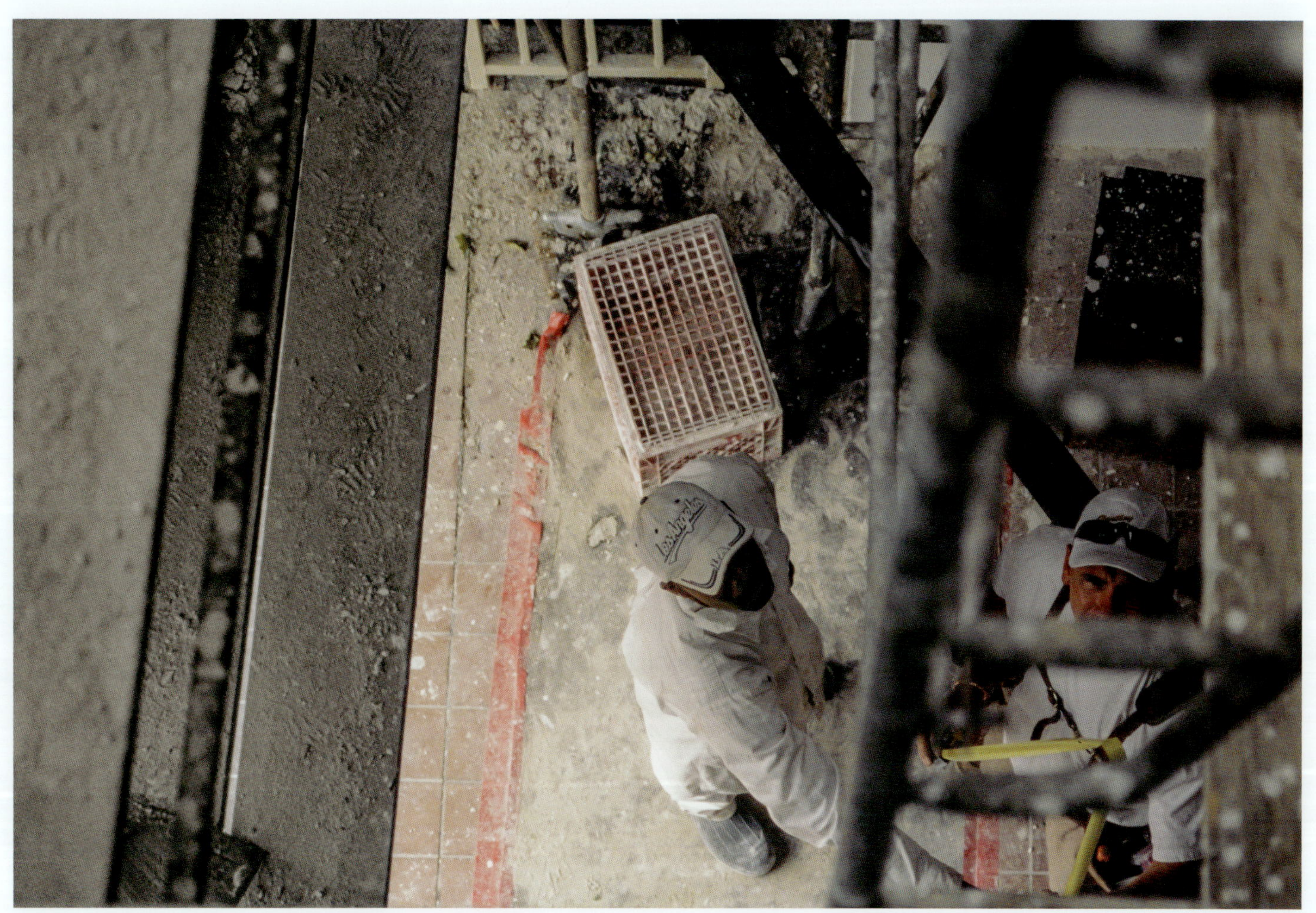

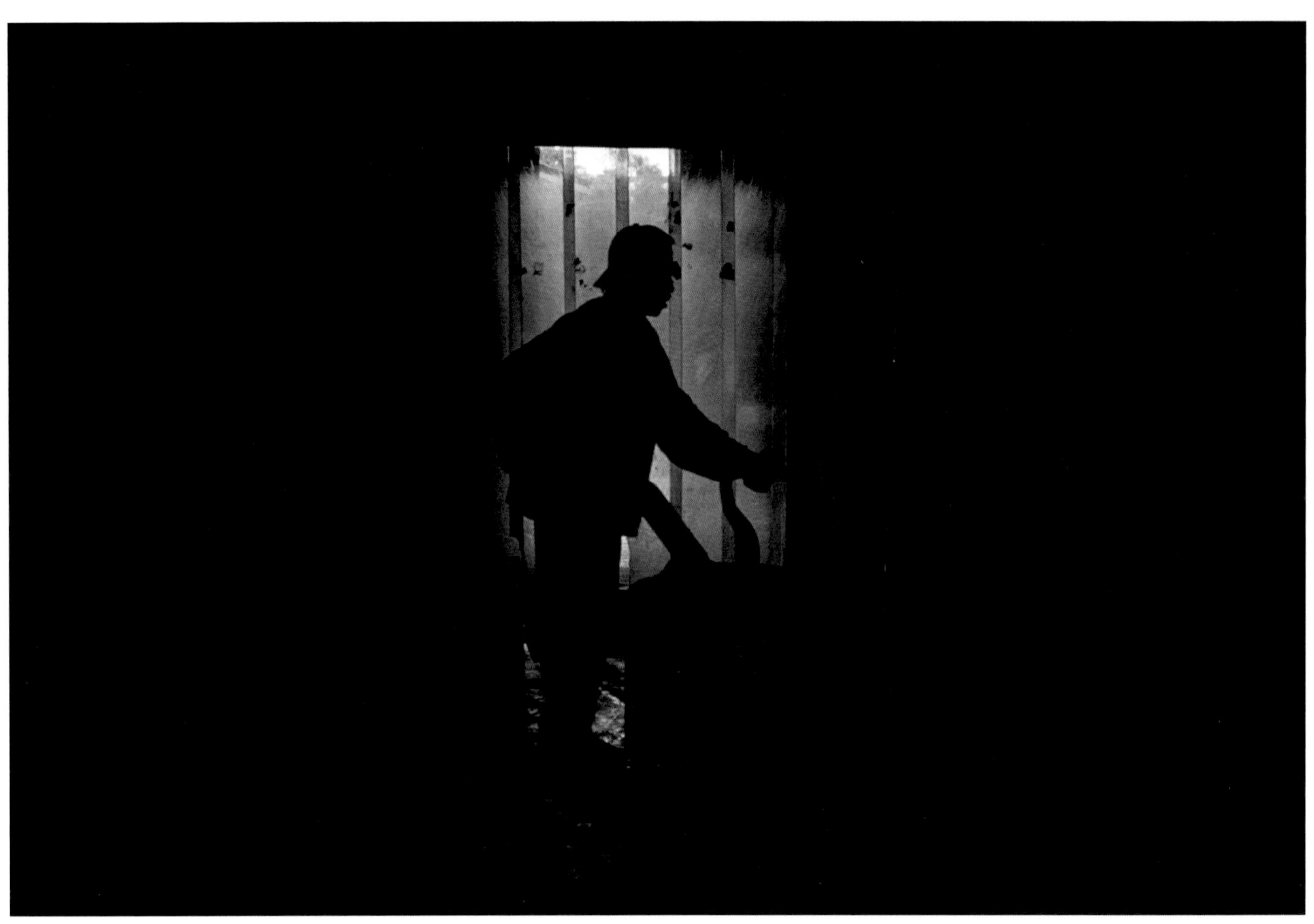

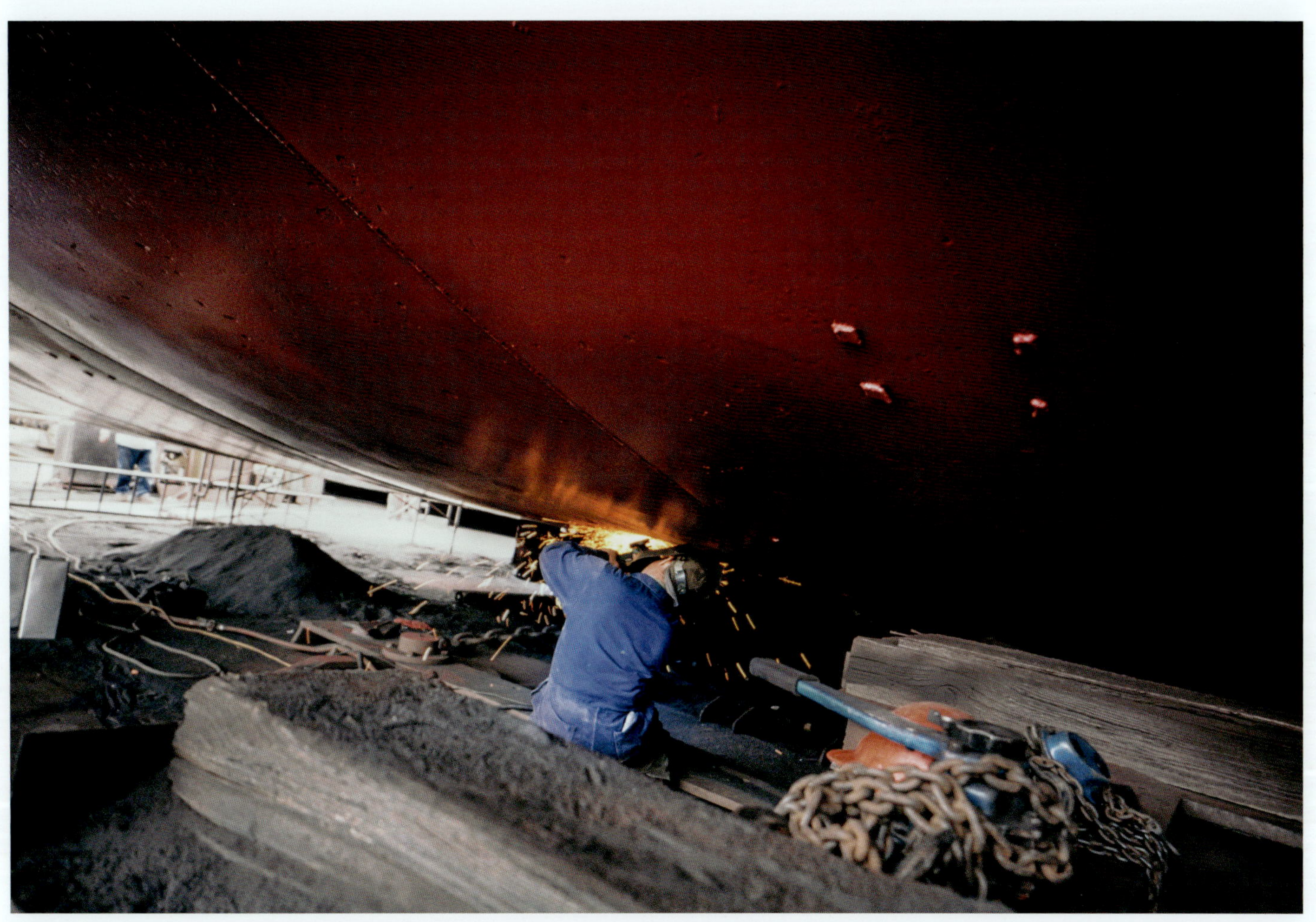

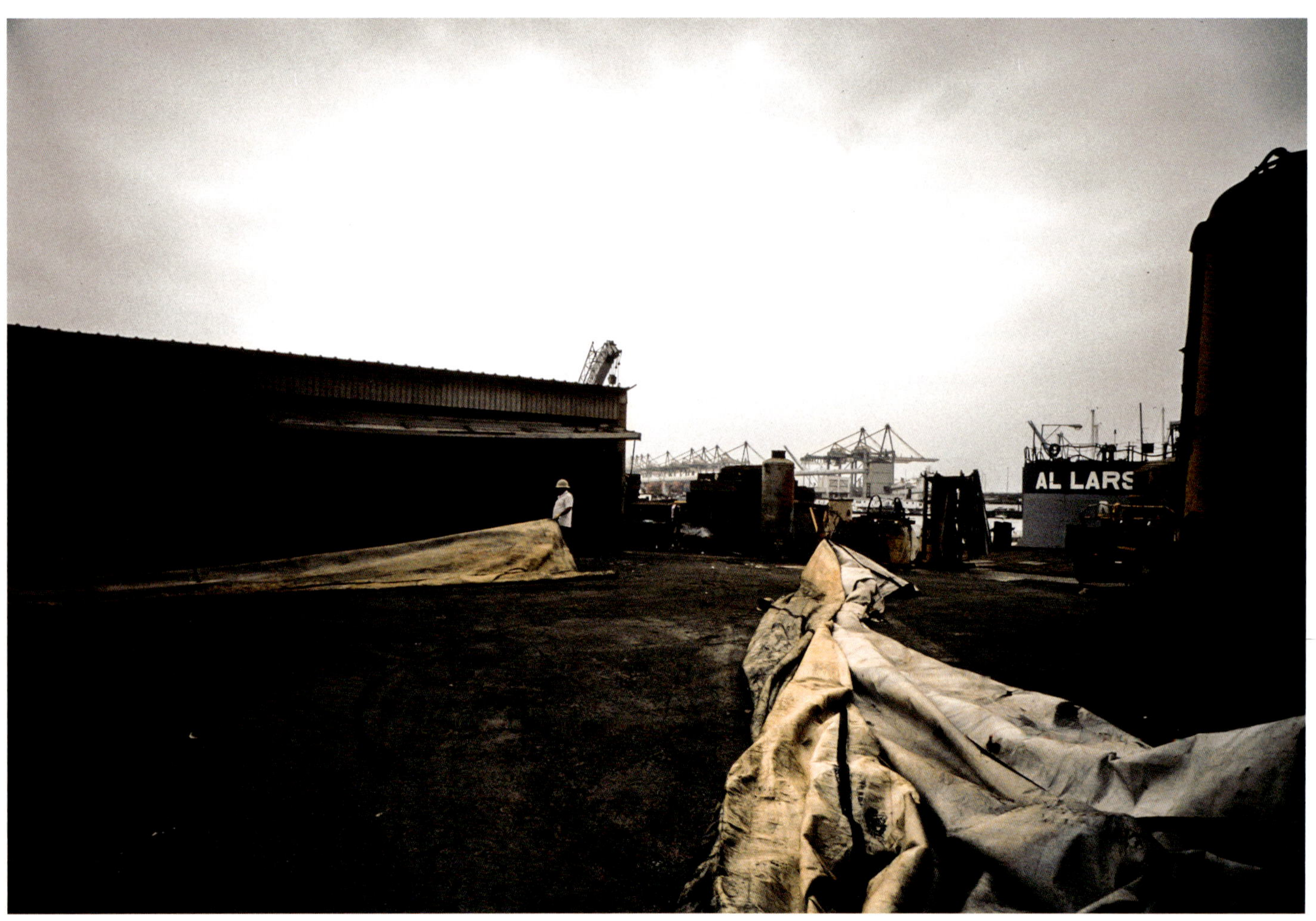

AL LARS

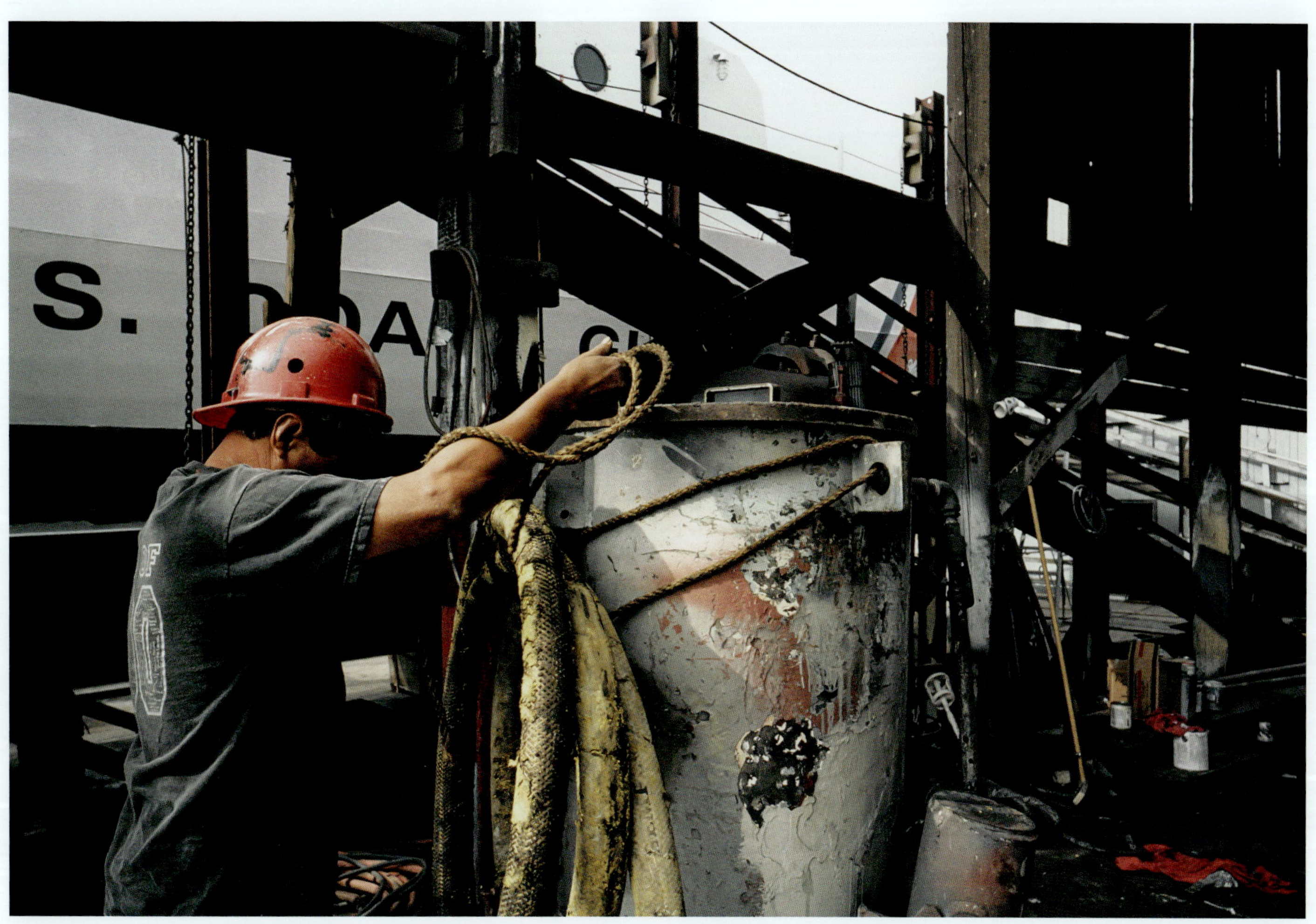
S. OA C

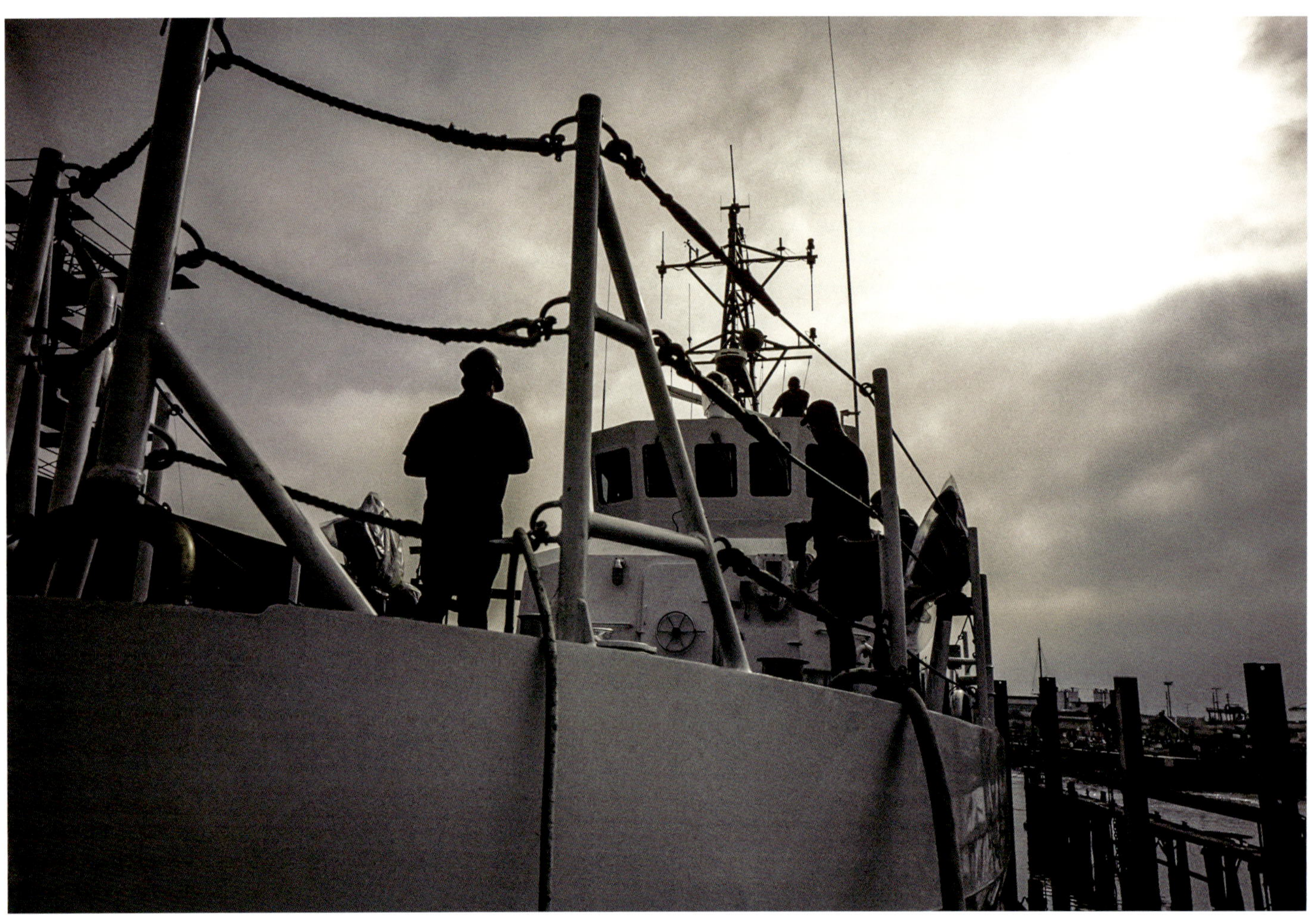

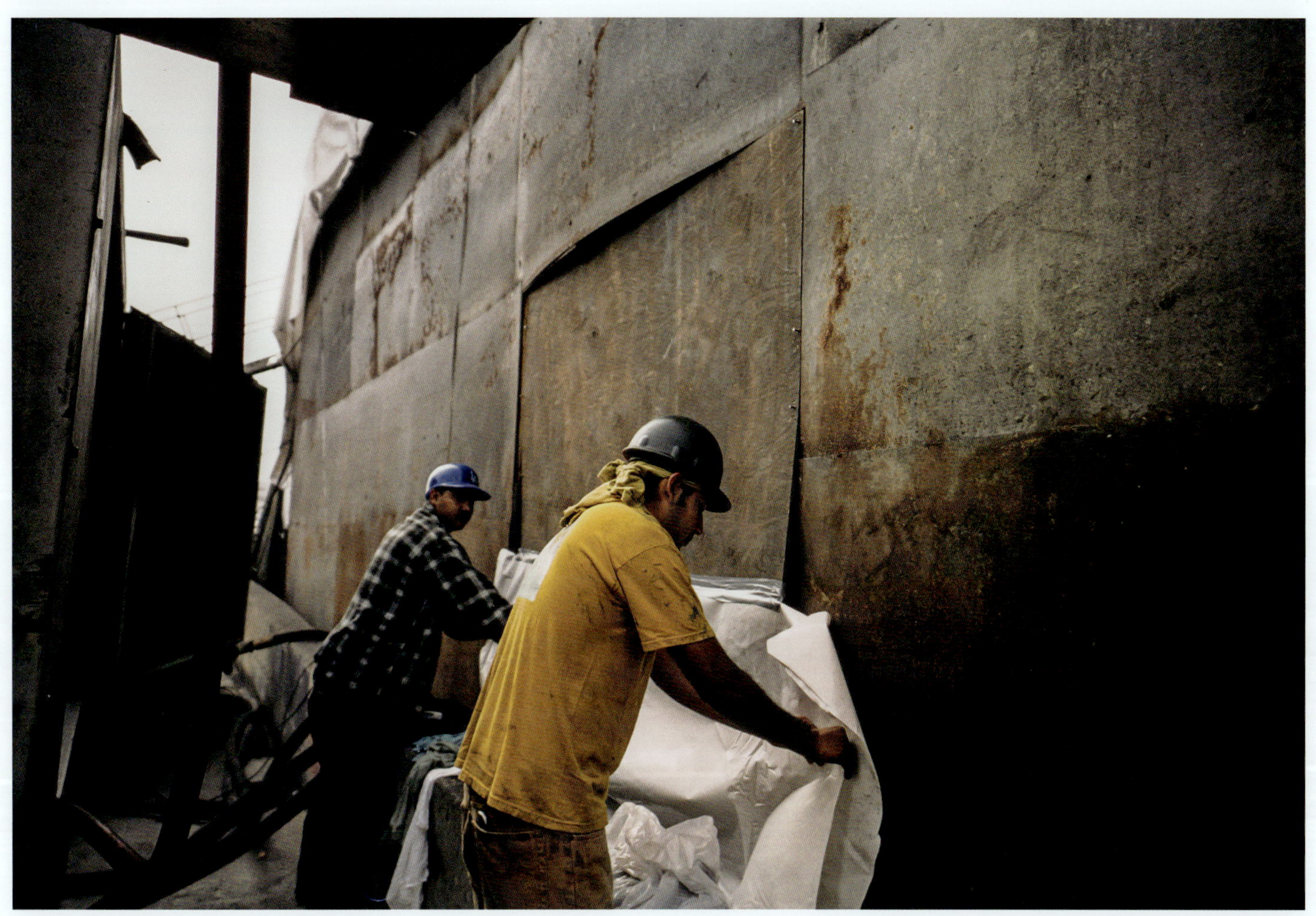

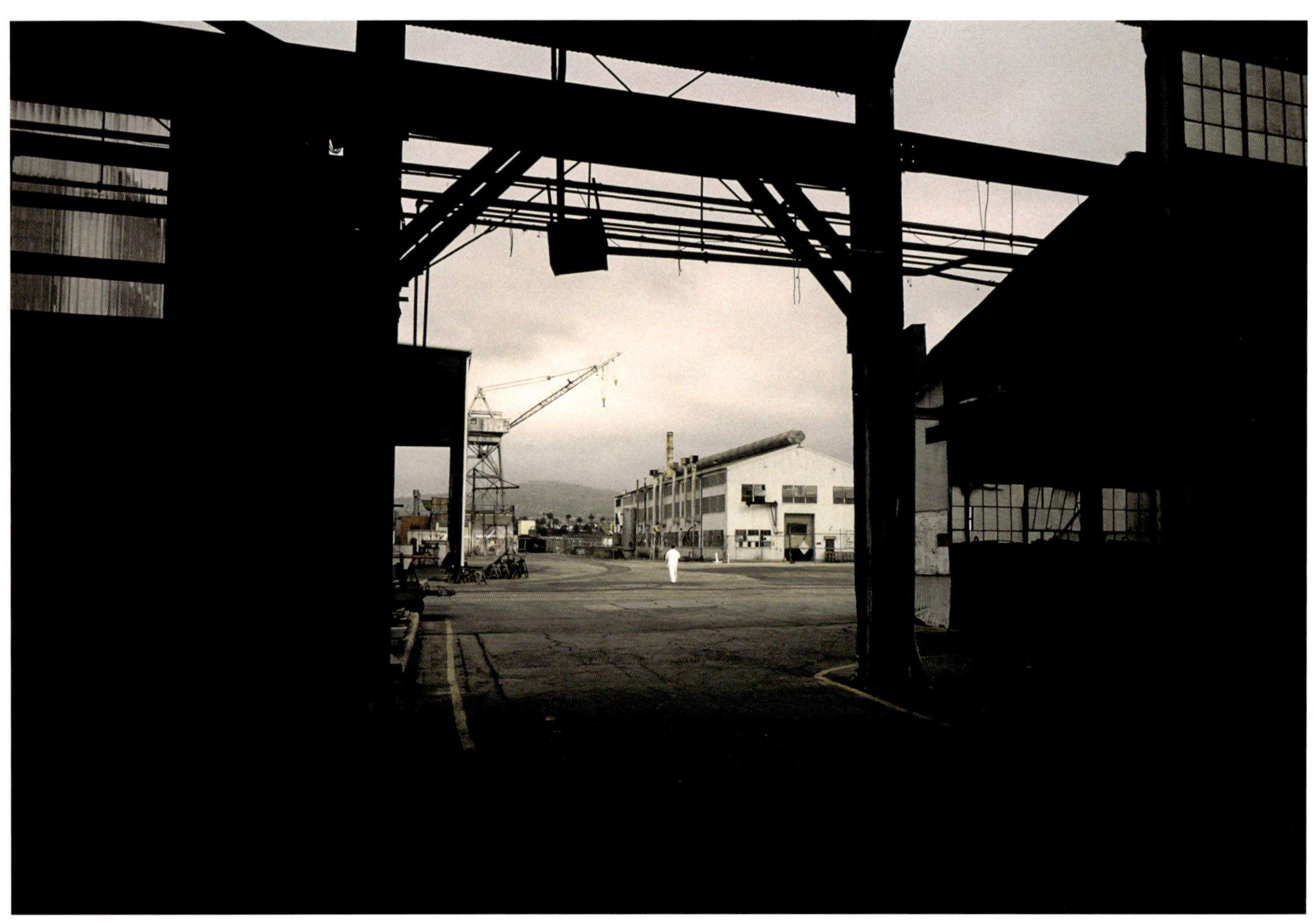

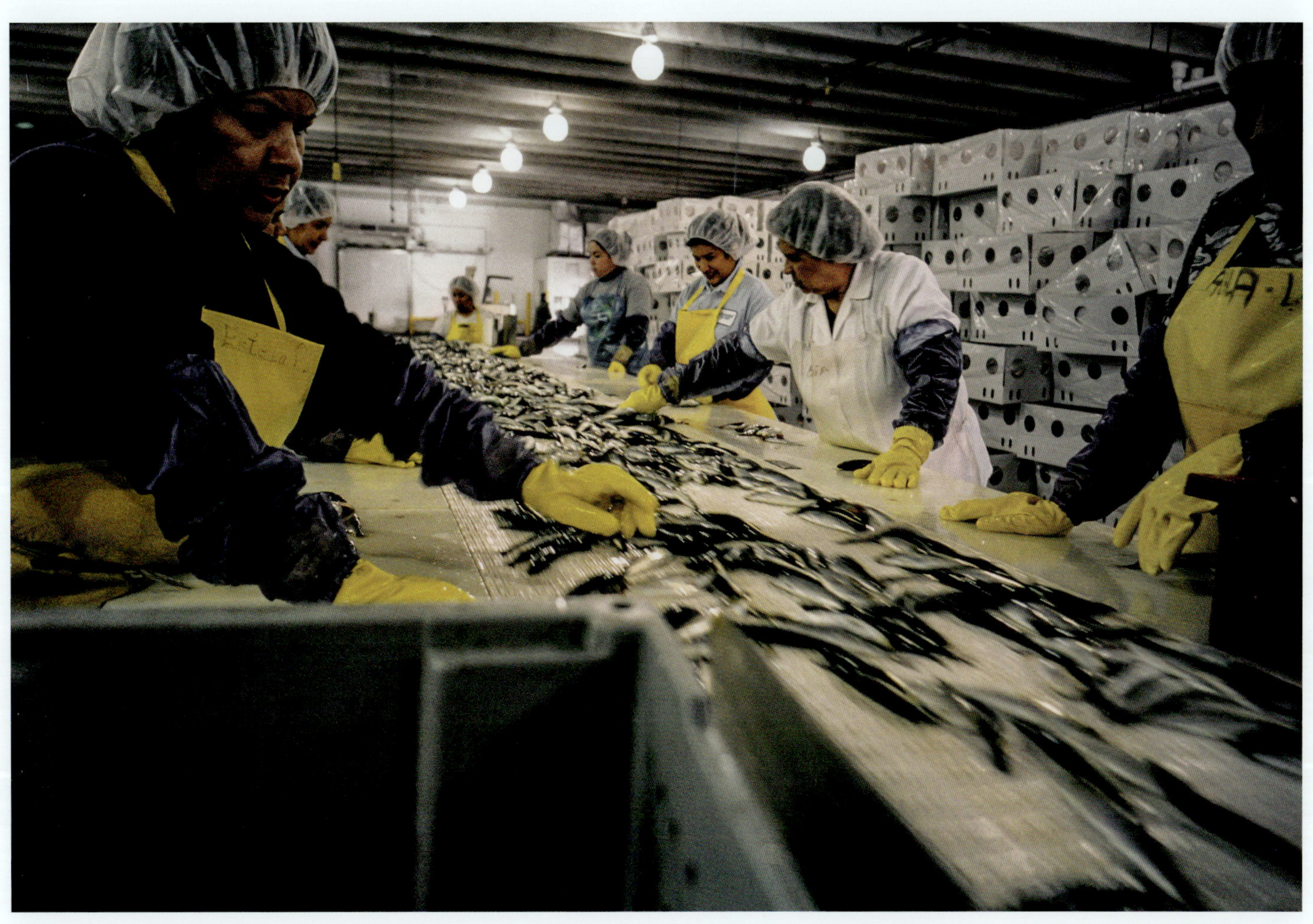

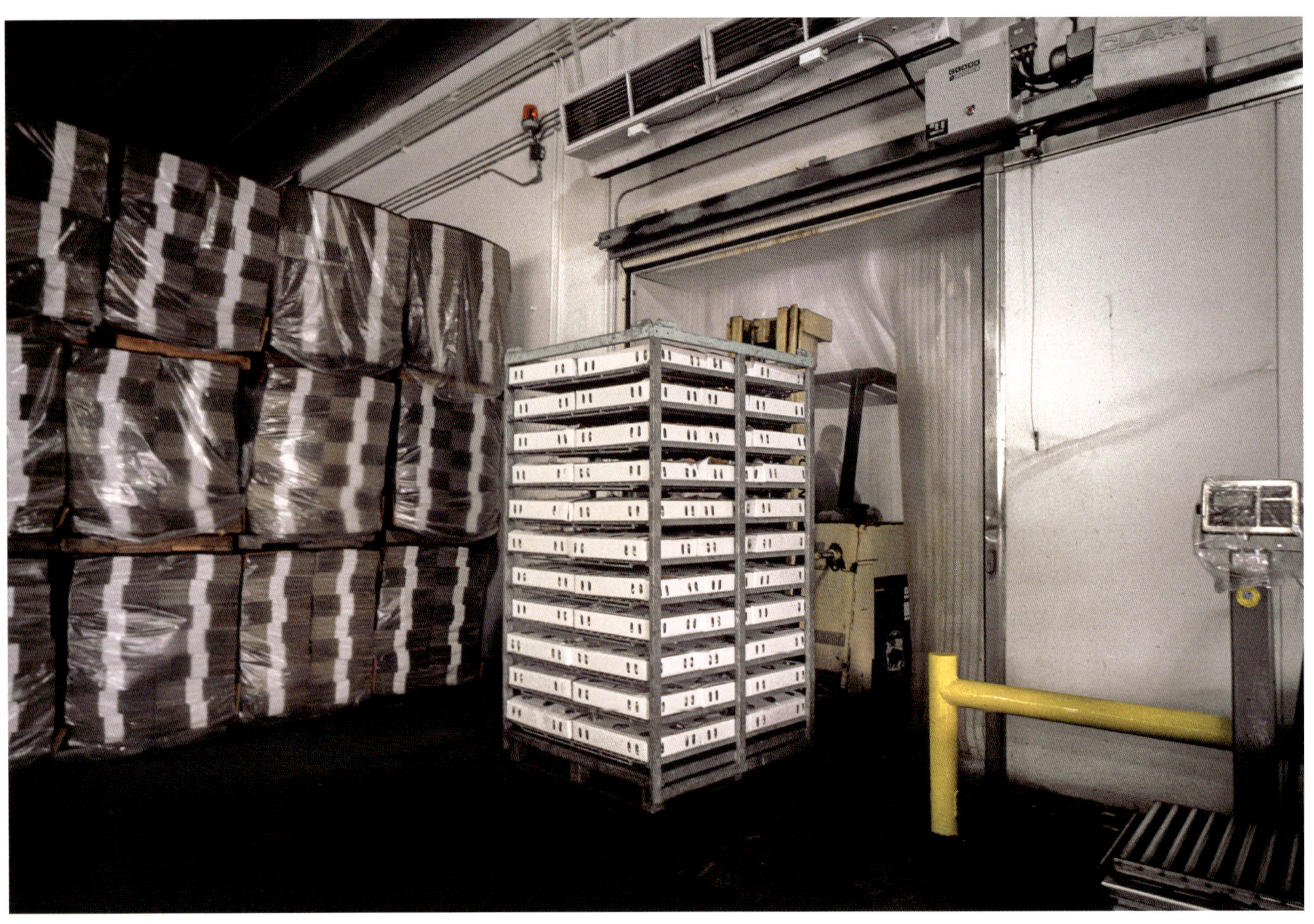

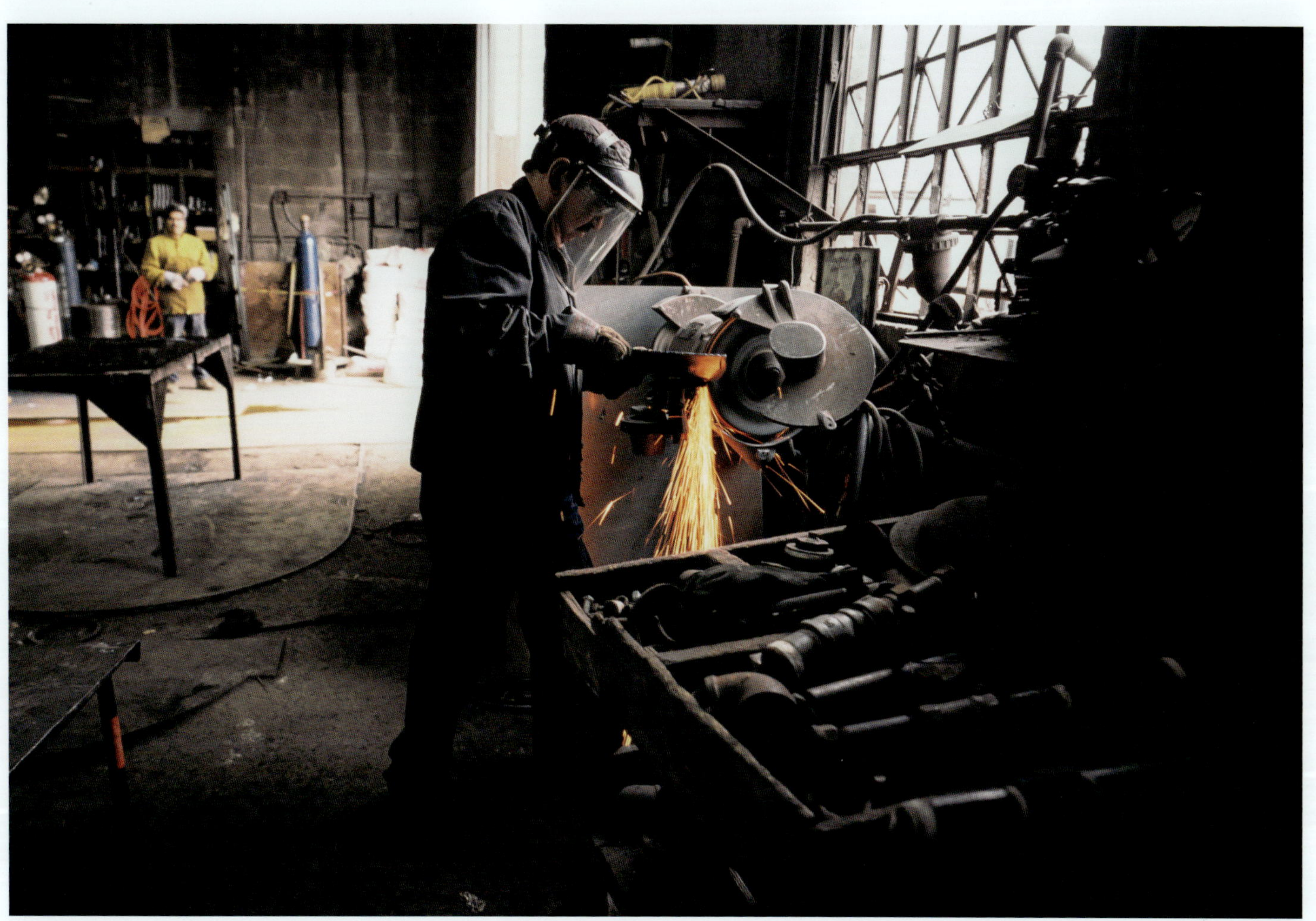

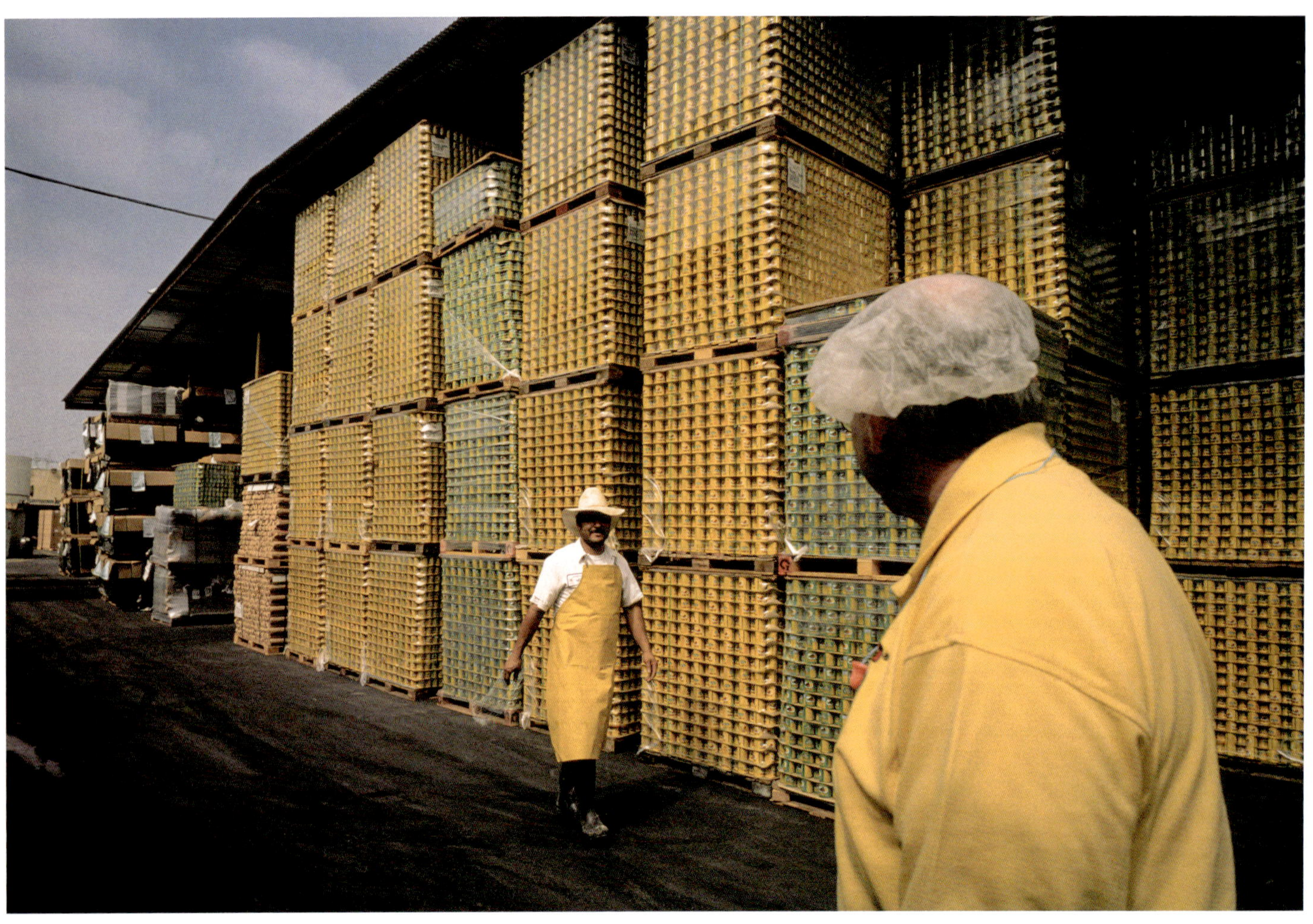

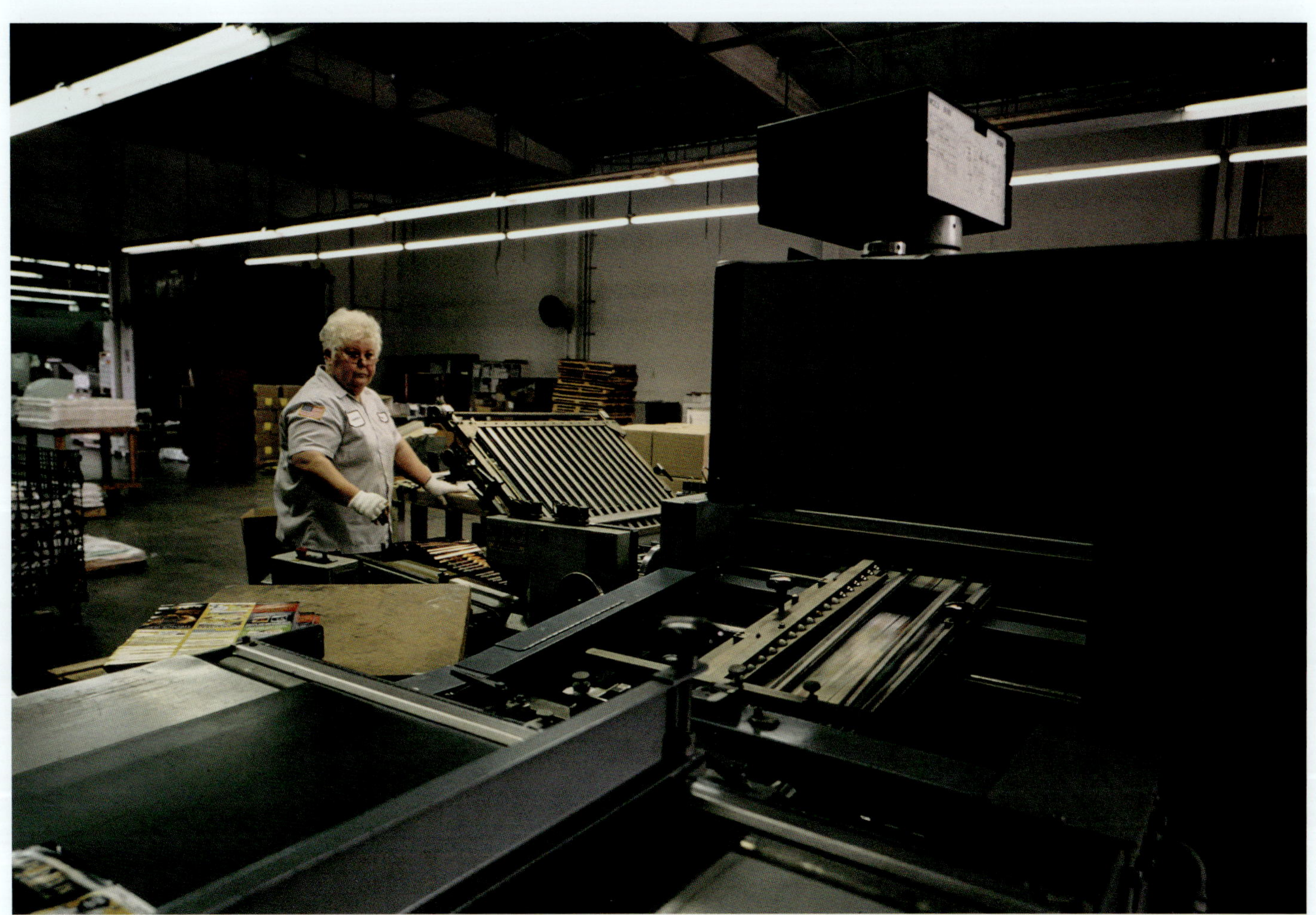

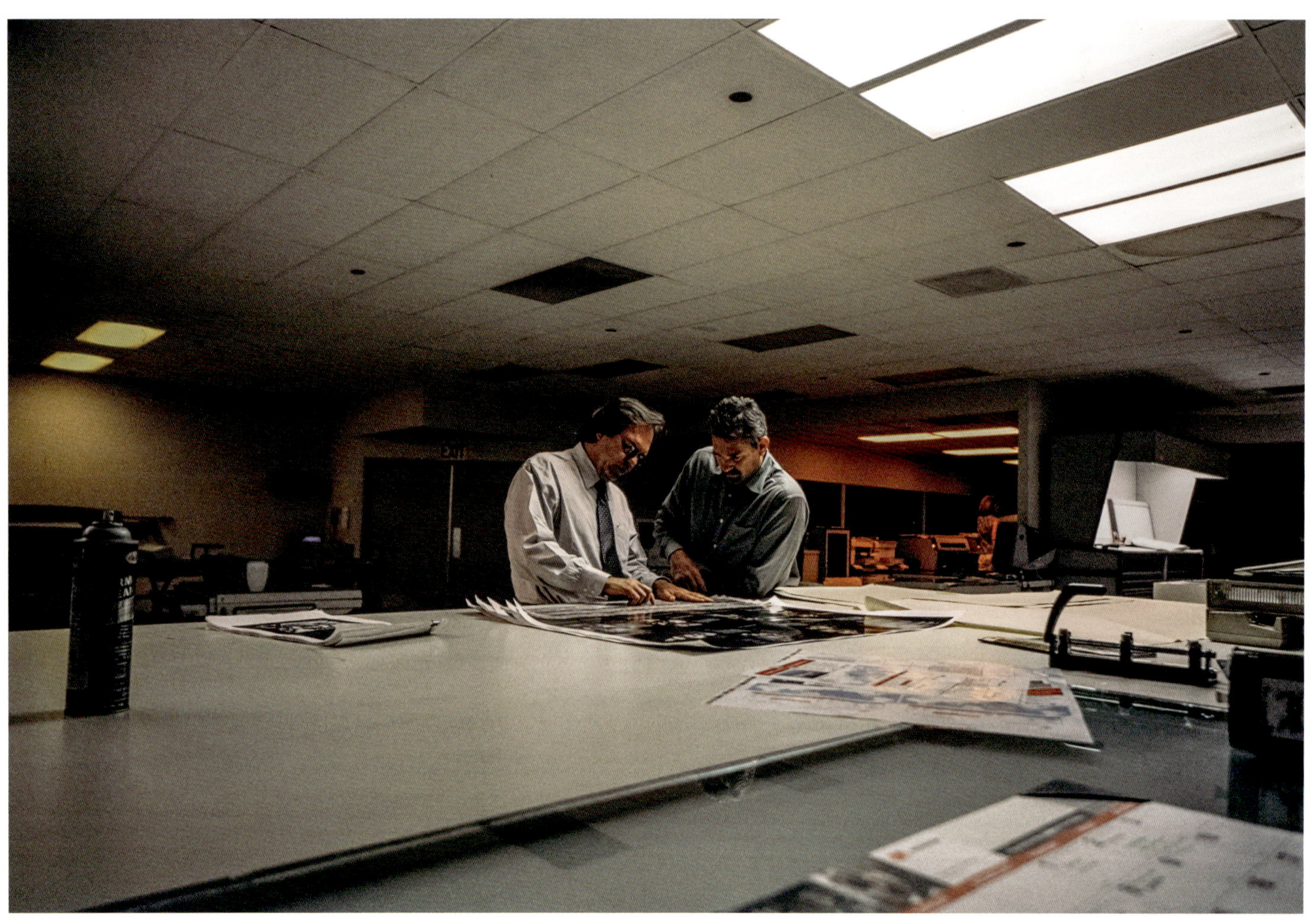

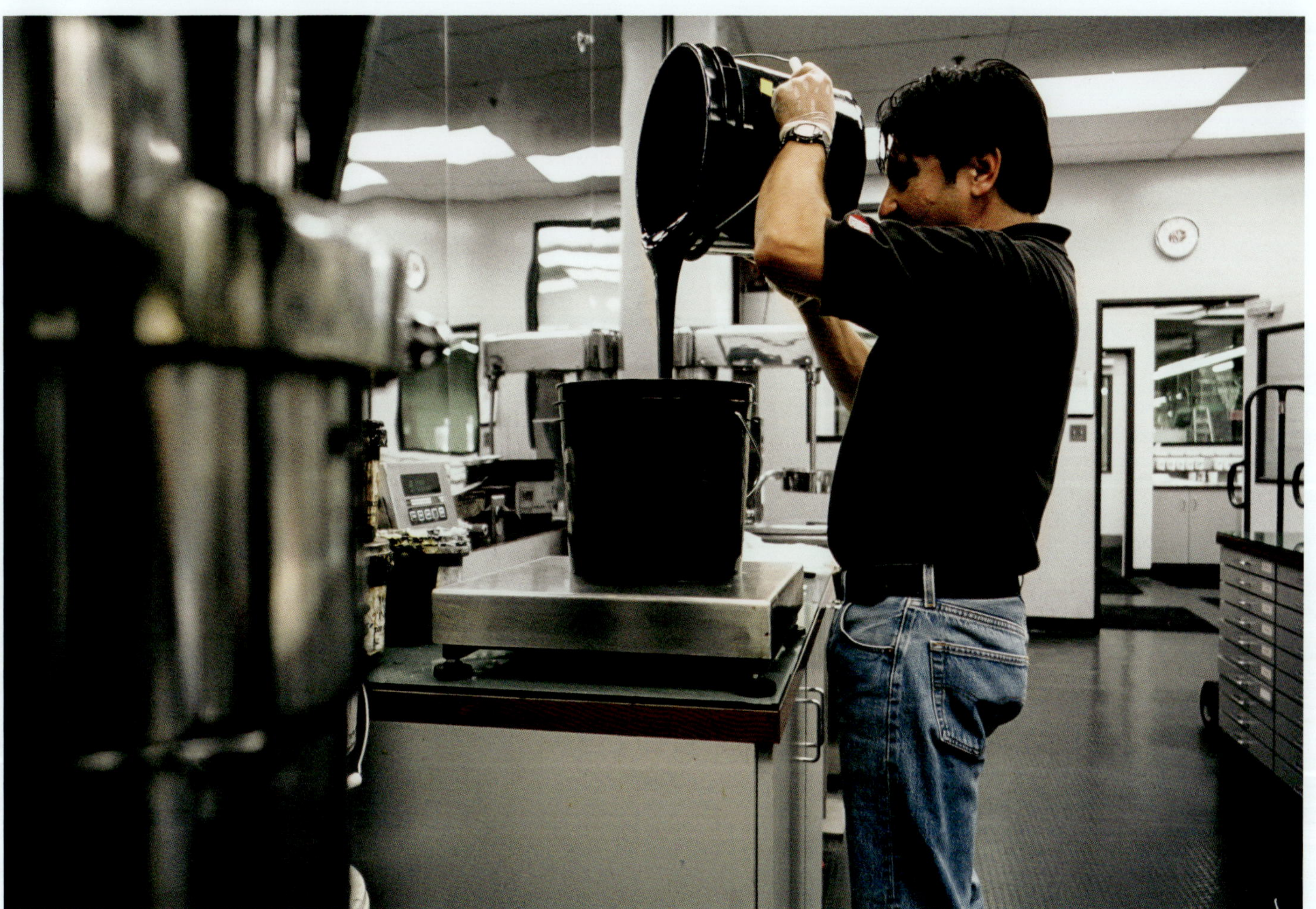

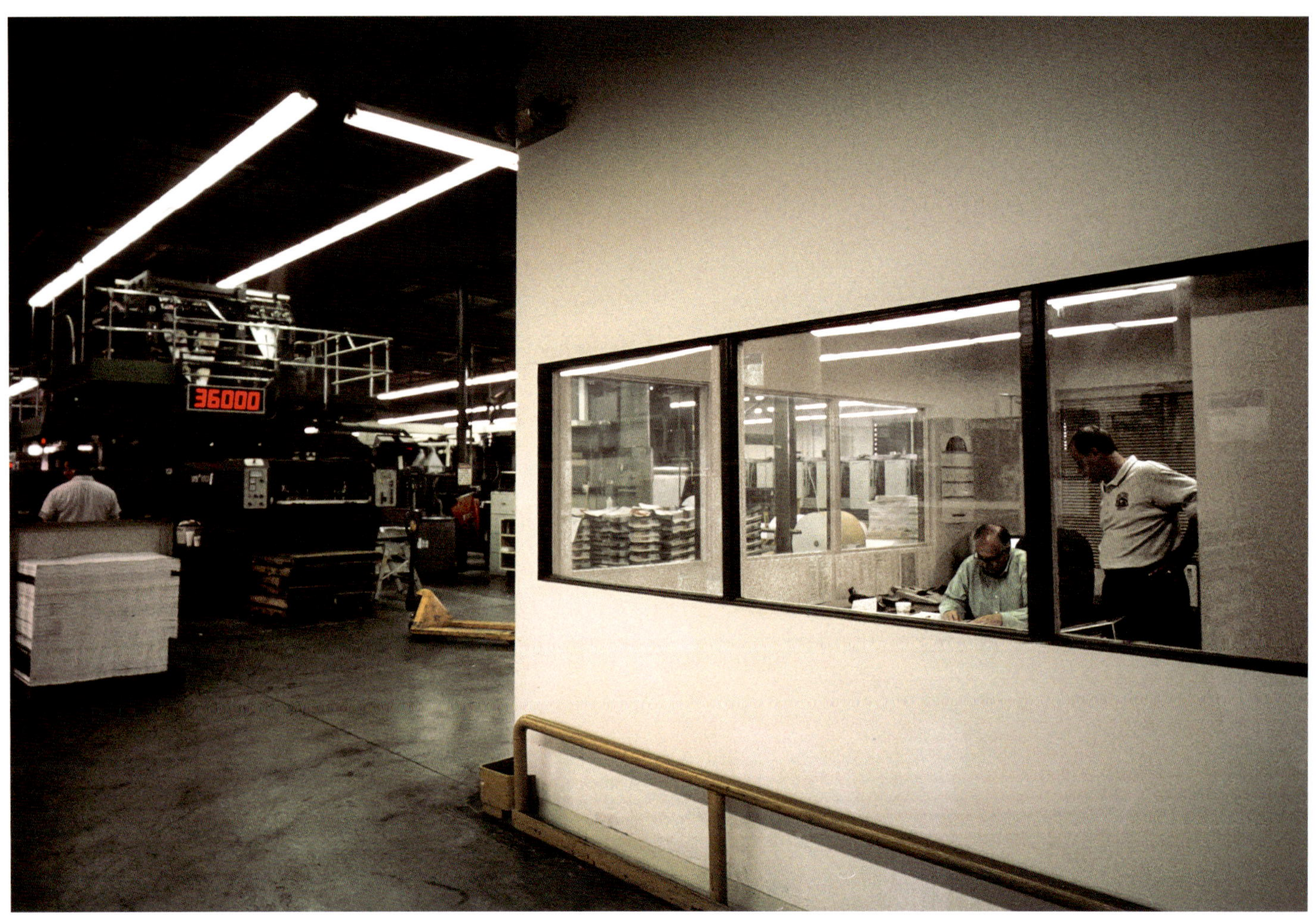

36000

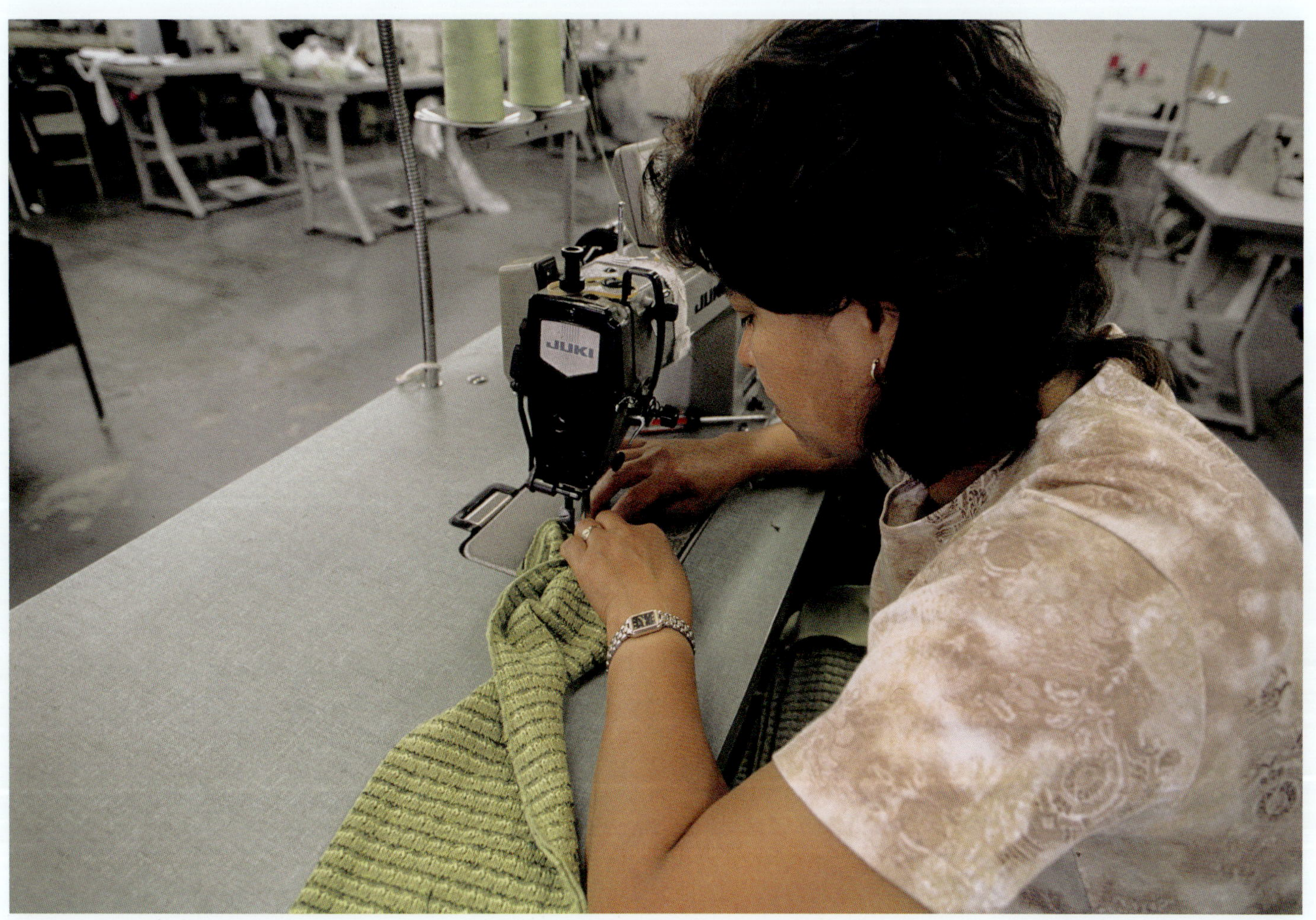

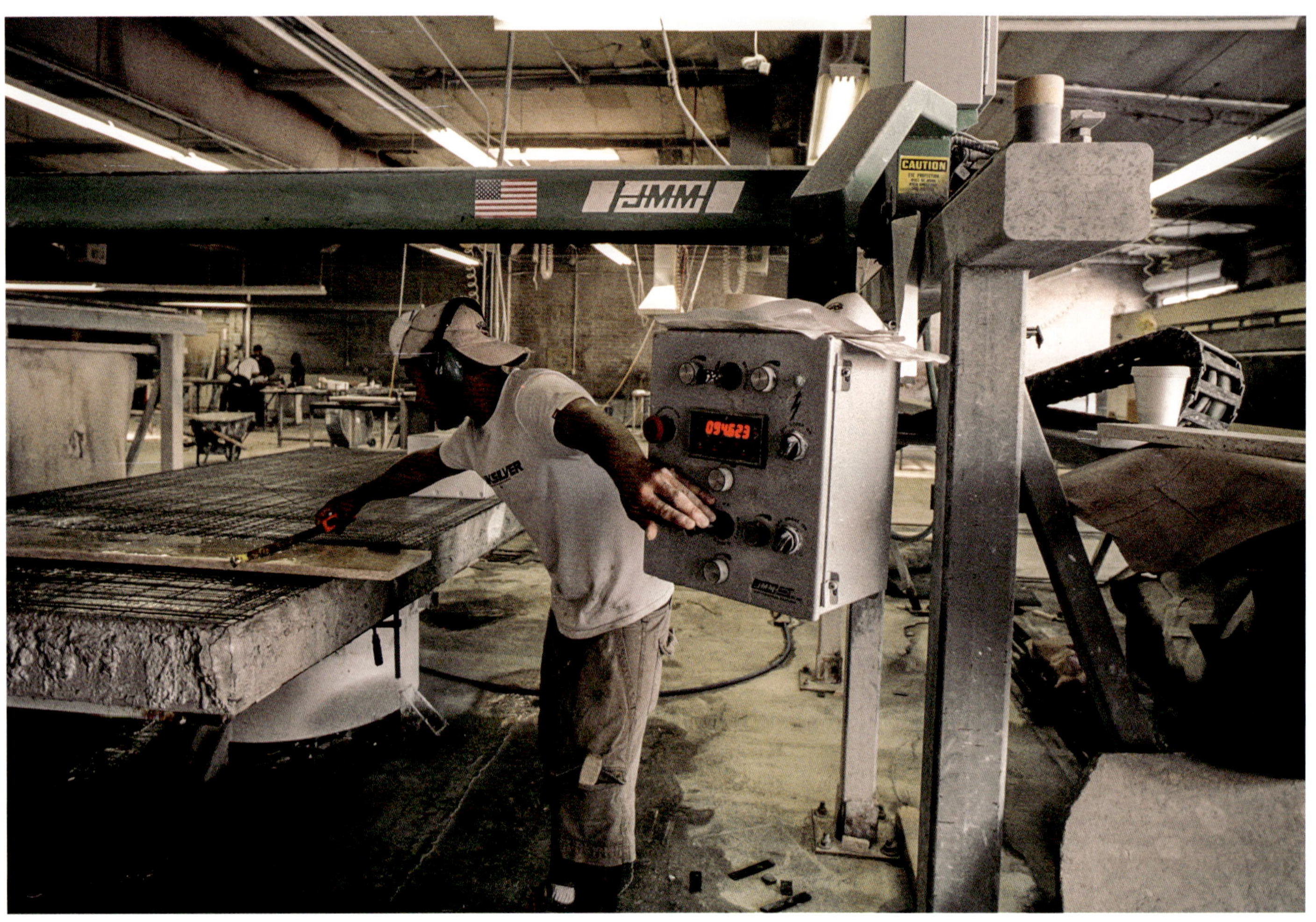
JMM
CAUTION
094623

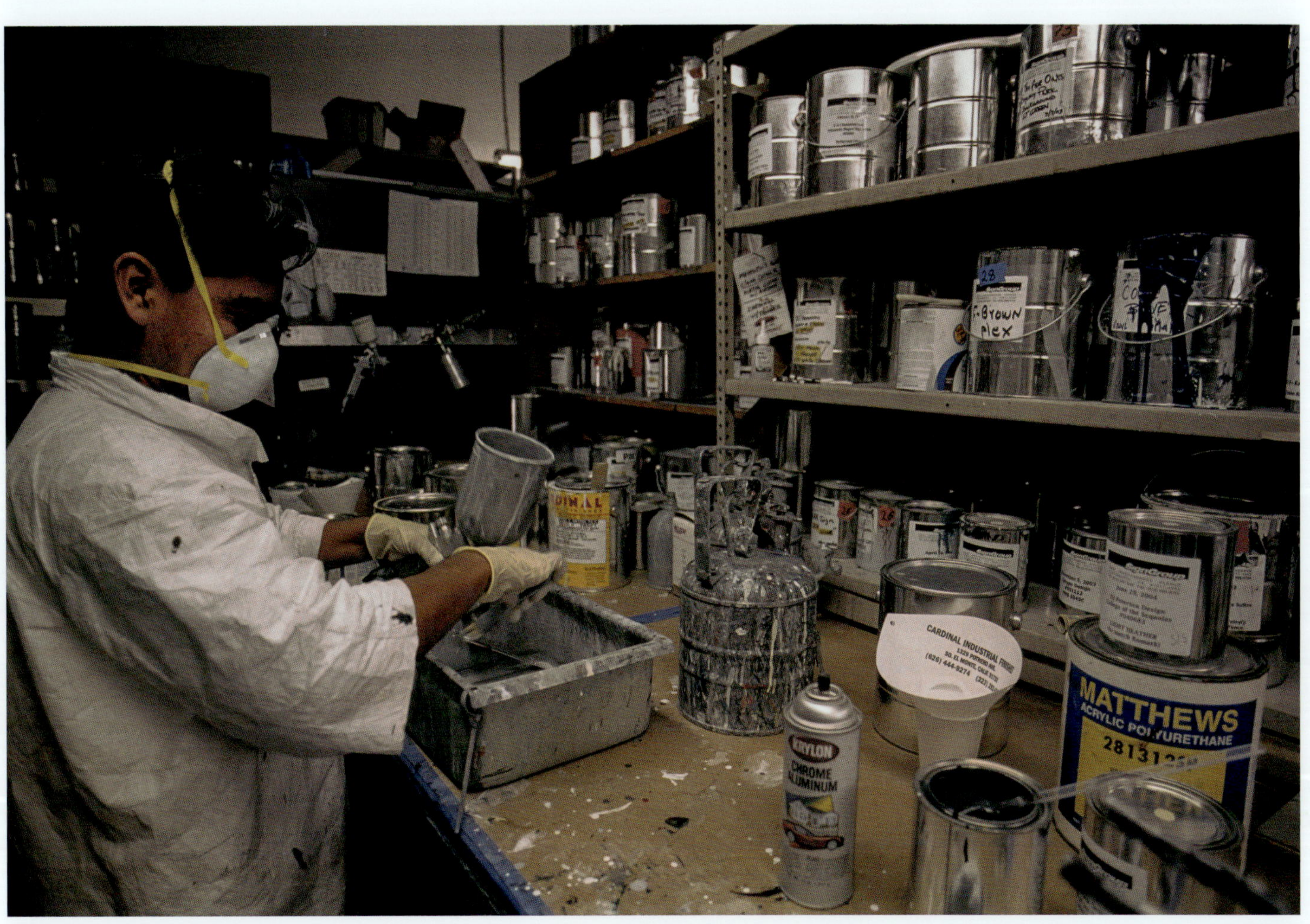

MATTHEWS
ACRYLIC POLYURETHANE
28131
KRYLON
CHROME
ALUMINUM
CARDINAL INDUSTRIAL FINISH
SO. EL MONTE, CALIF.
(626) 444-9274

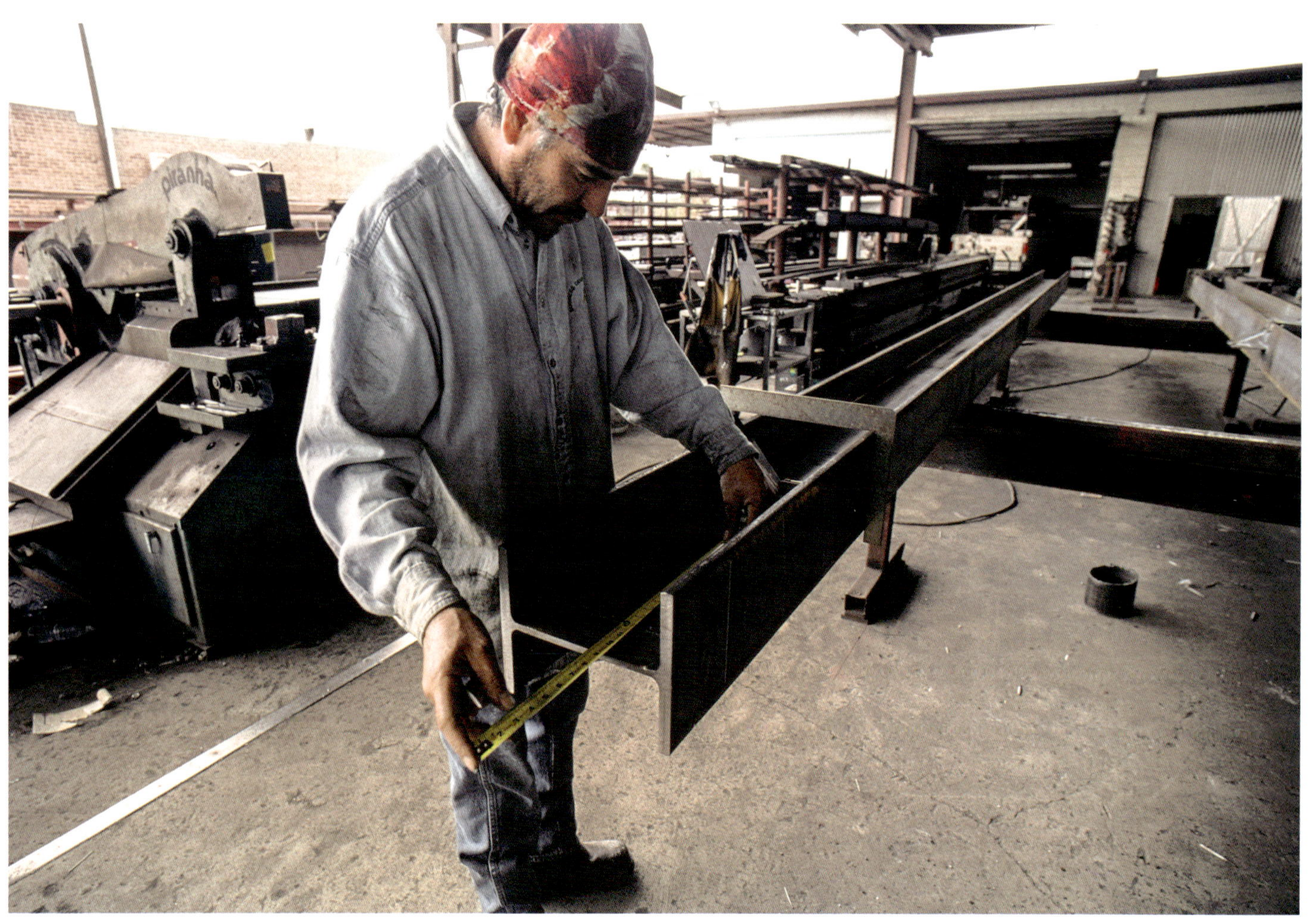

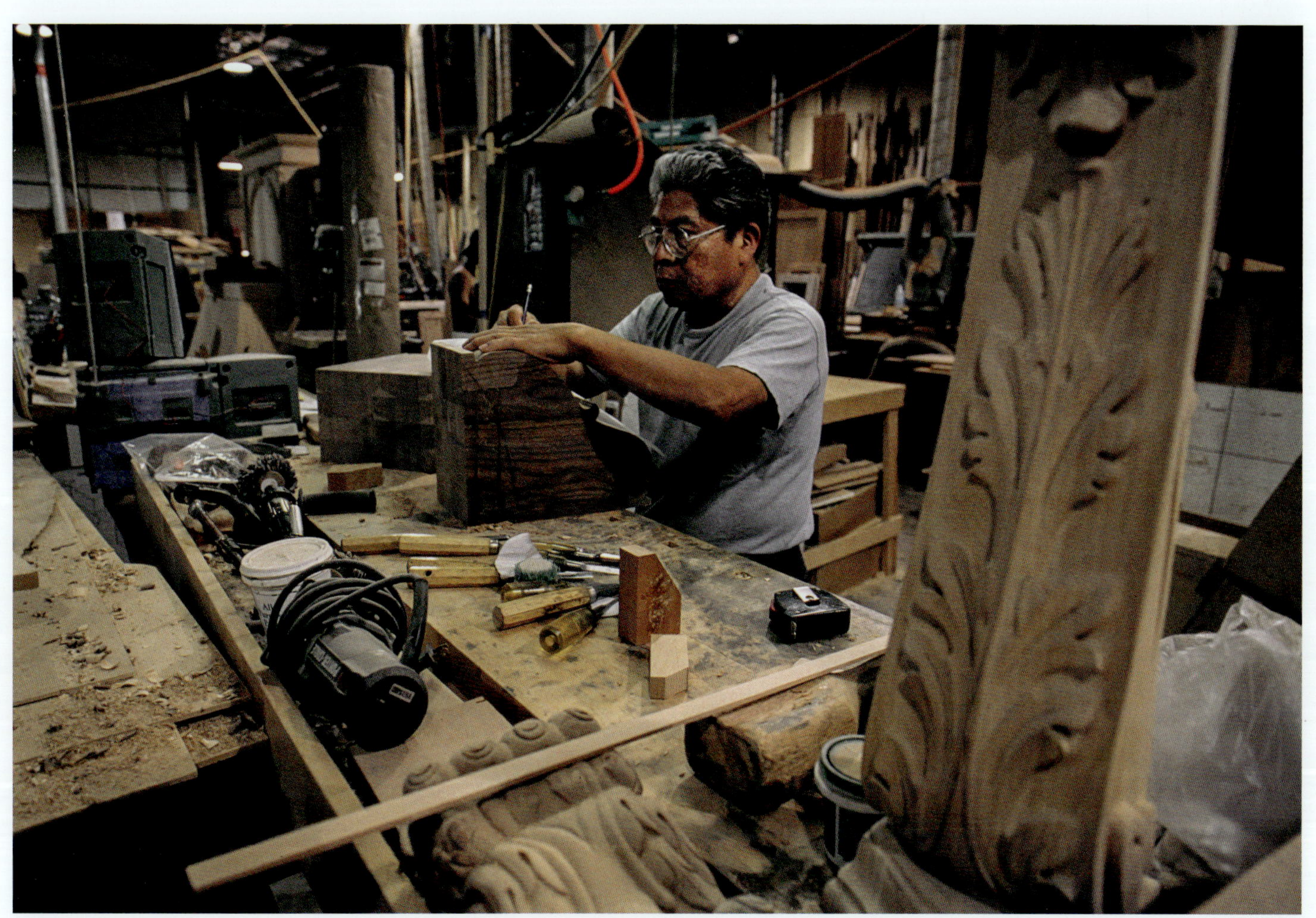

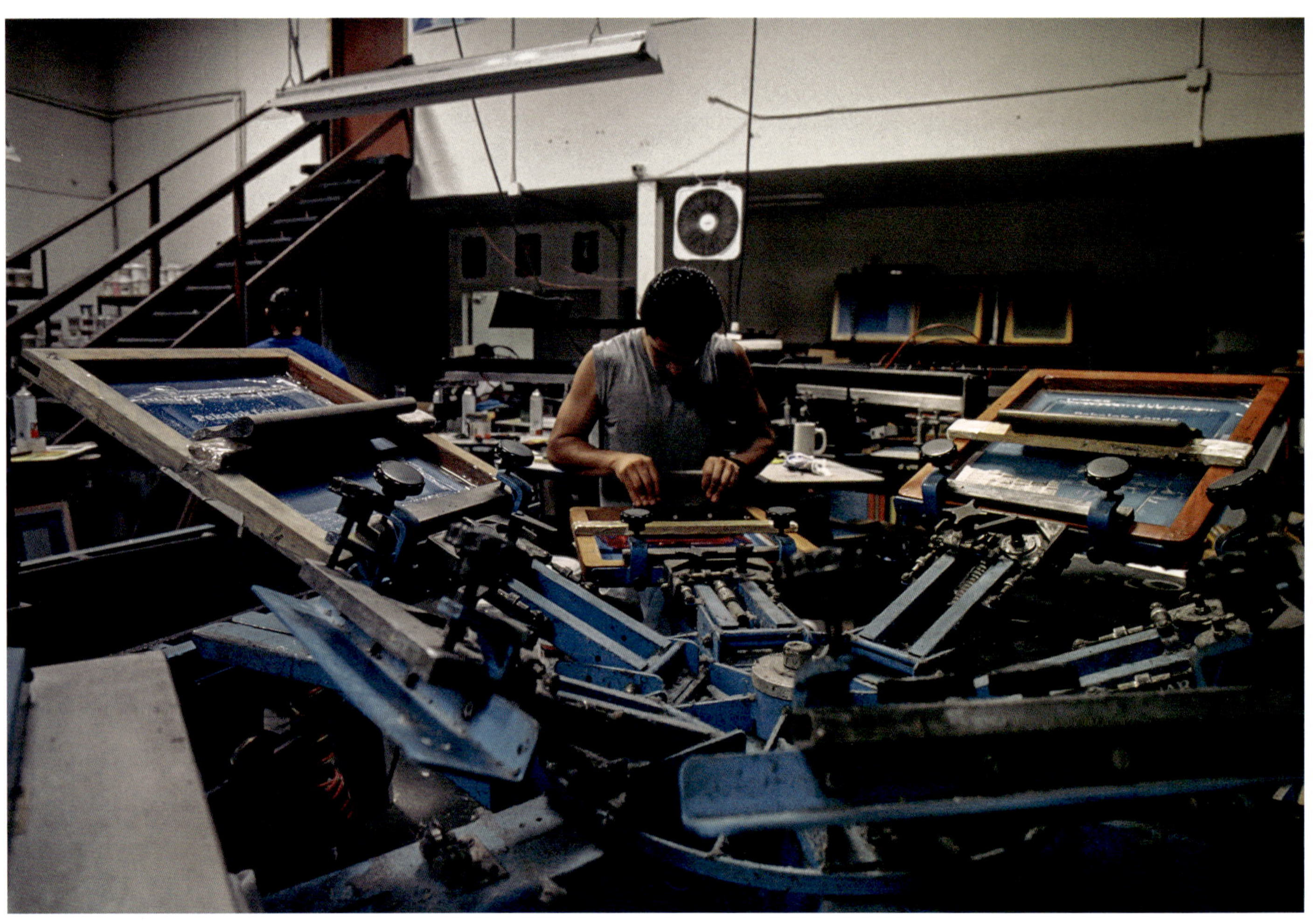

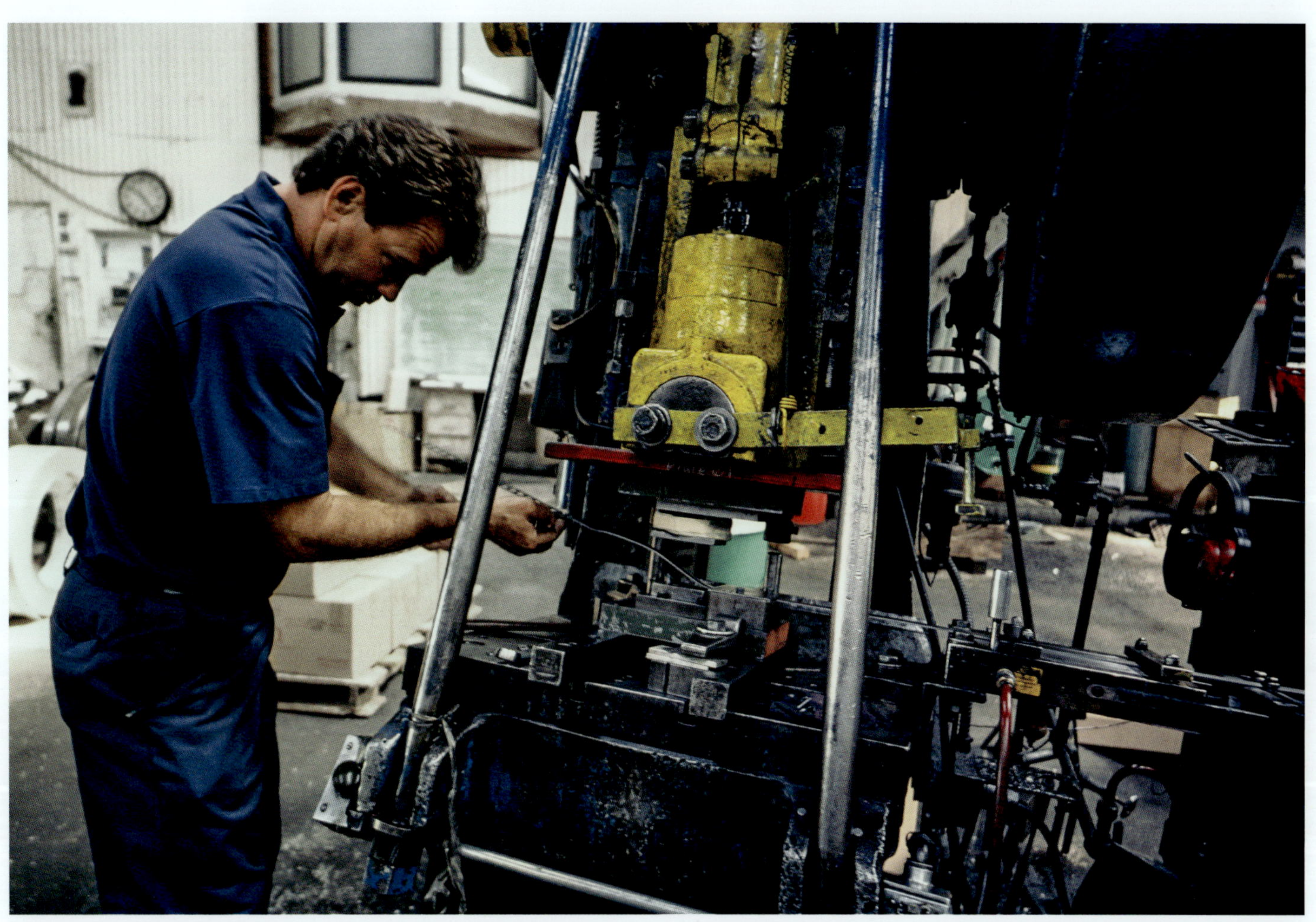

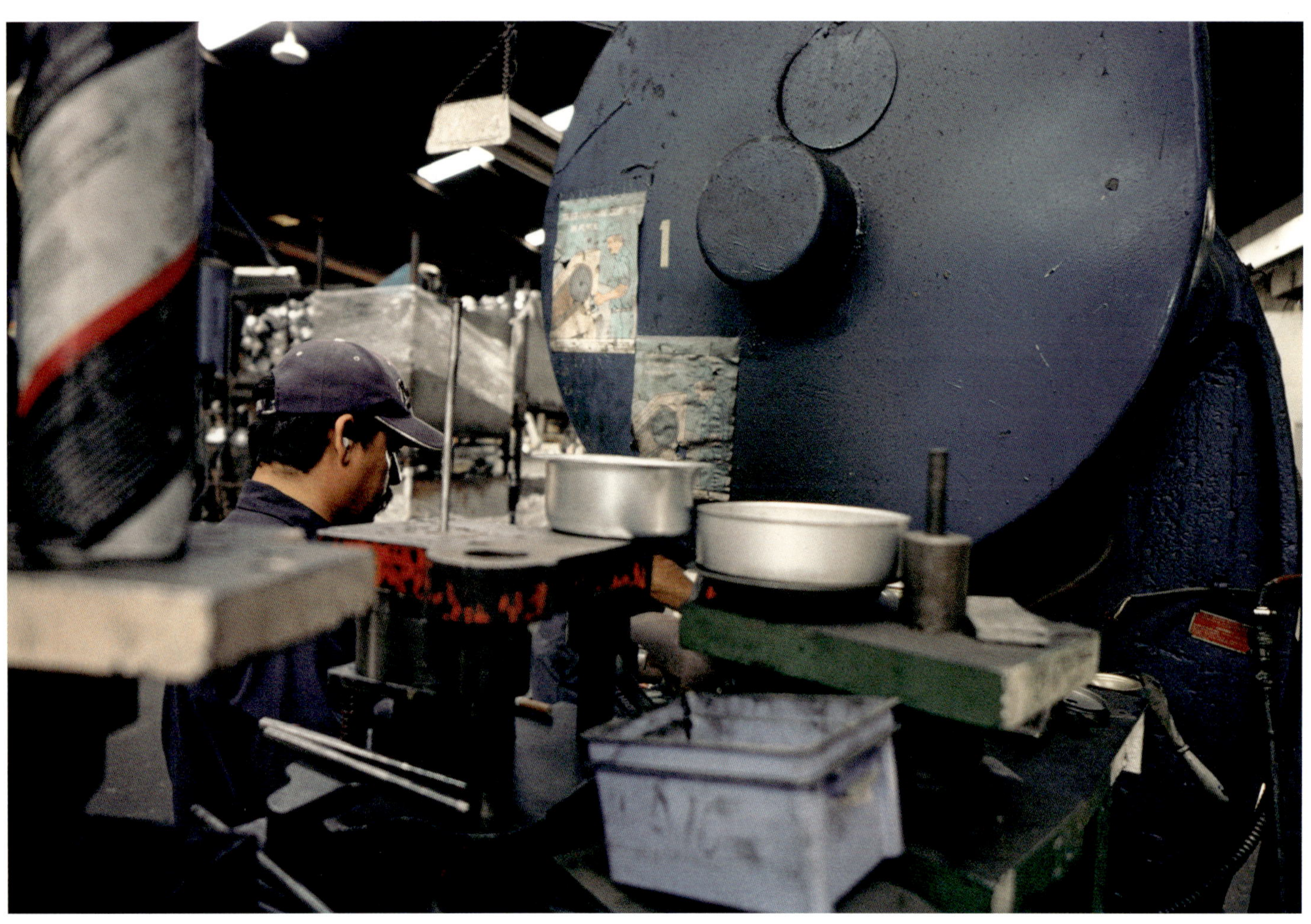

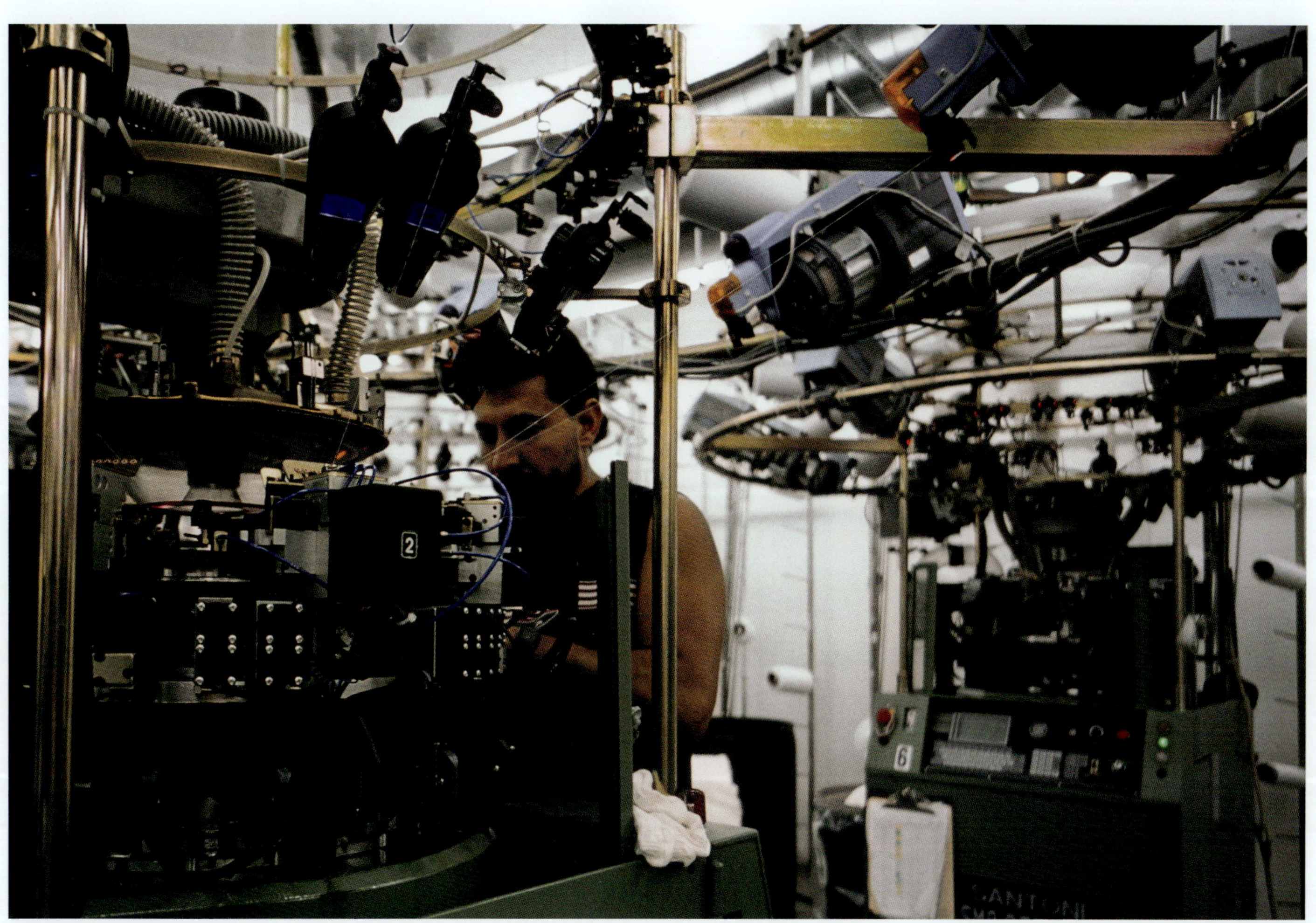

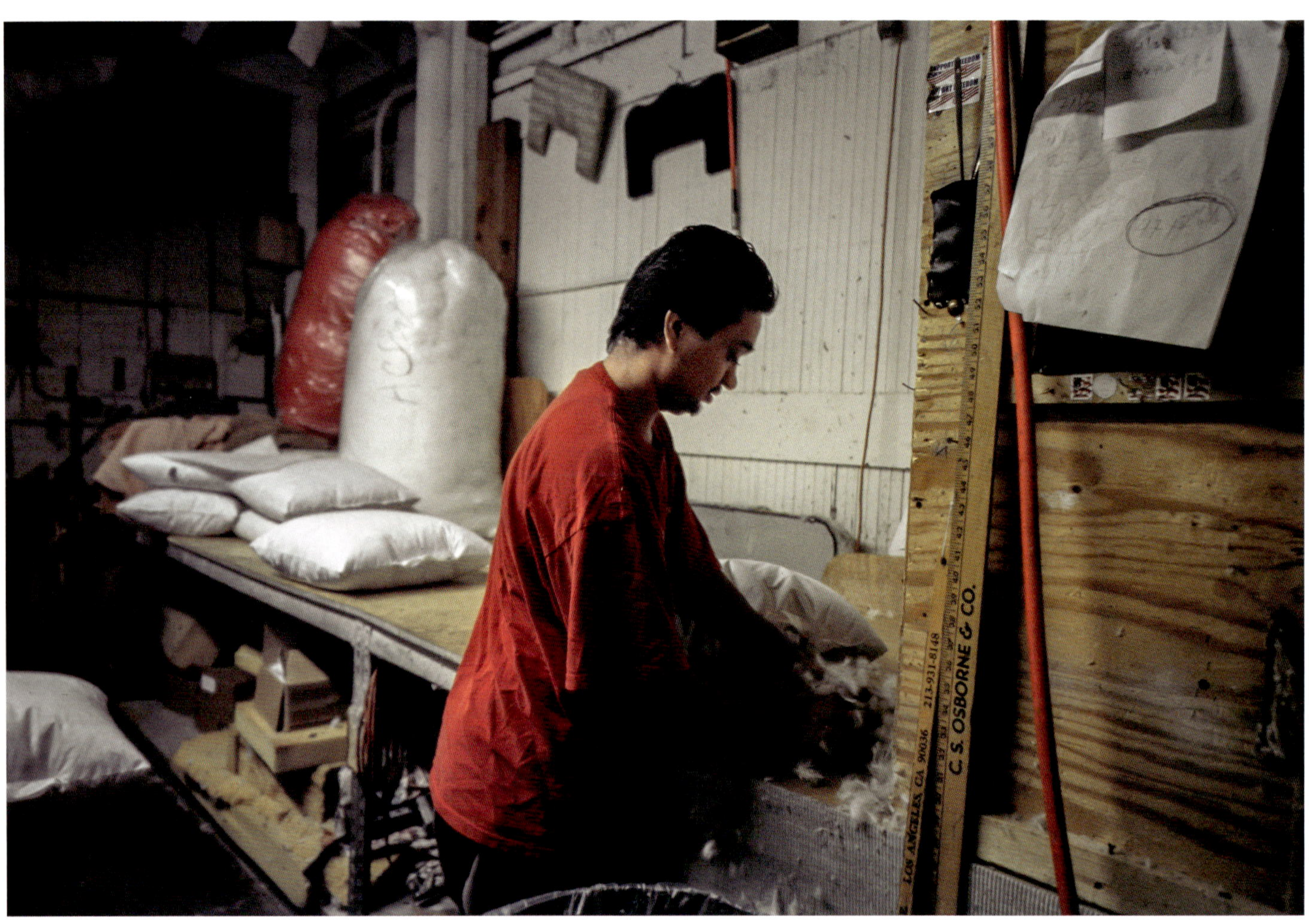

C. S. OSBORNE & CO.
213-931-8148
LOS ANGELES, CA 90036

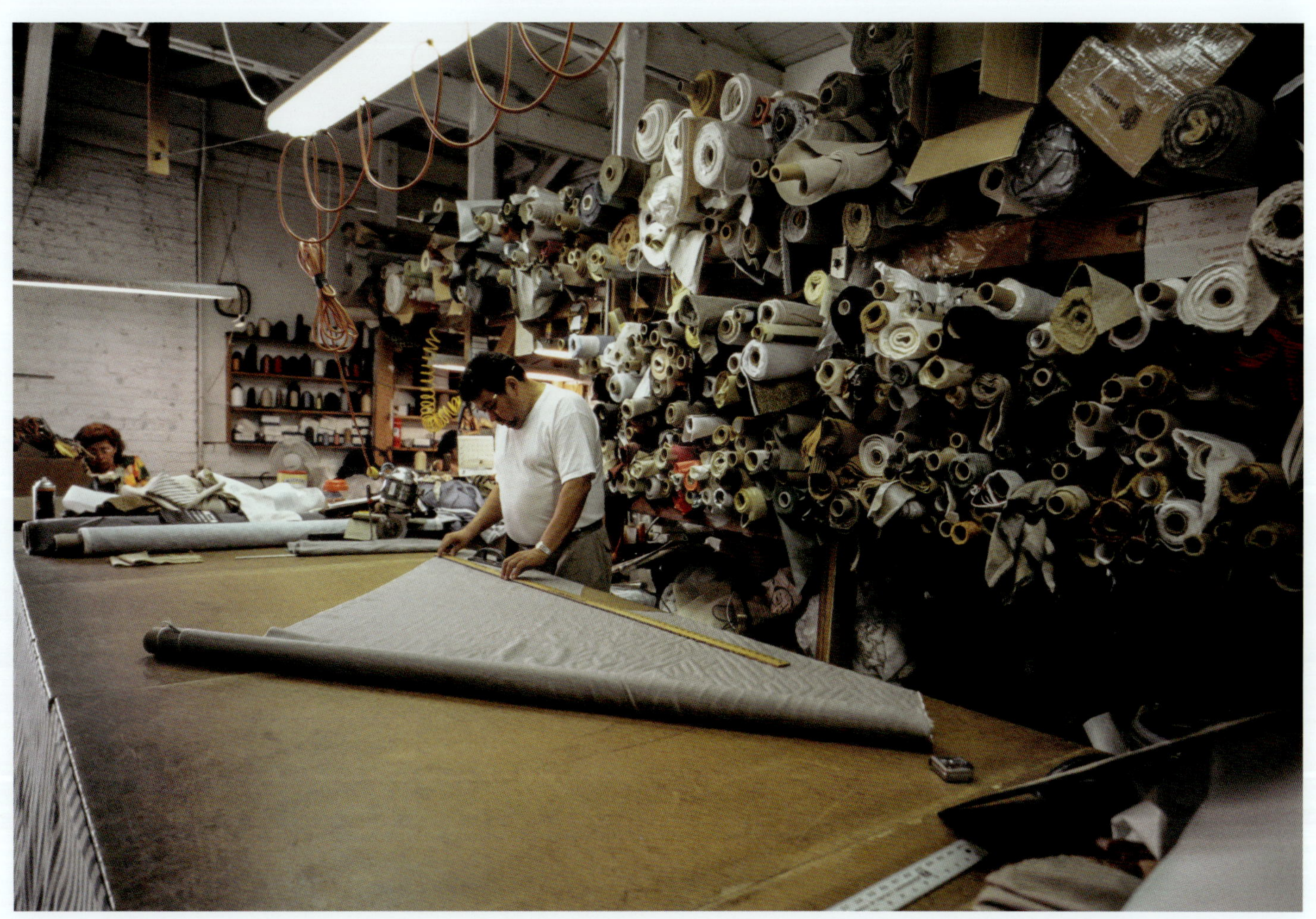

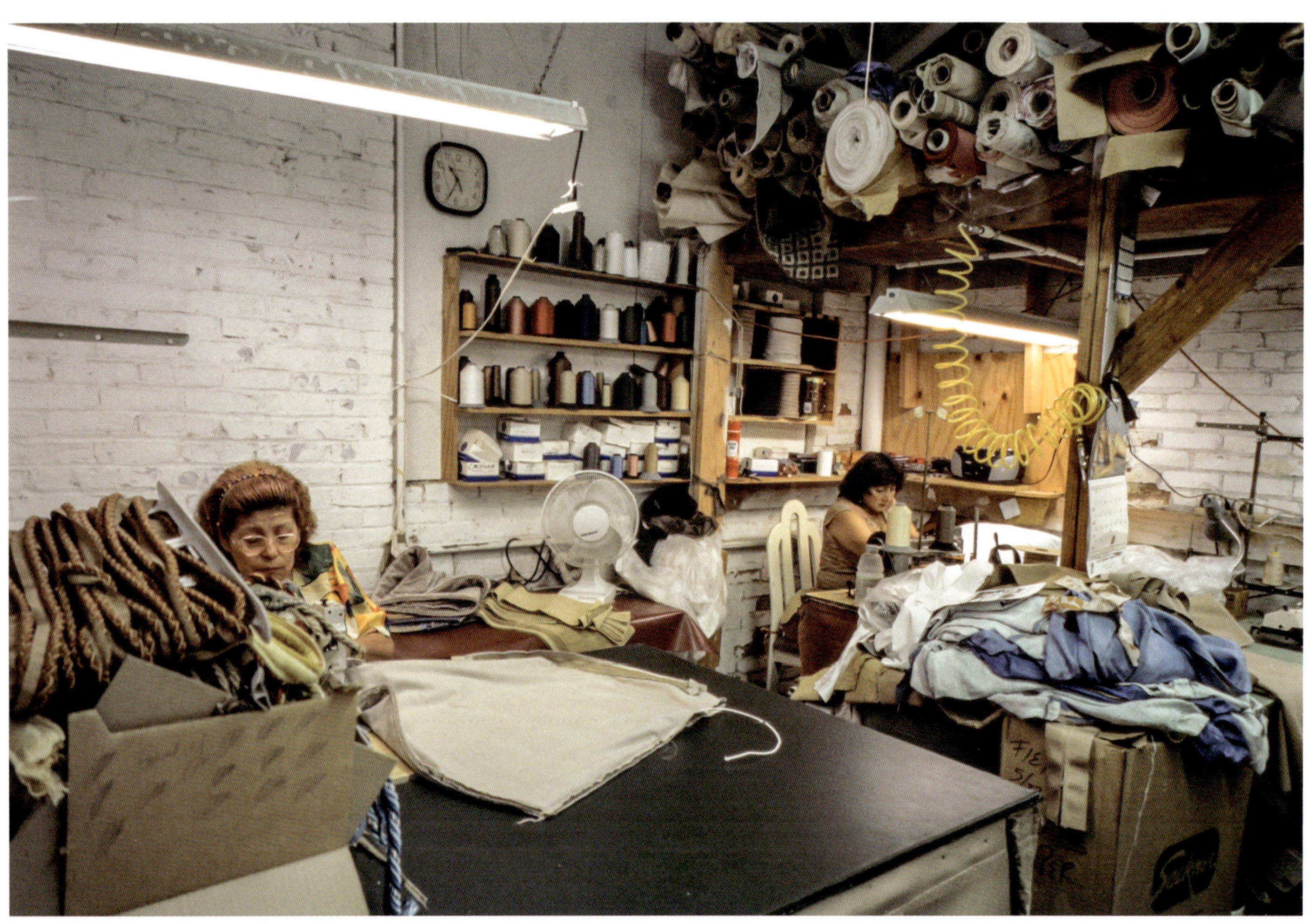

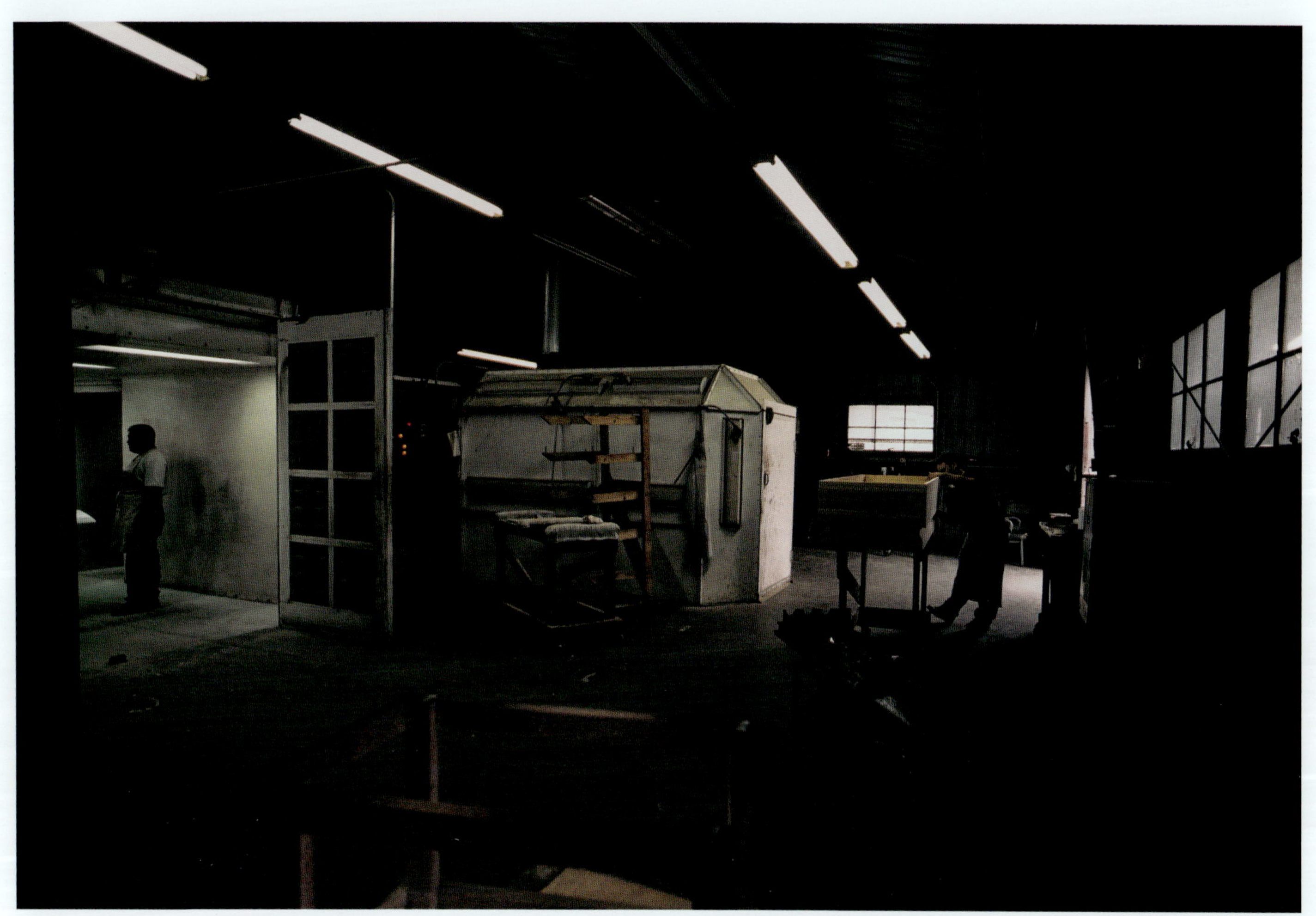

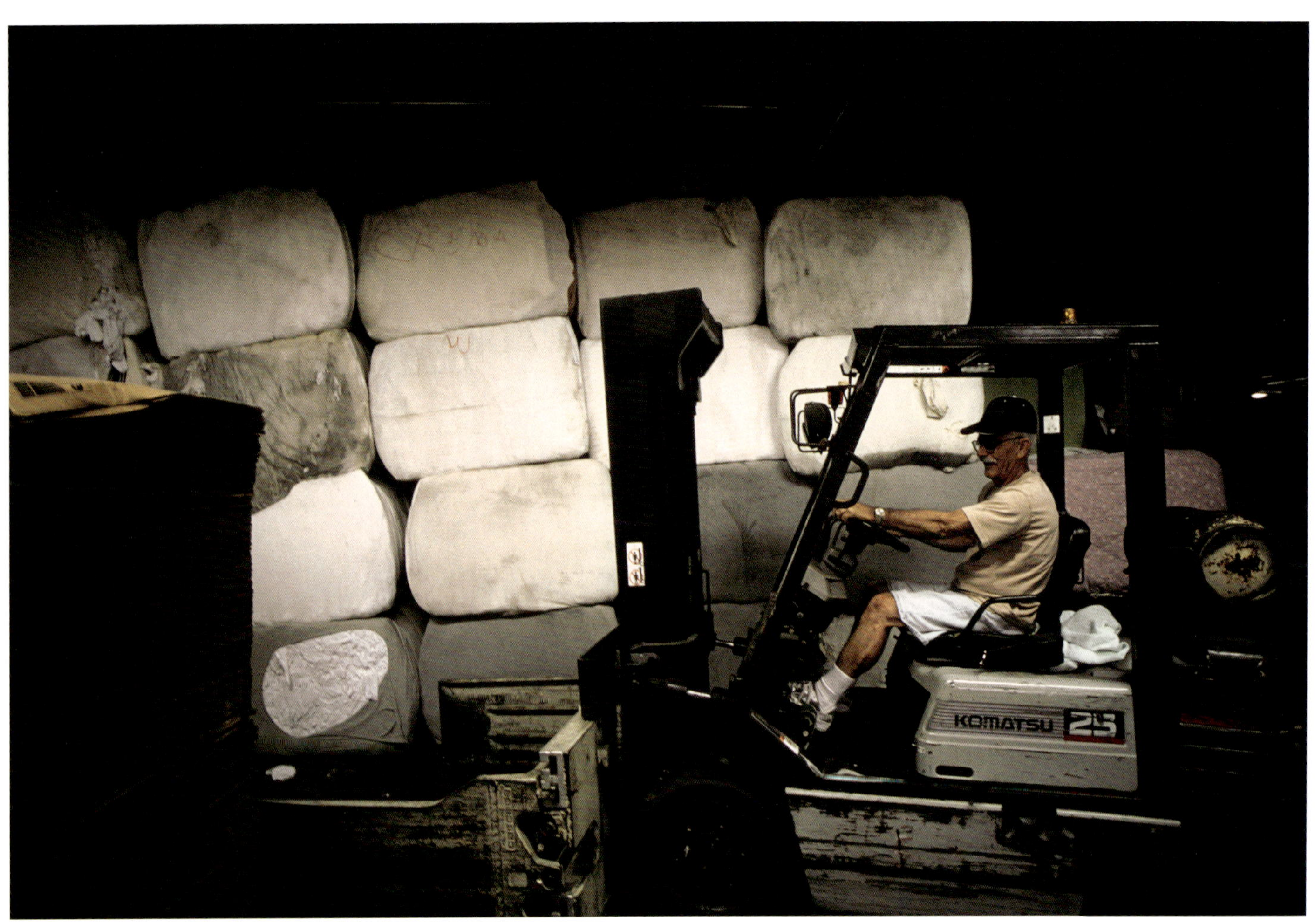

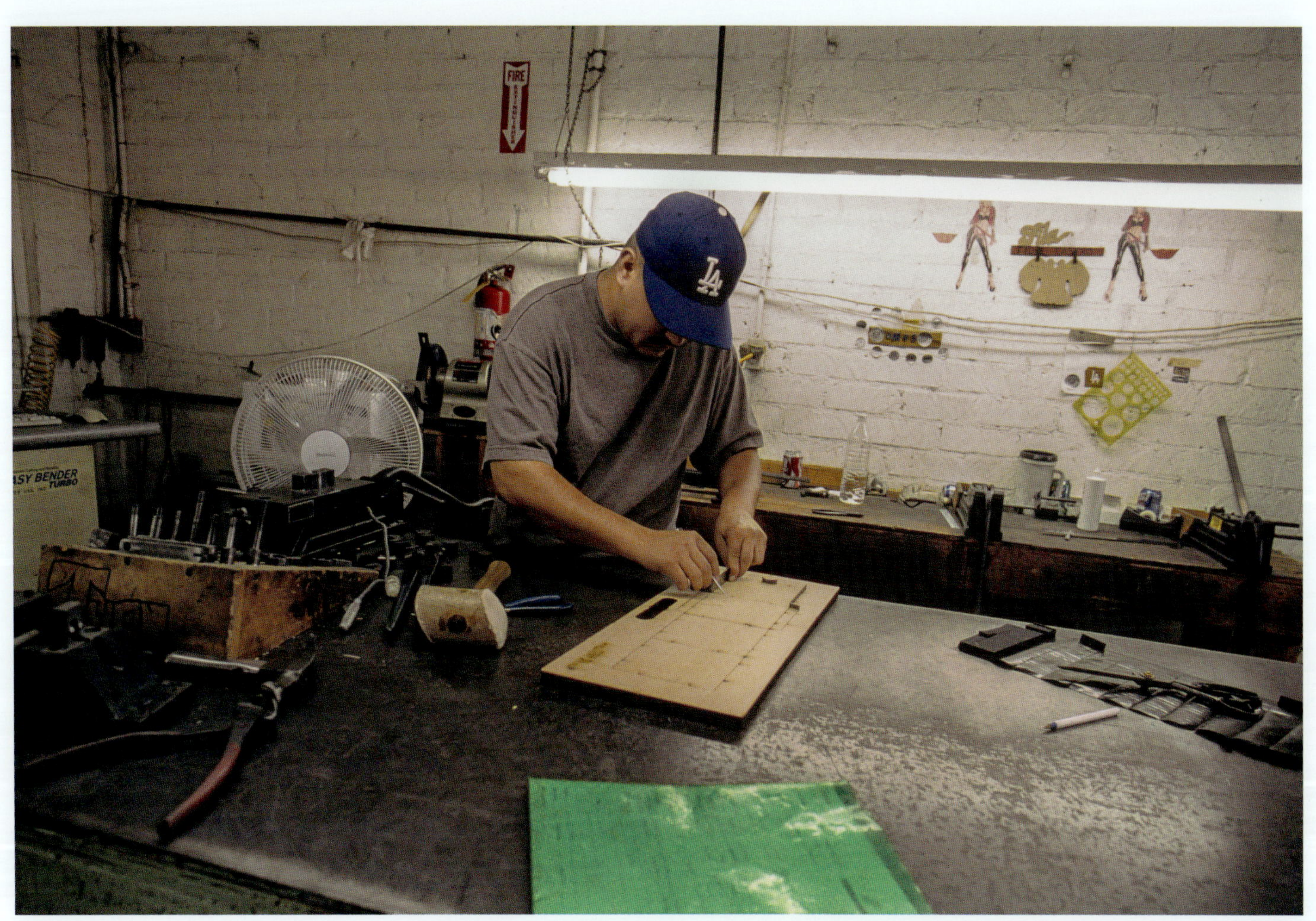

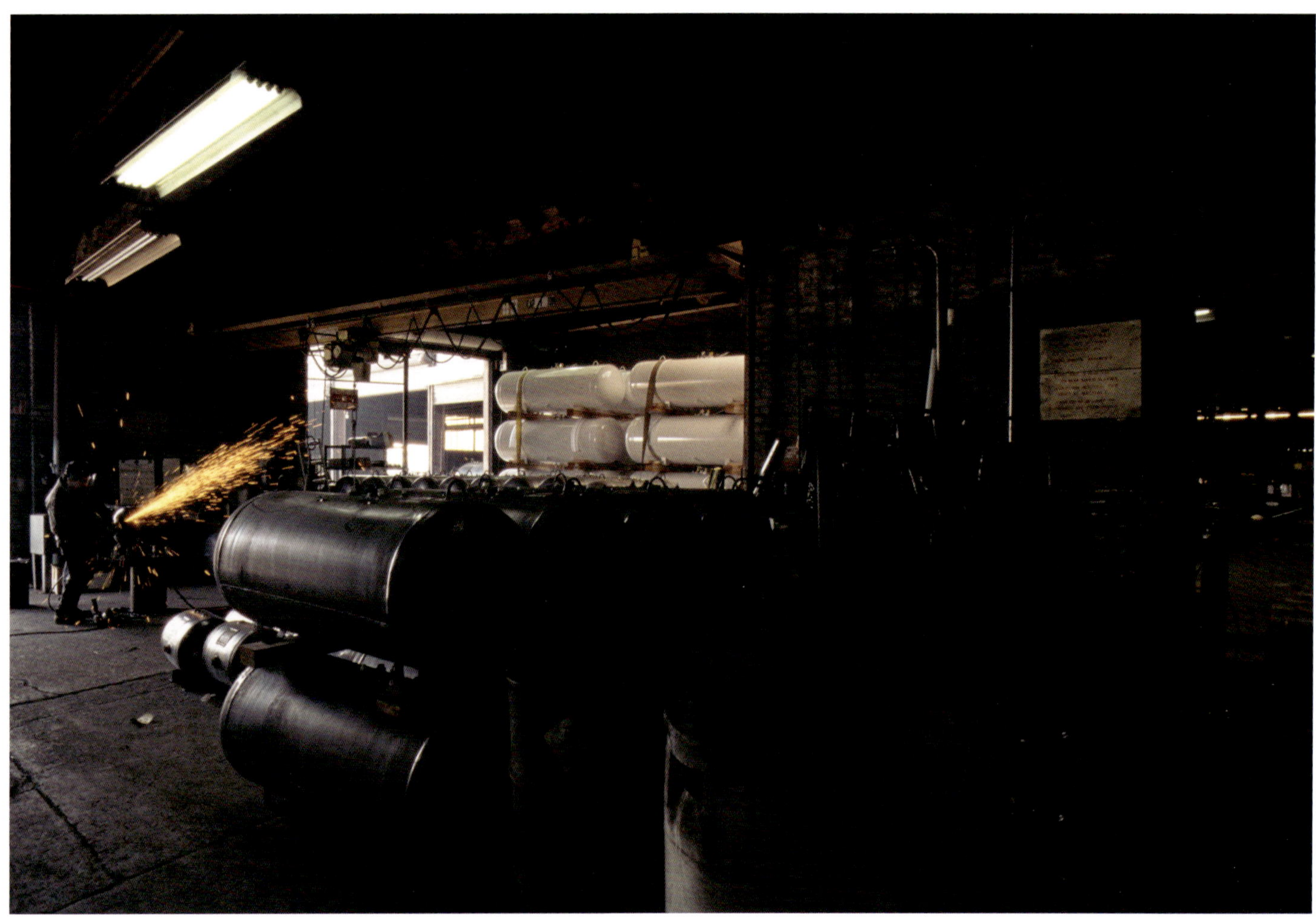

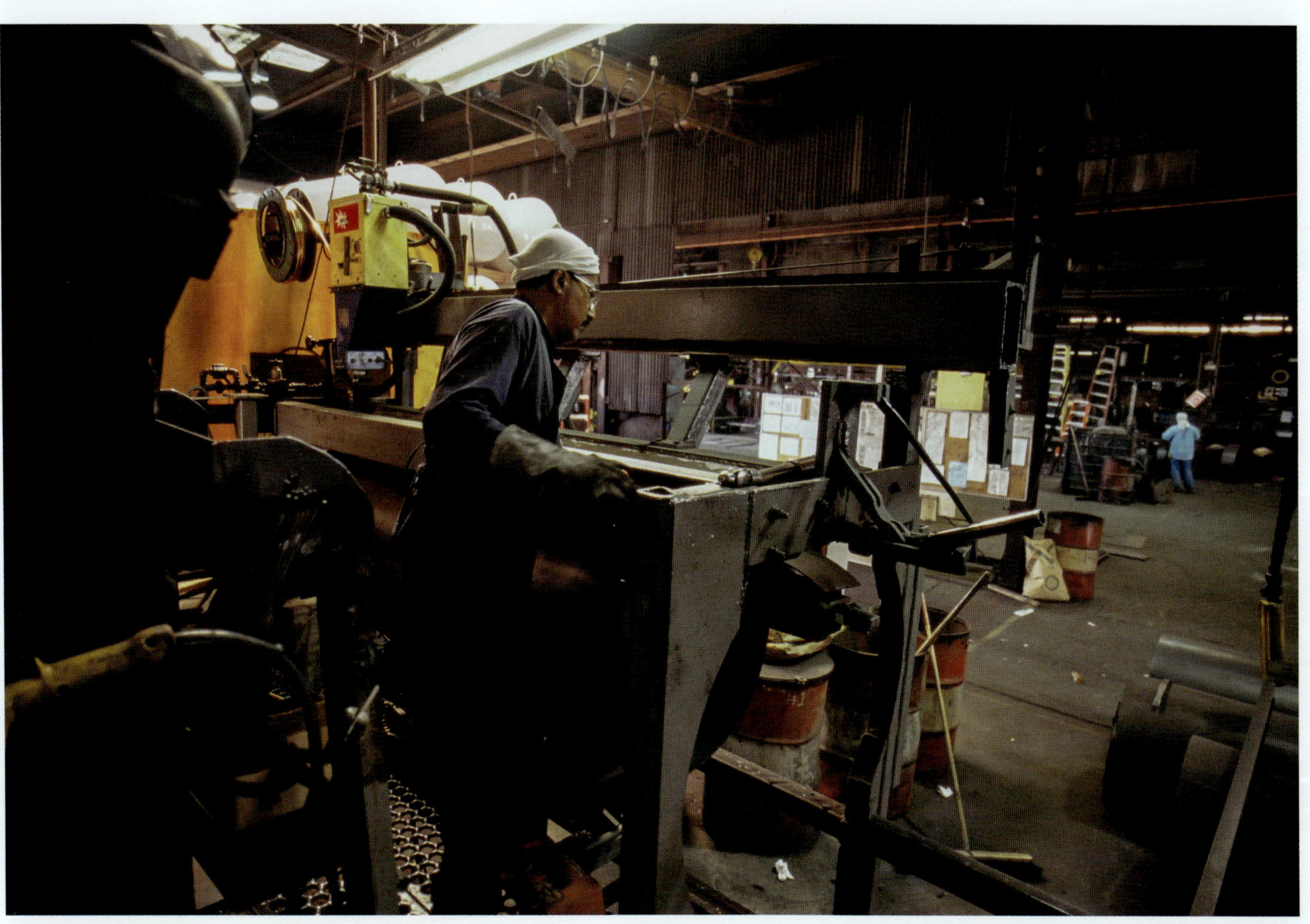

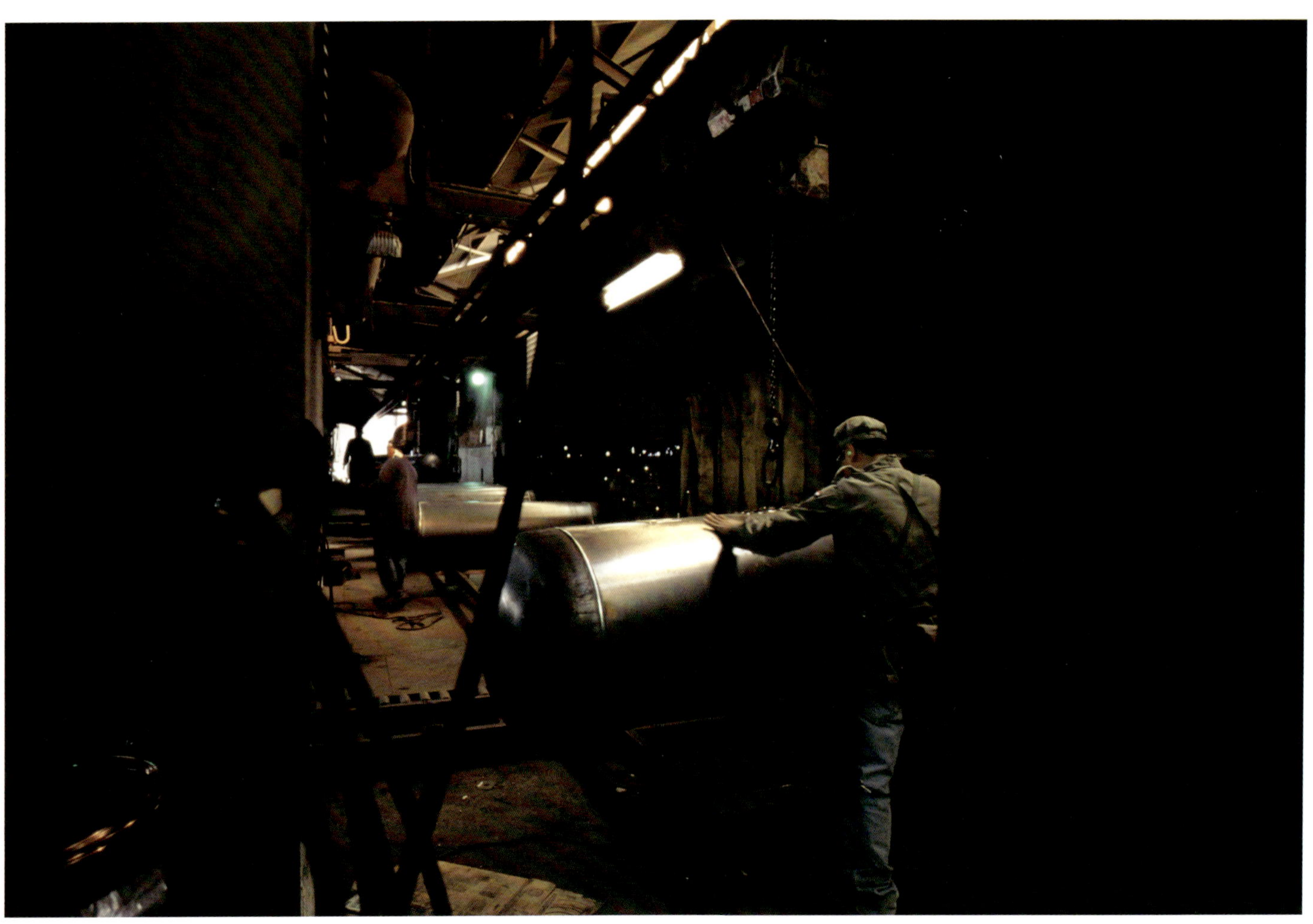

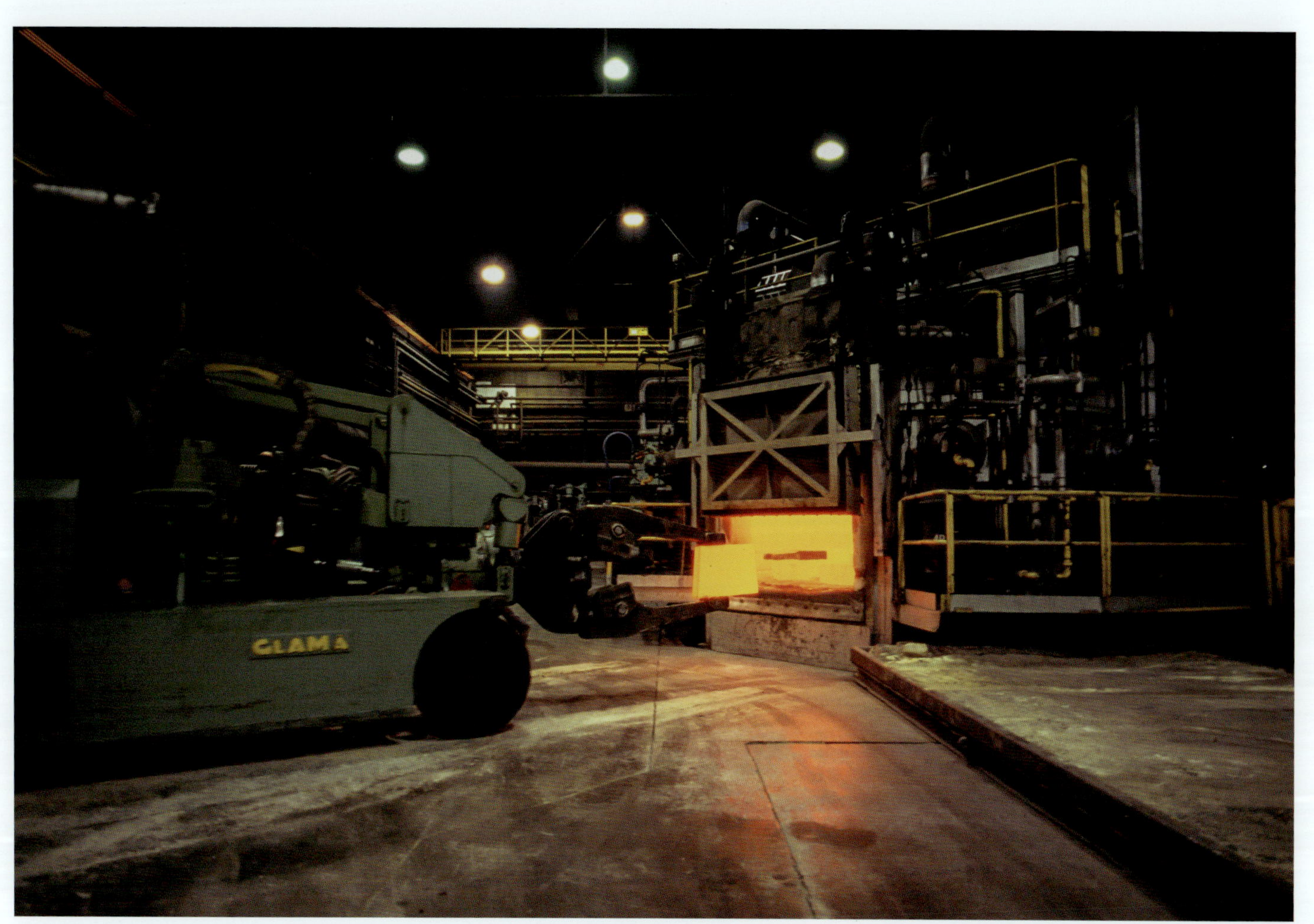
GLAMA

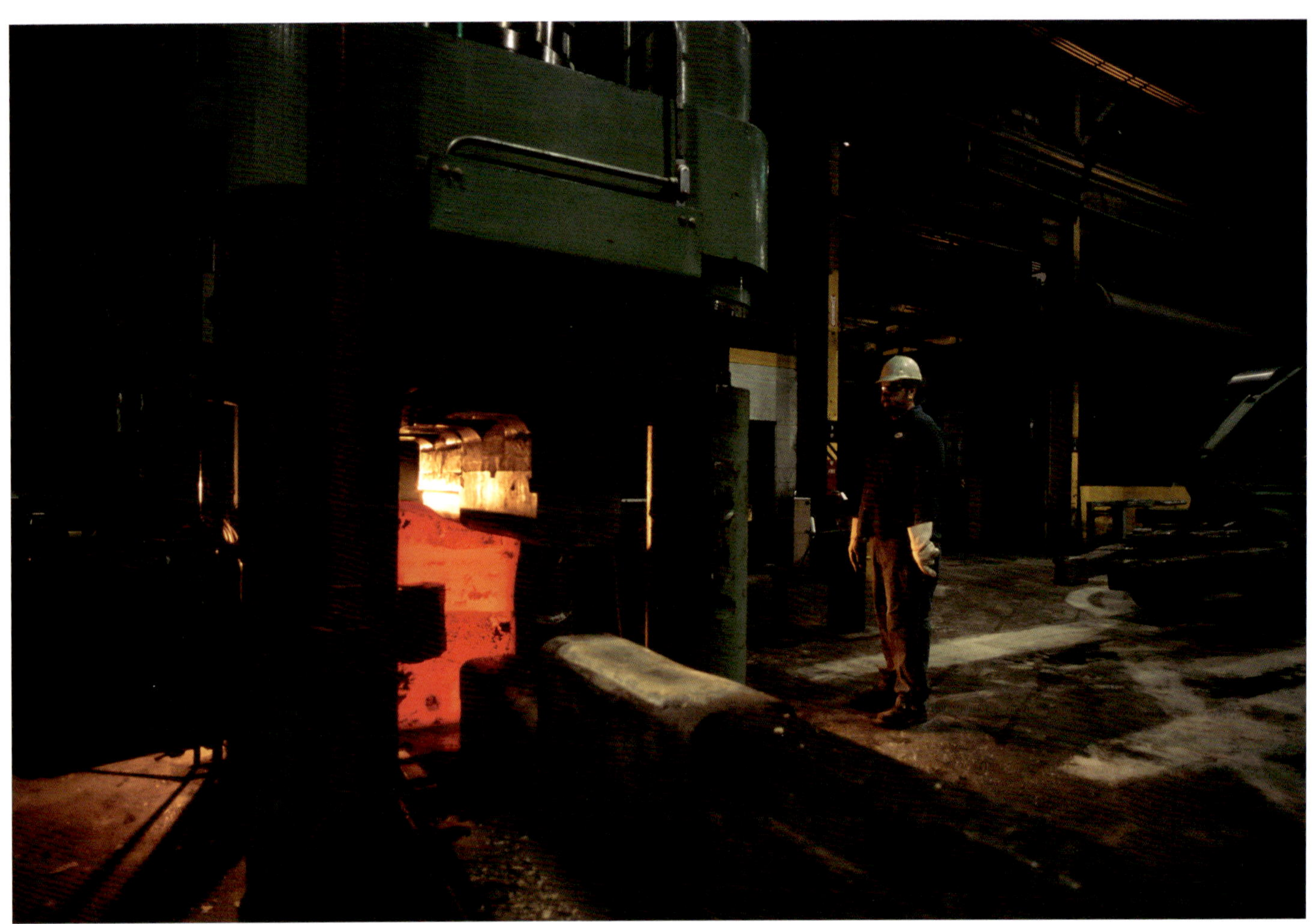

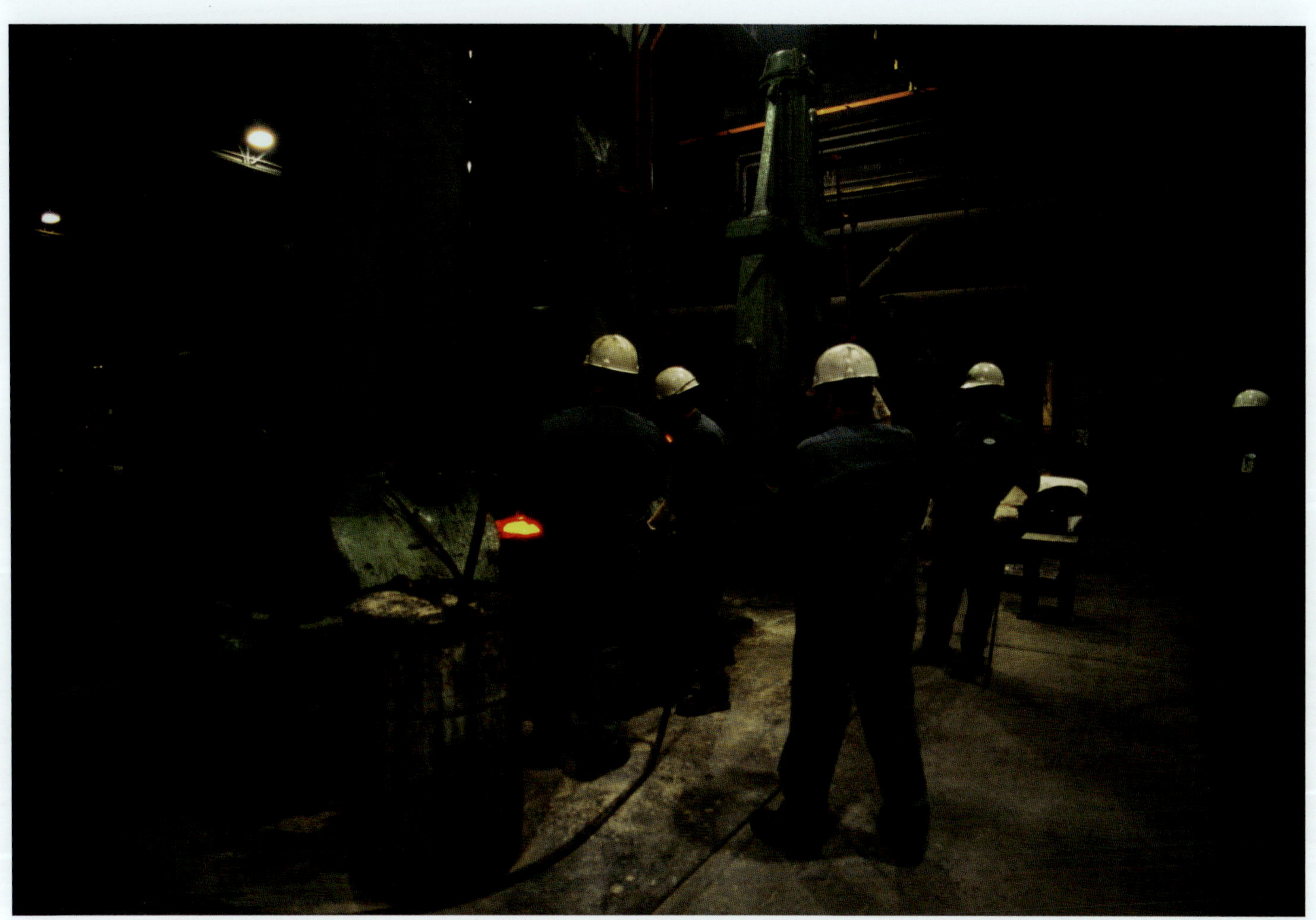

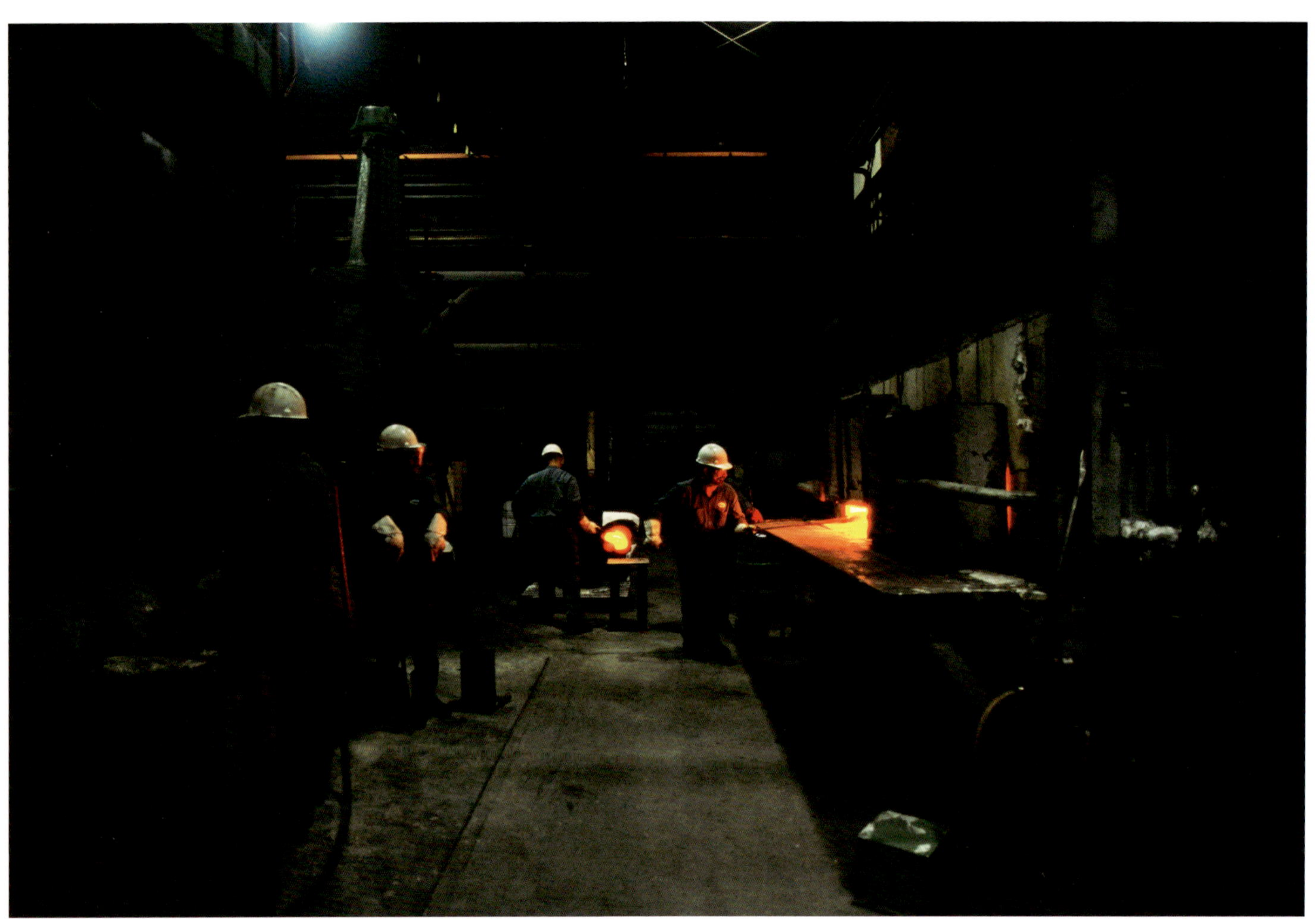

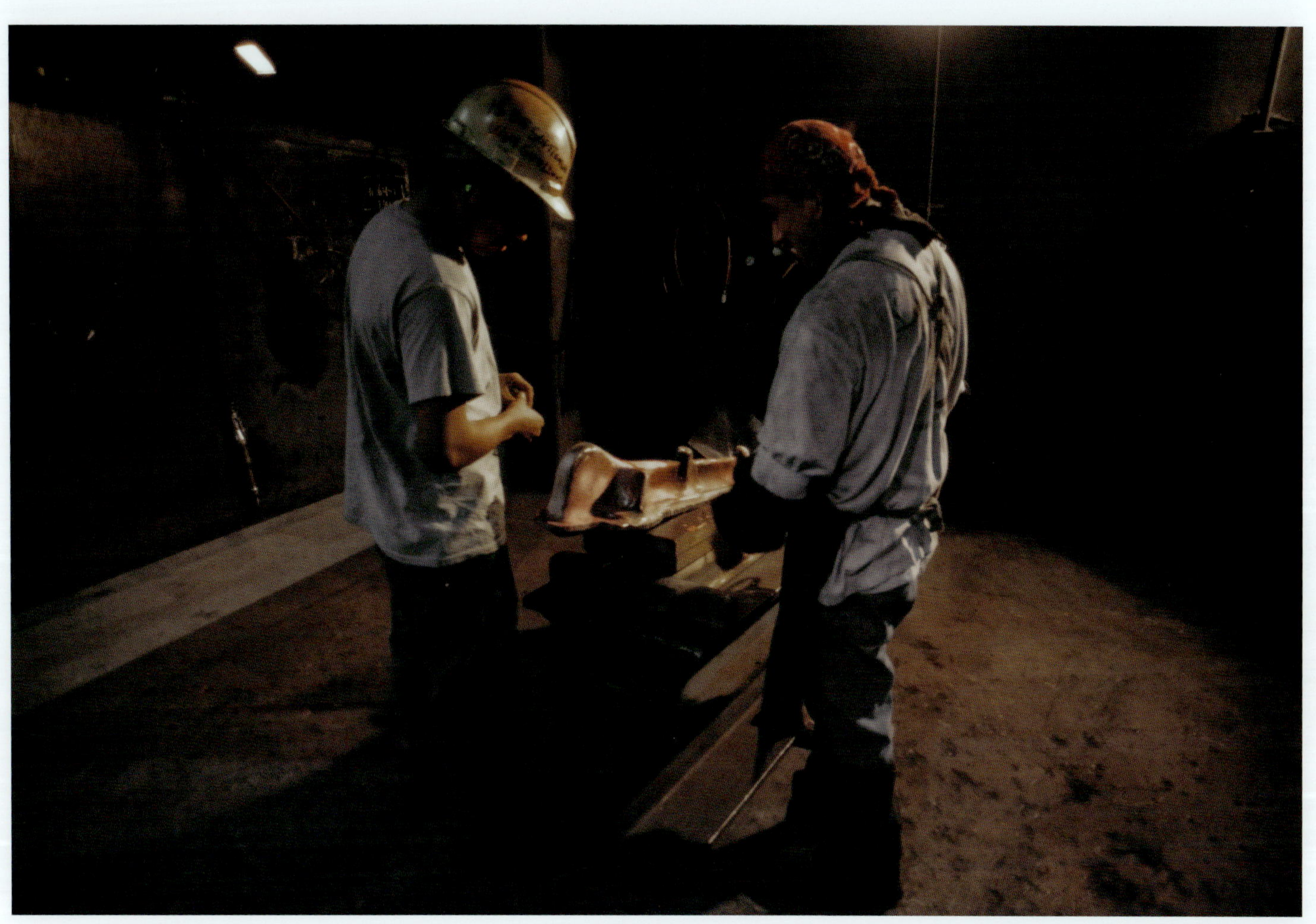

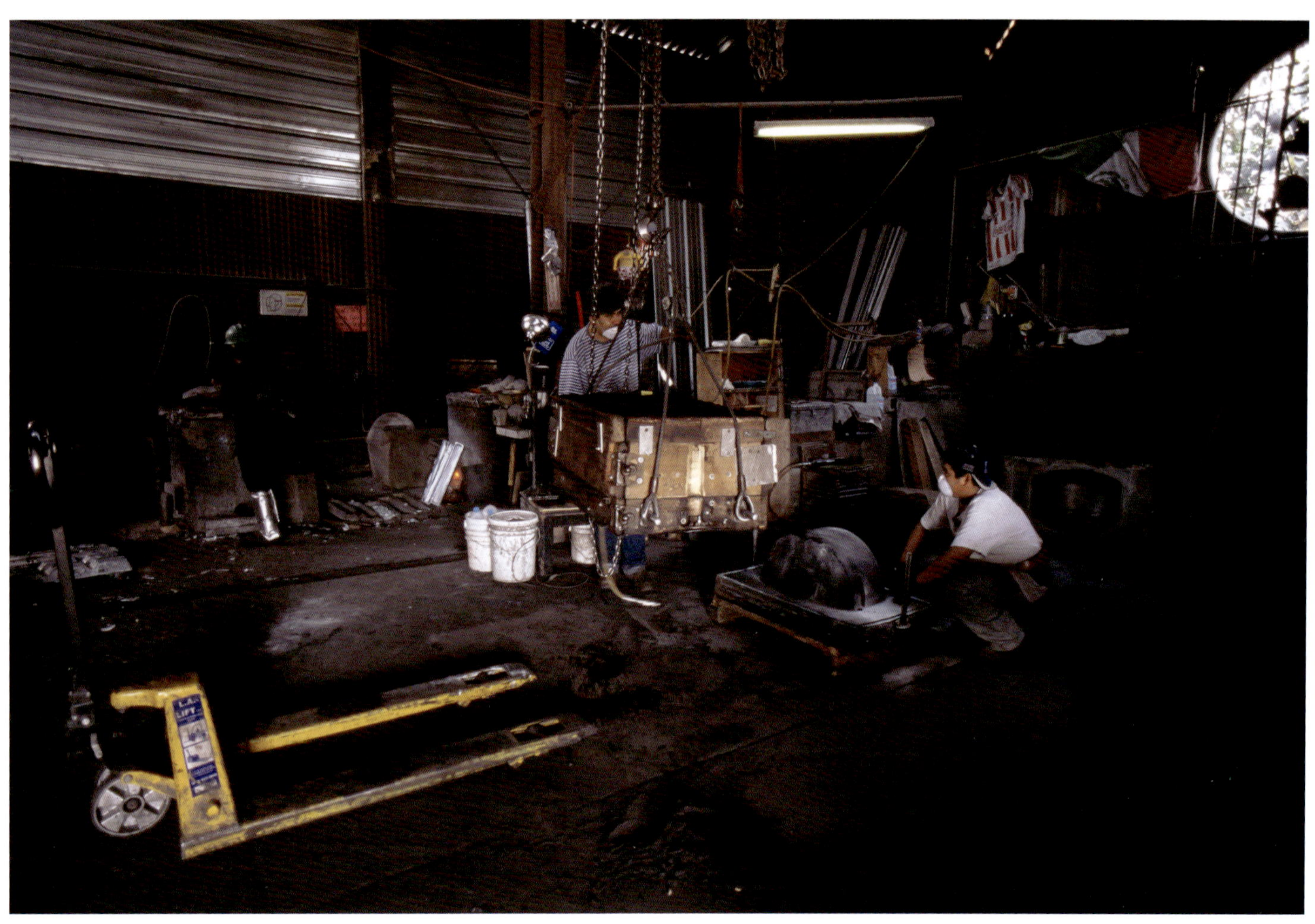

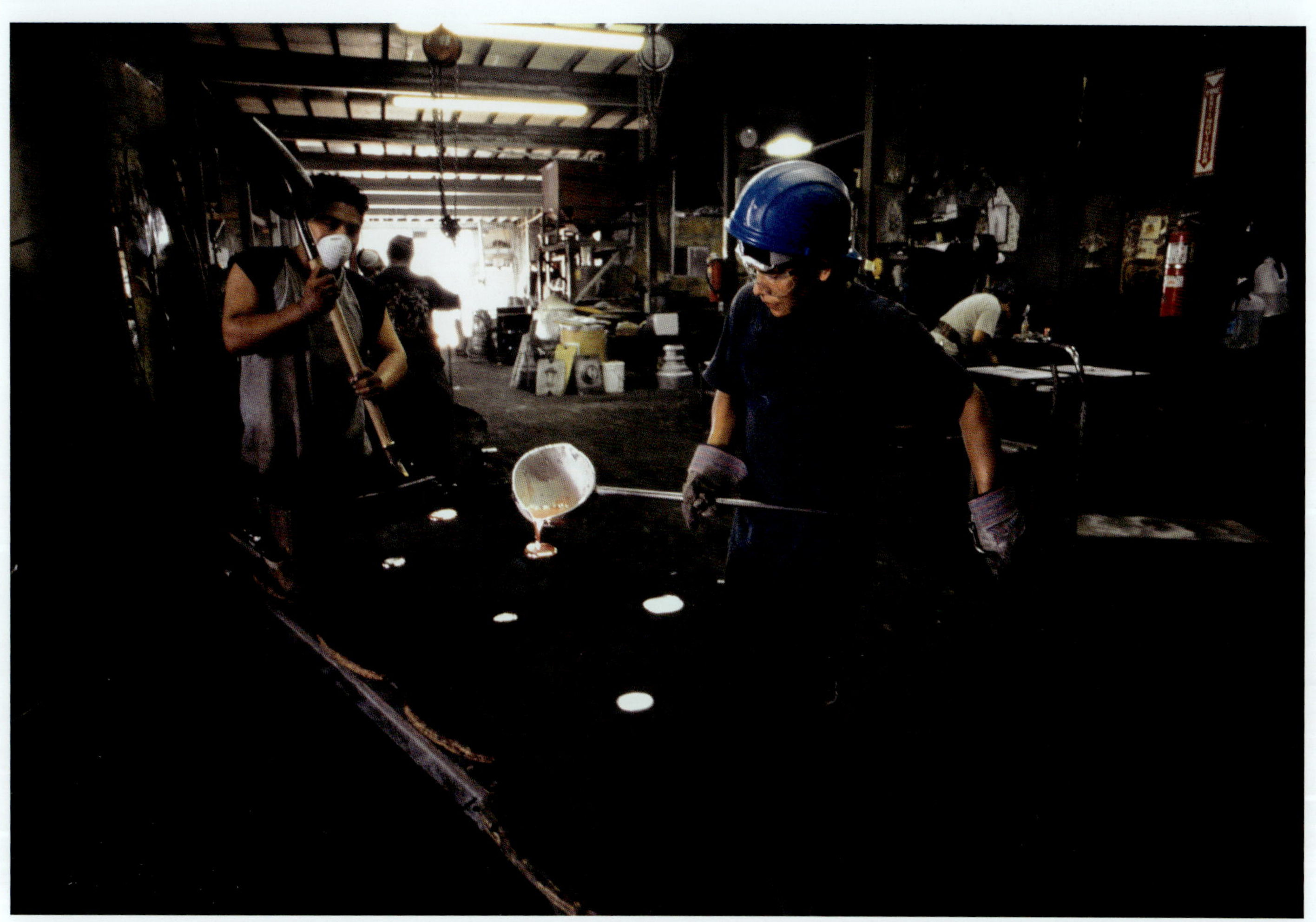

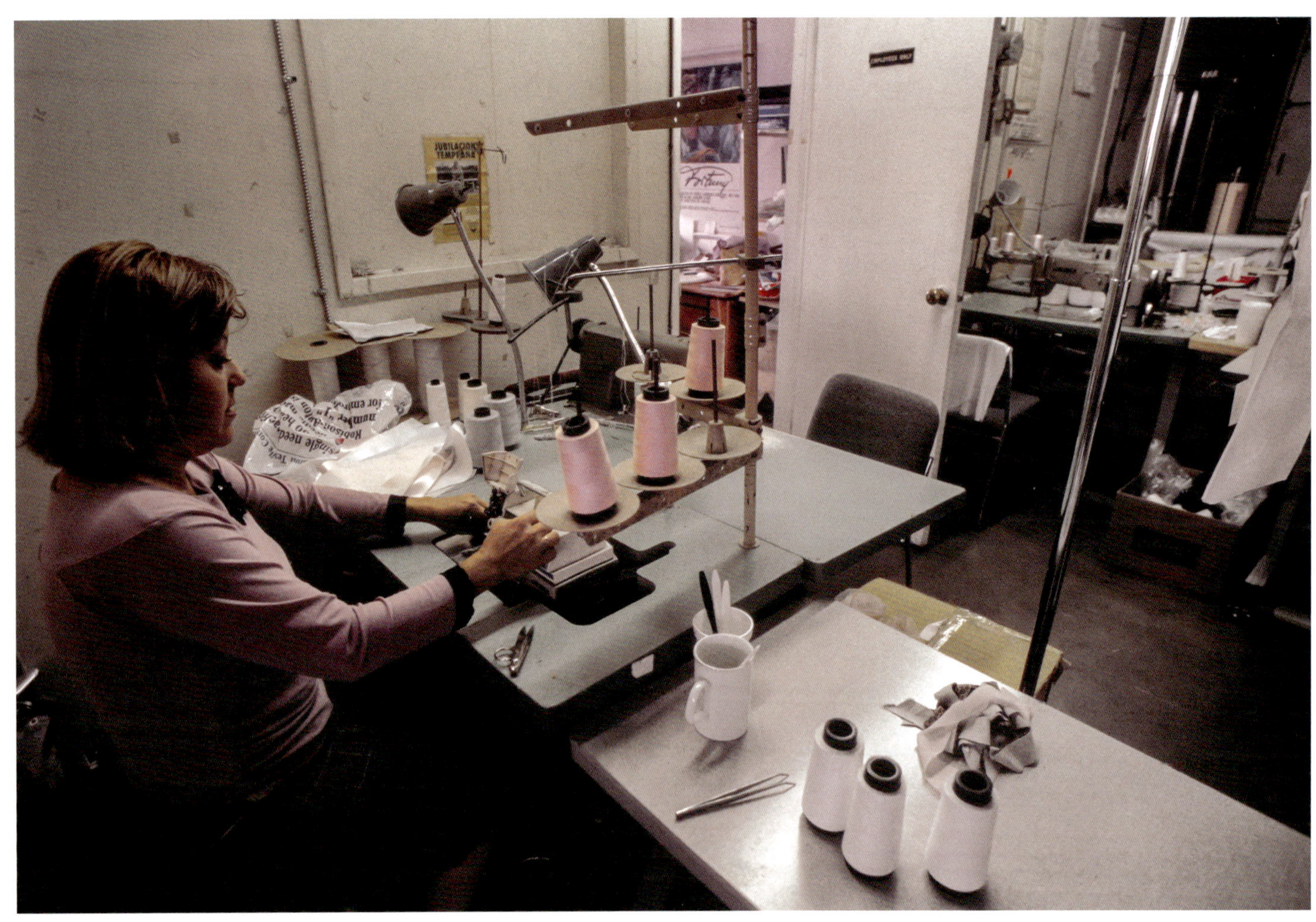

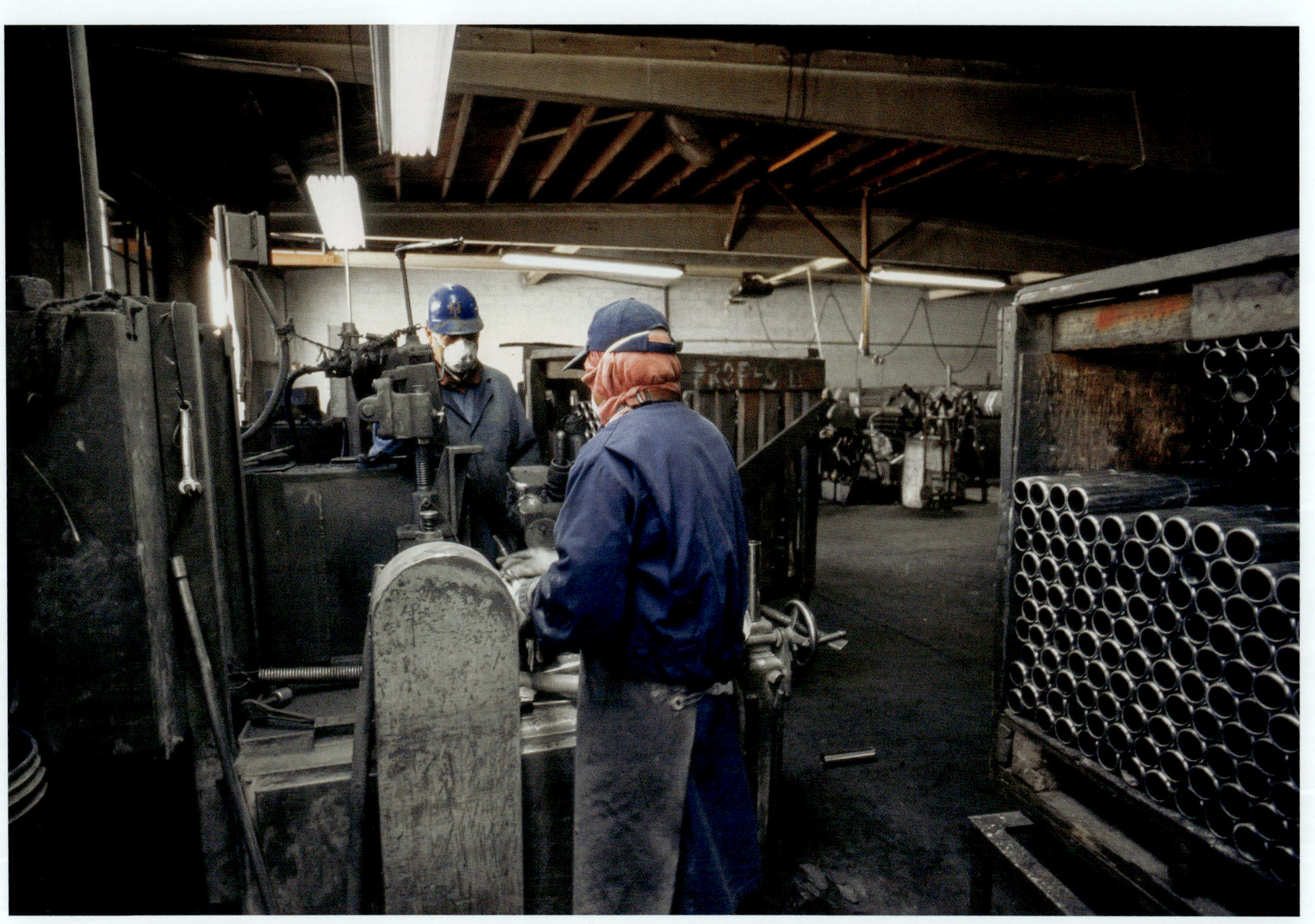

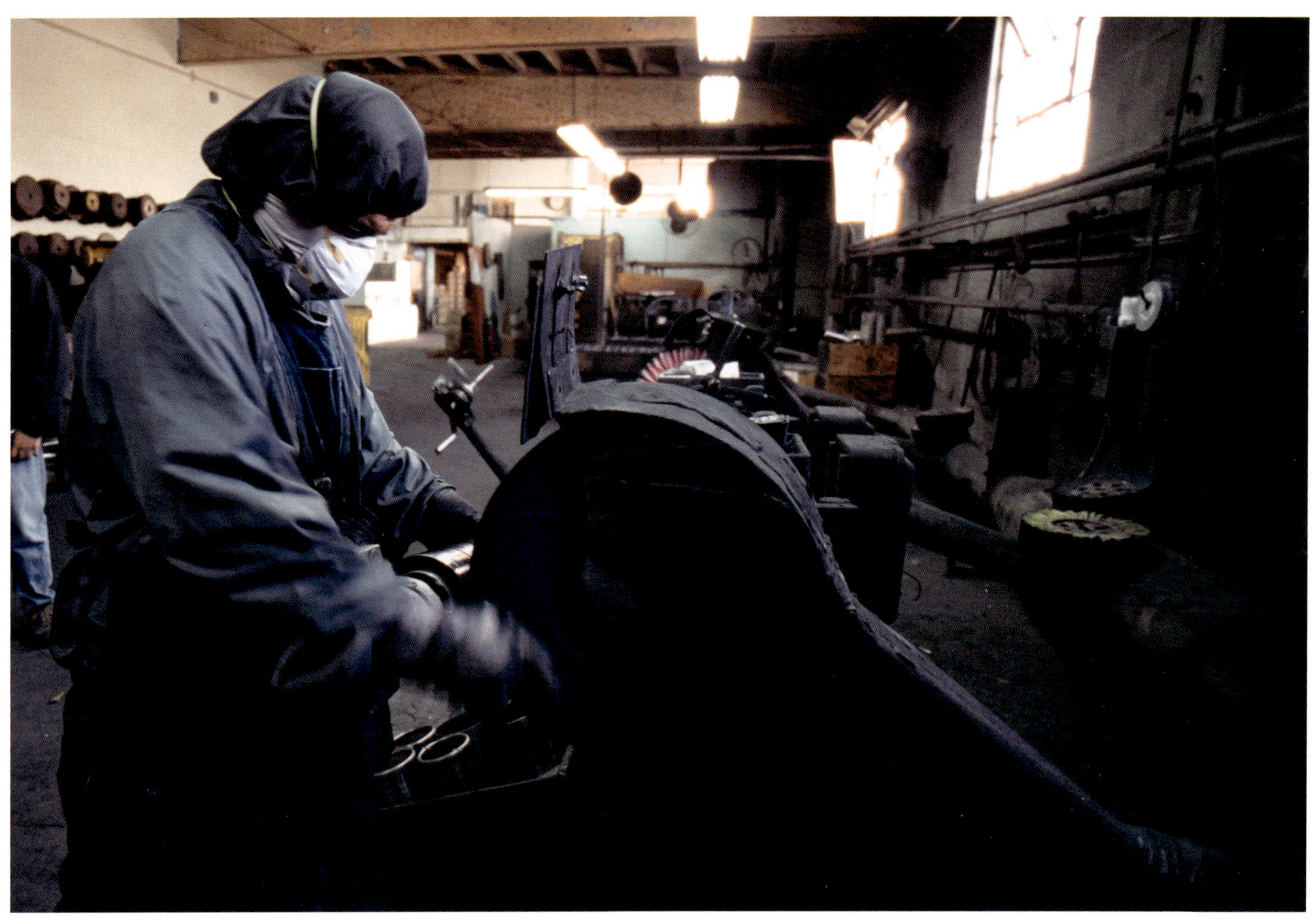

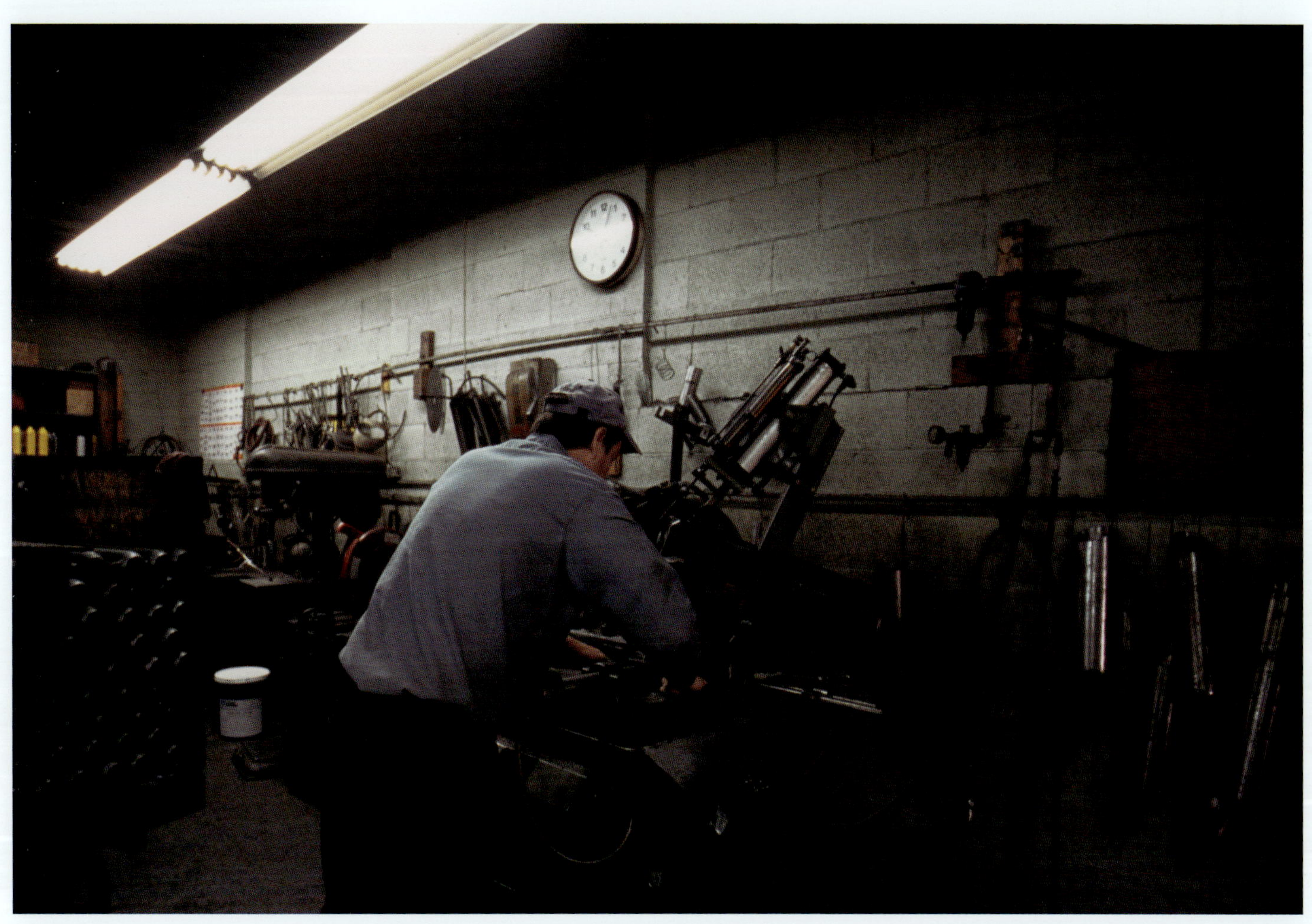

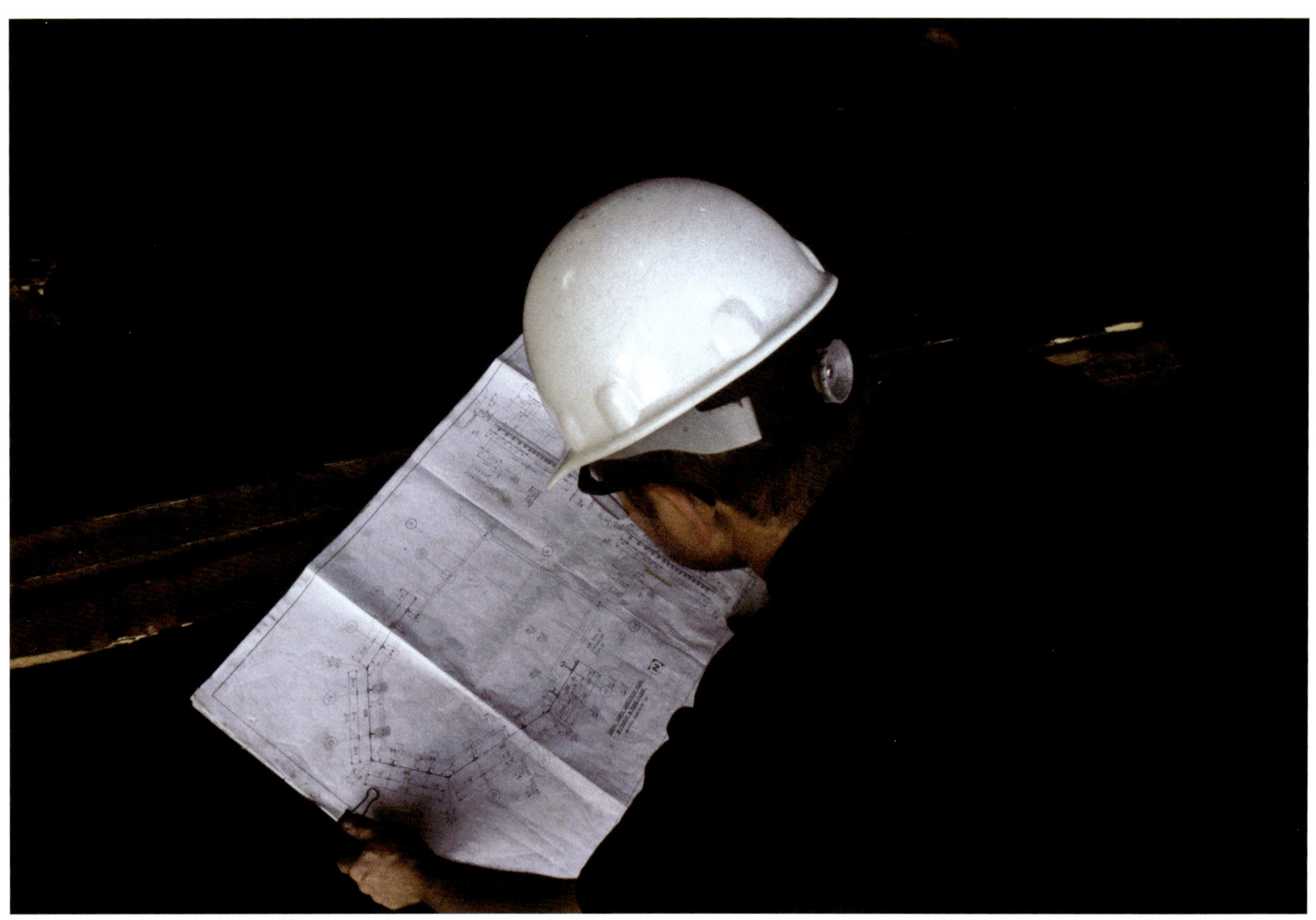

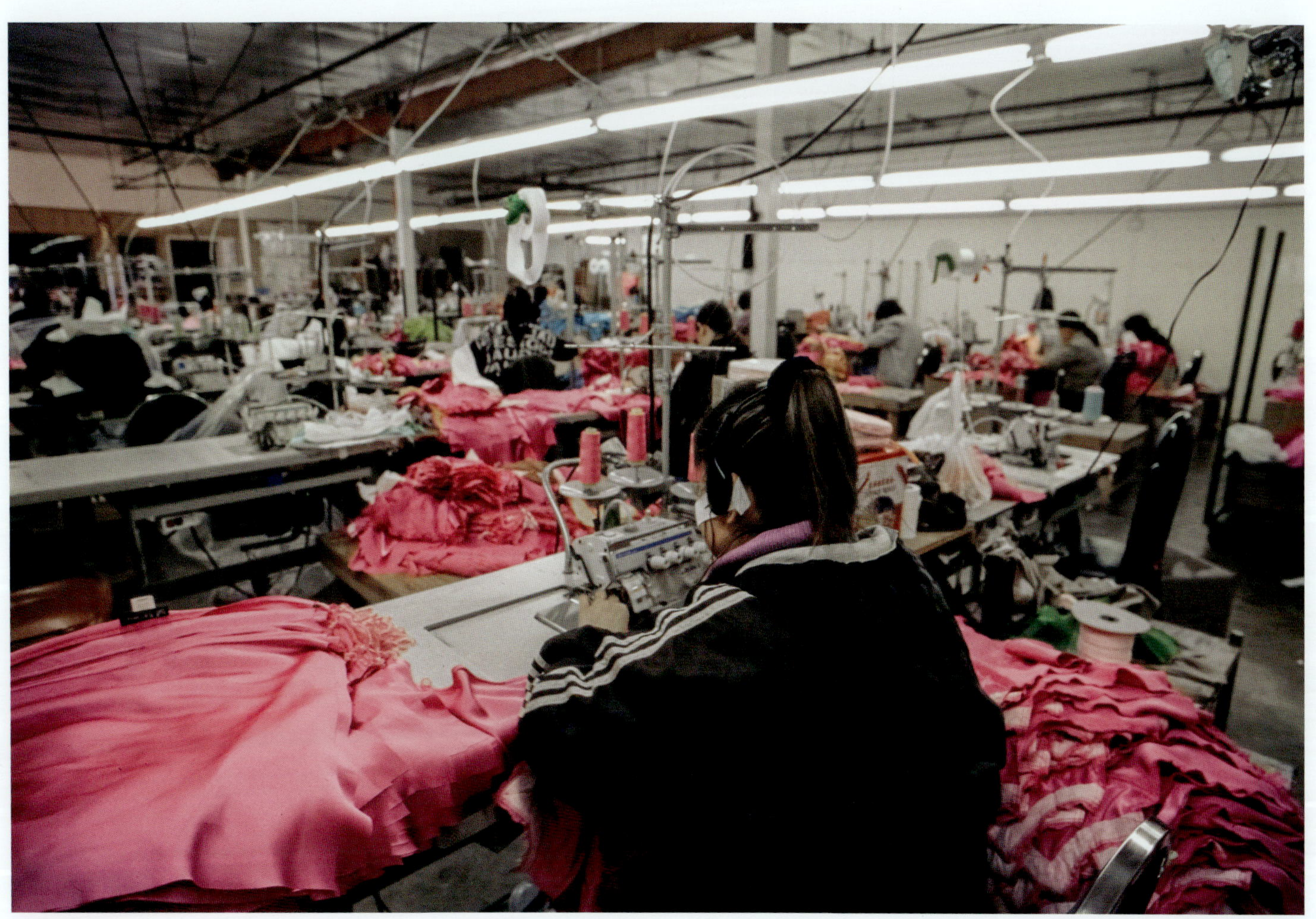

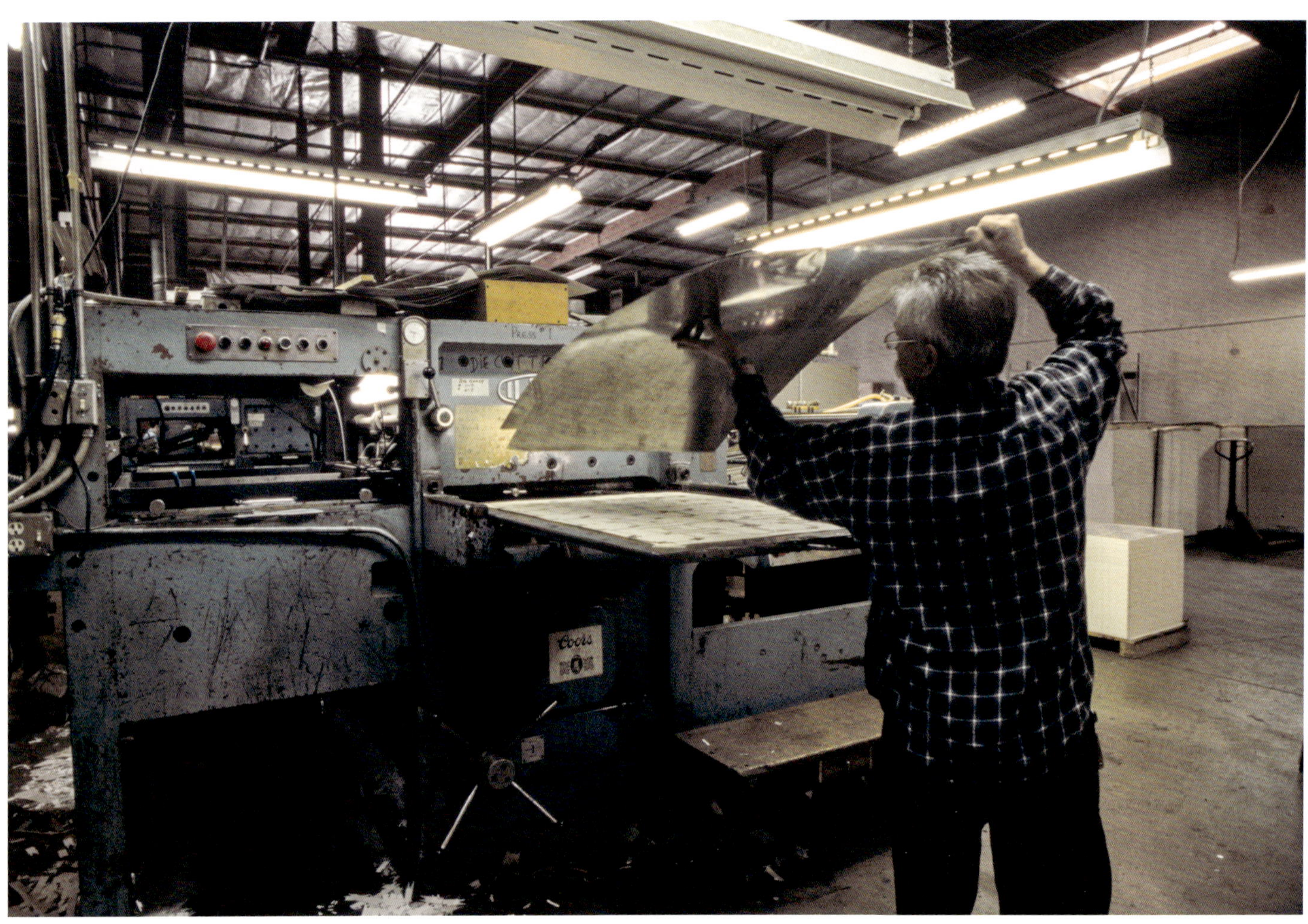

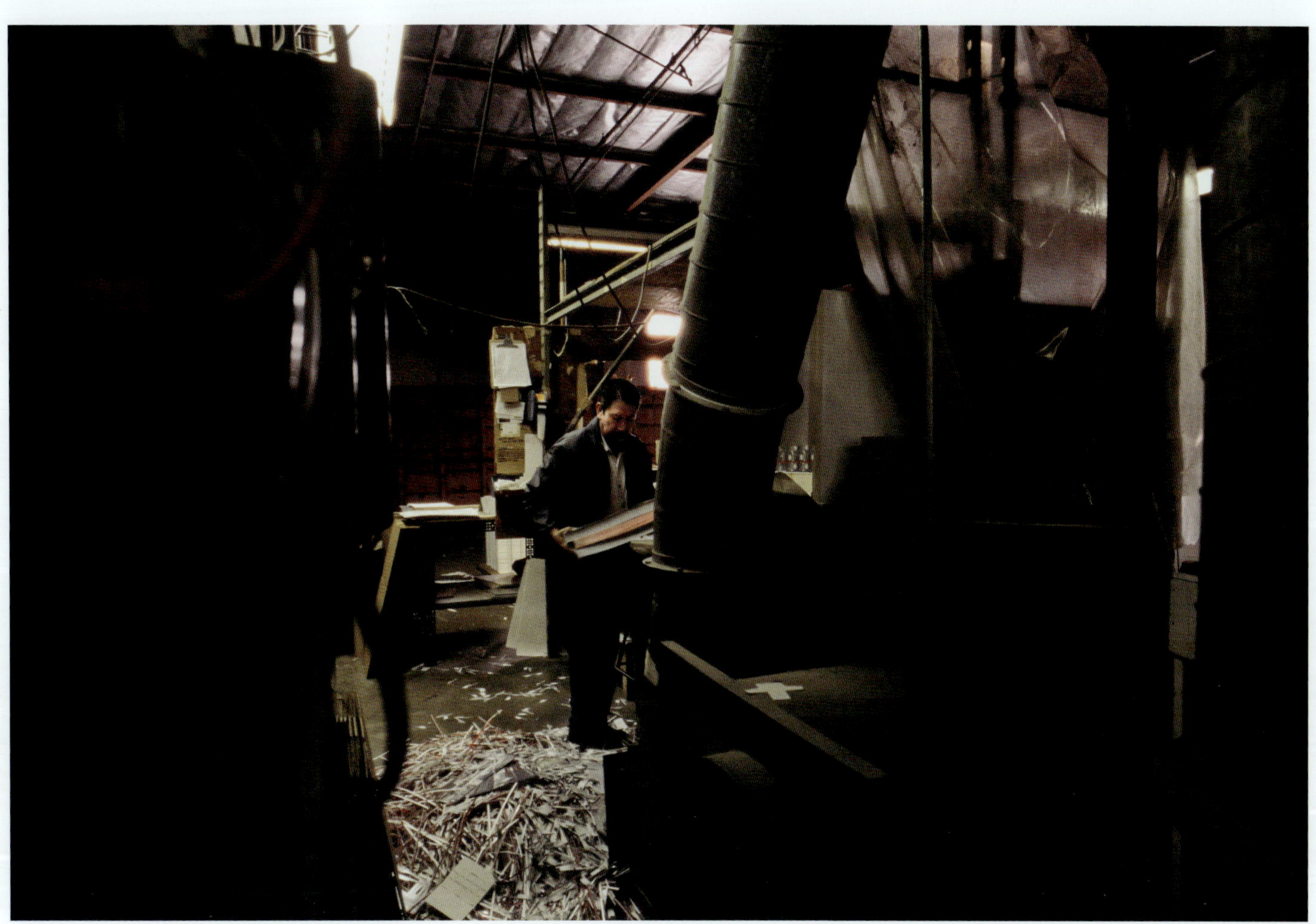

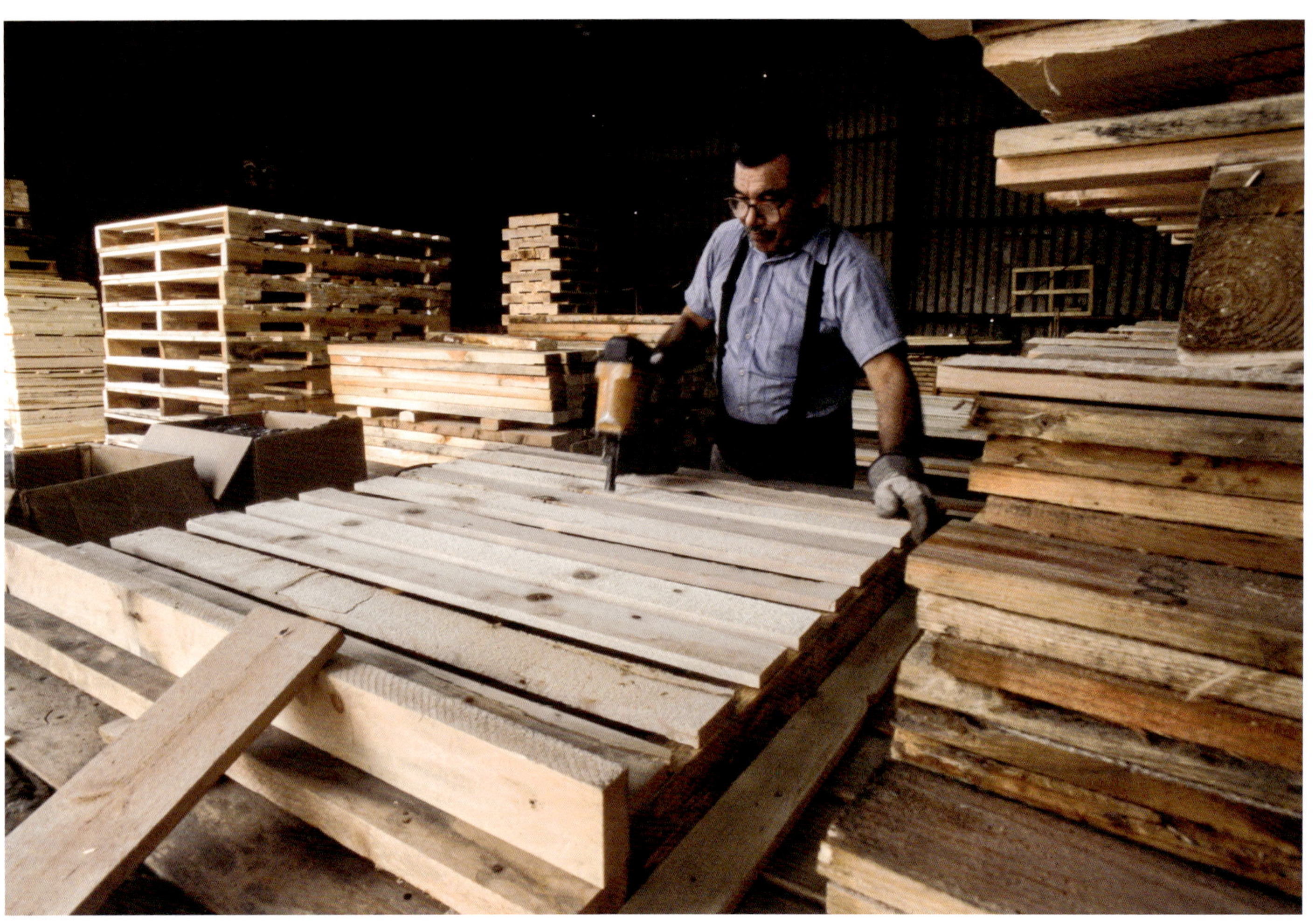

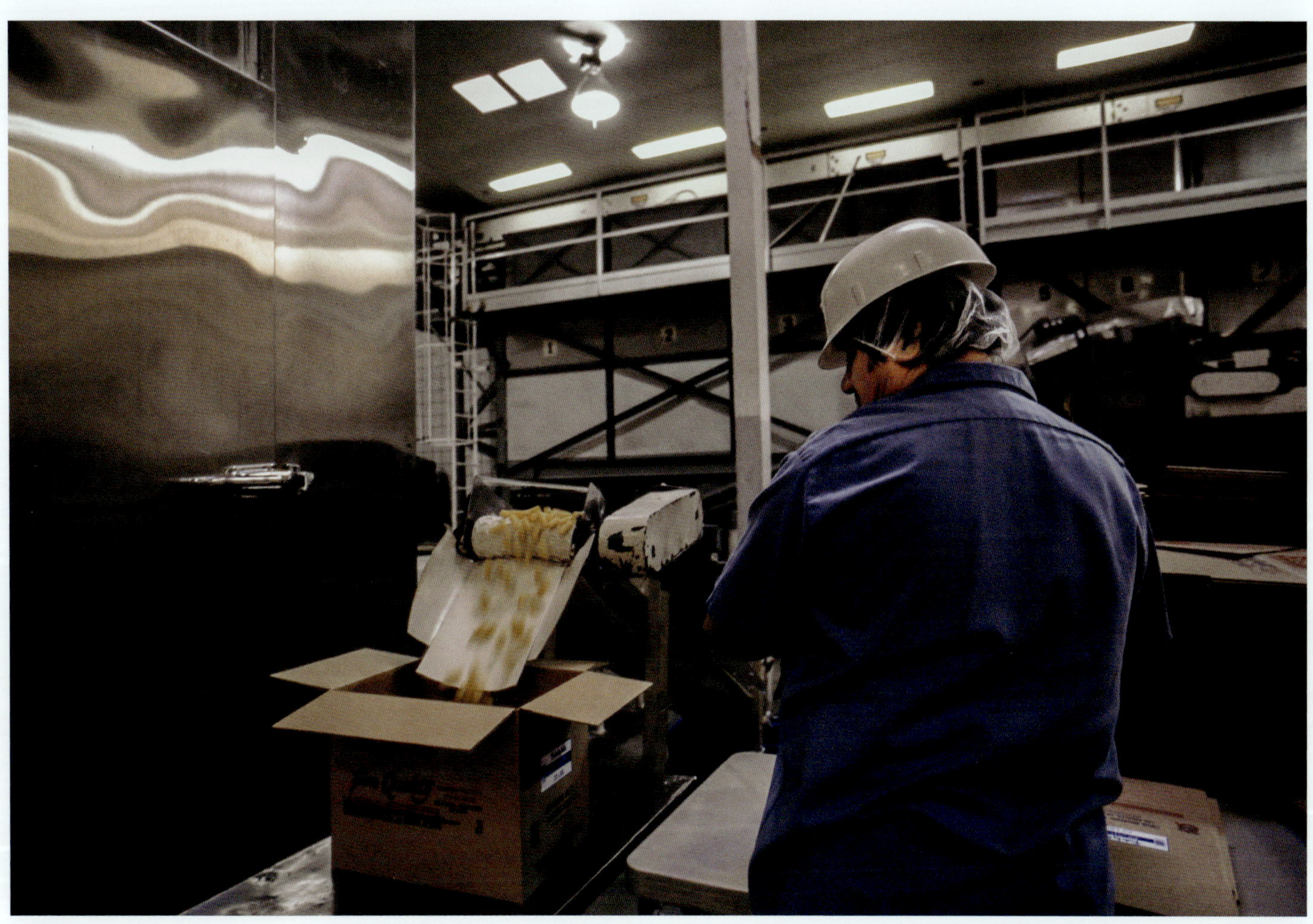

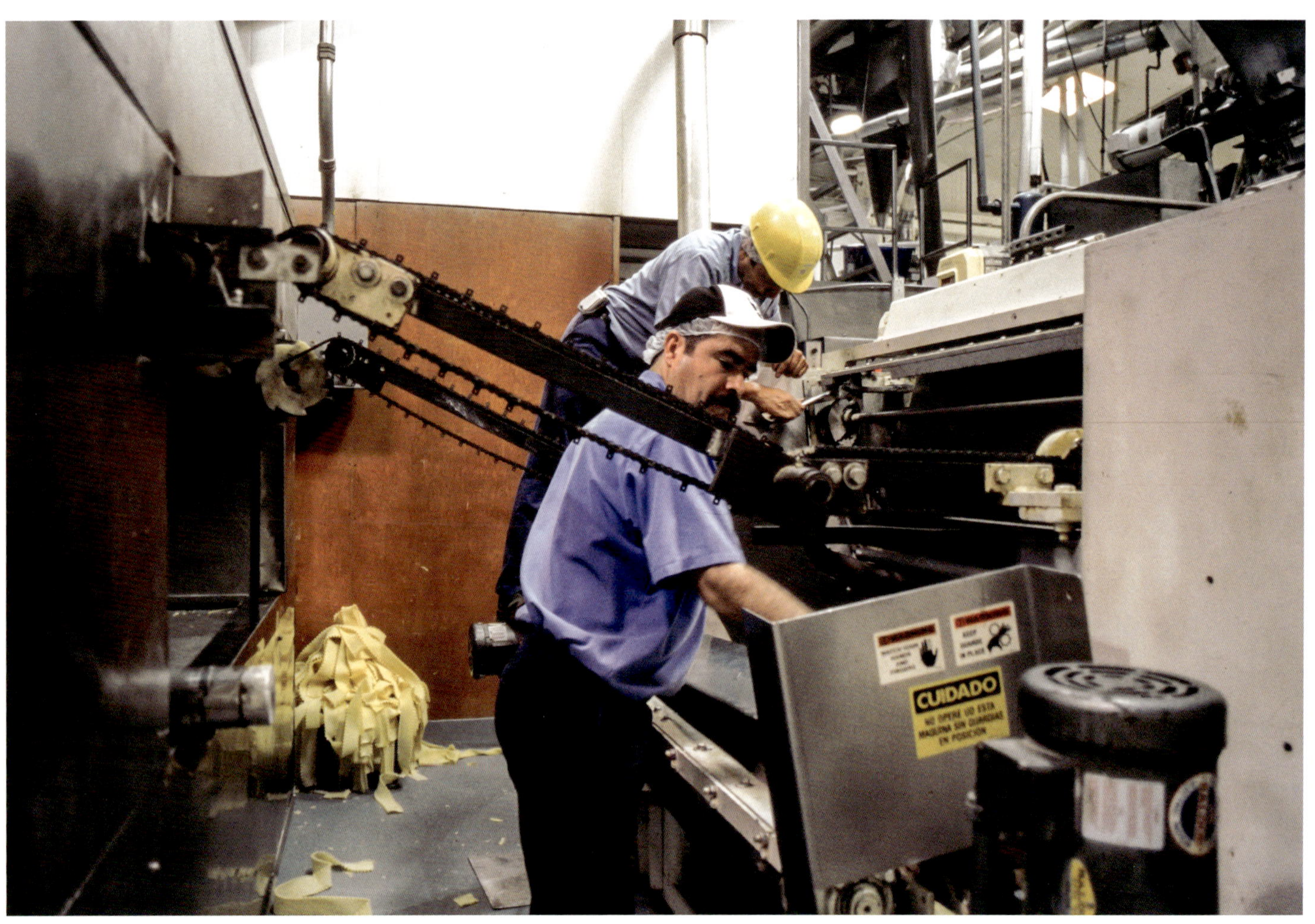
CUIDADO
NO OPERE UD ESTA
MAQUINA SIN GUARDAS
EN POSICIÓN

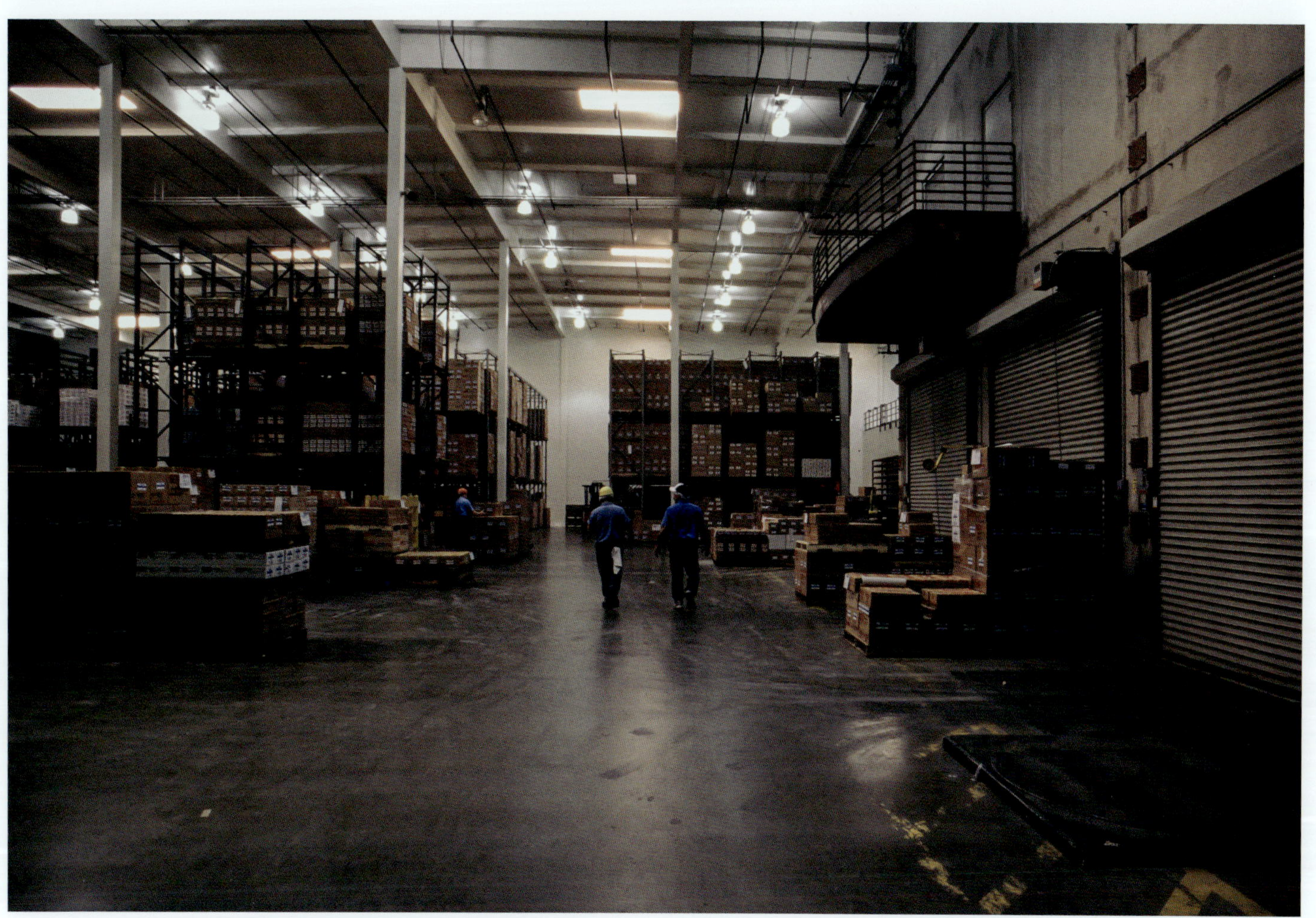

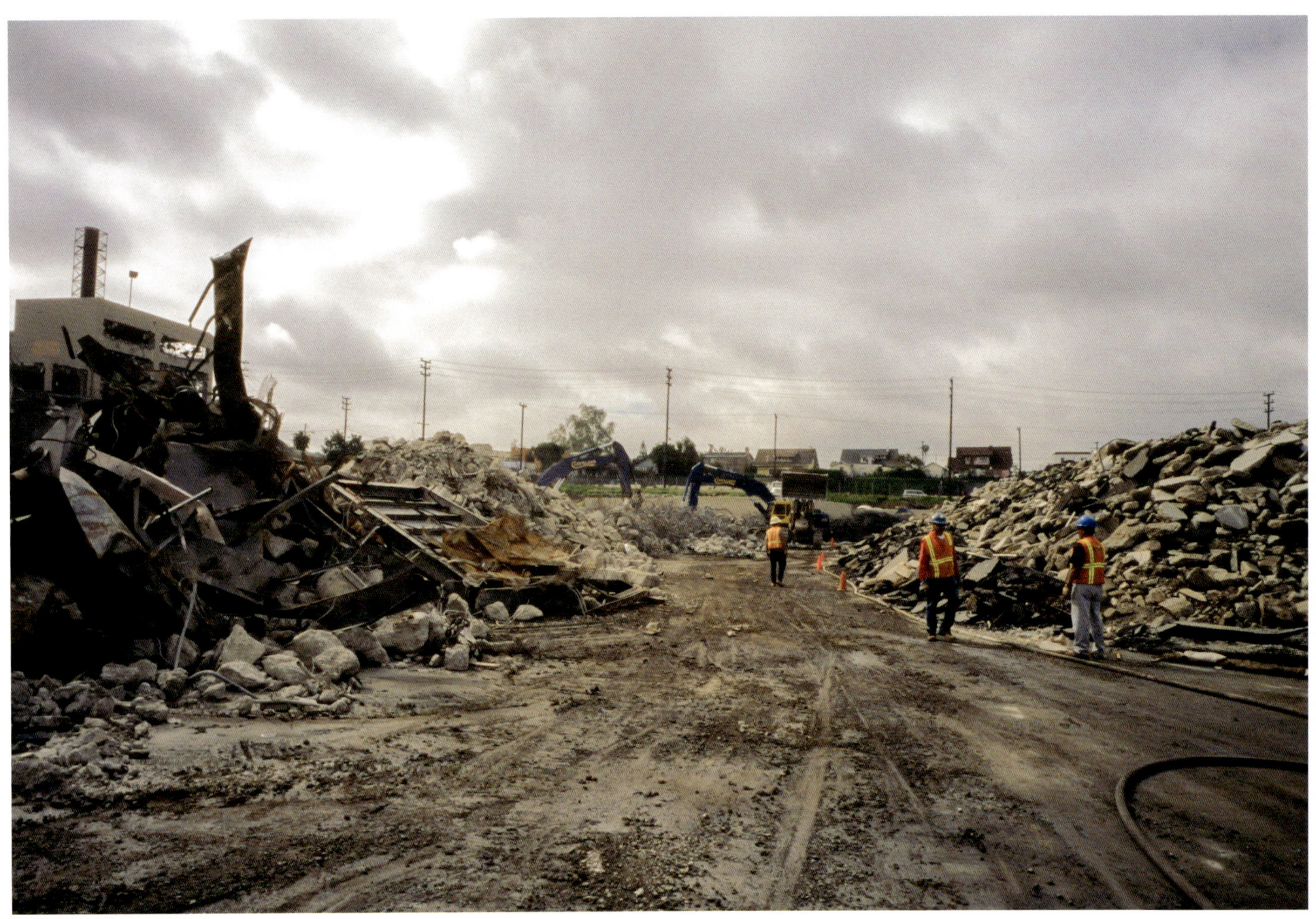

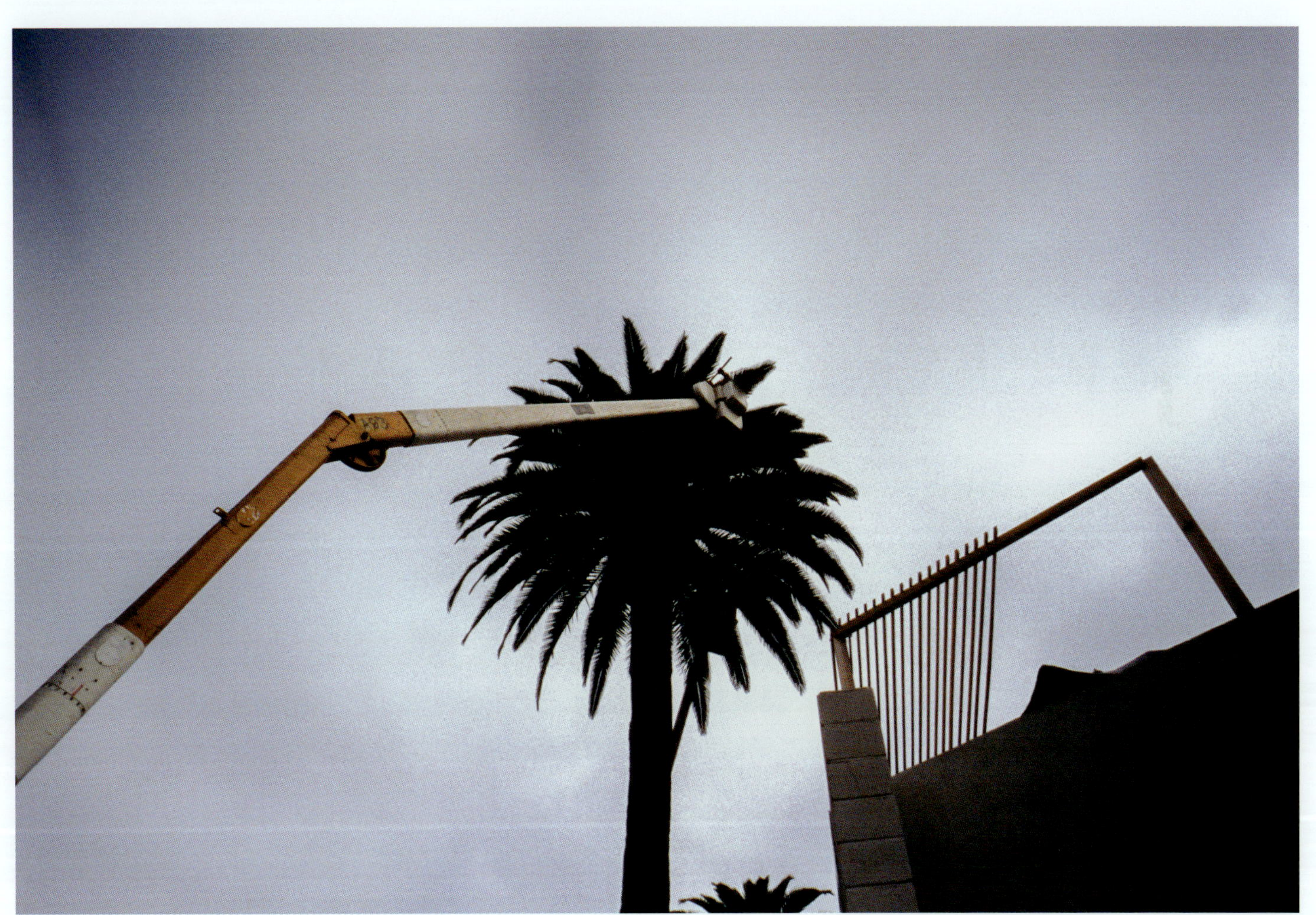

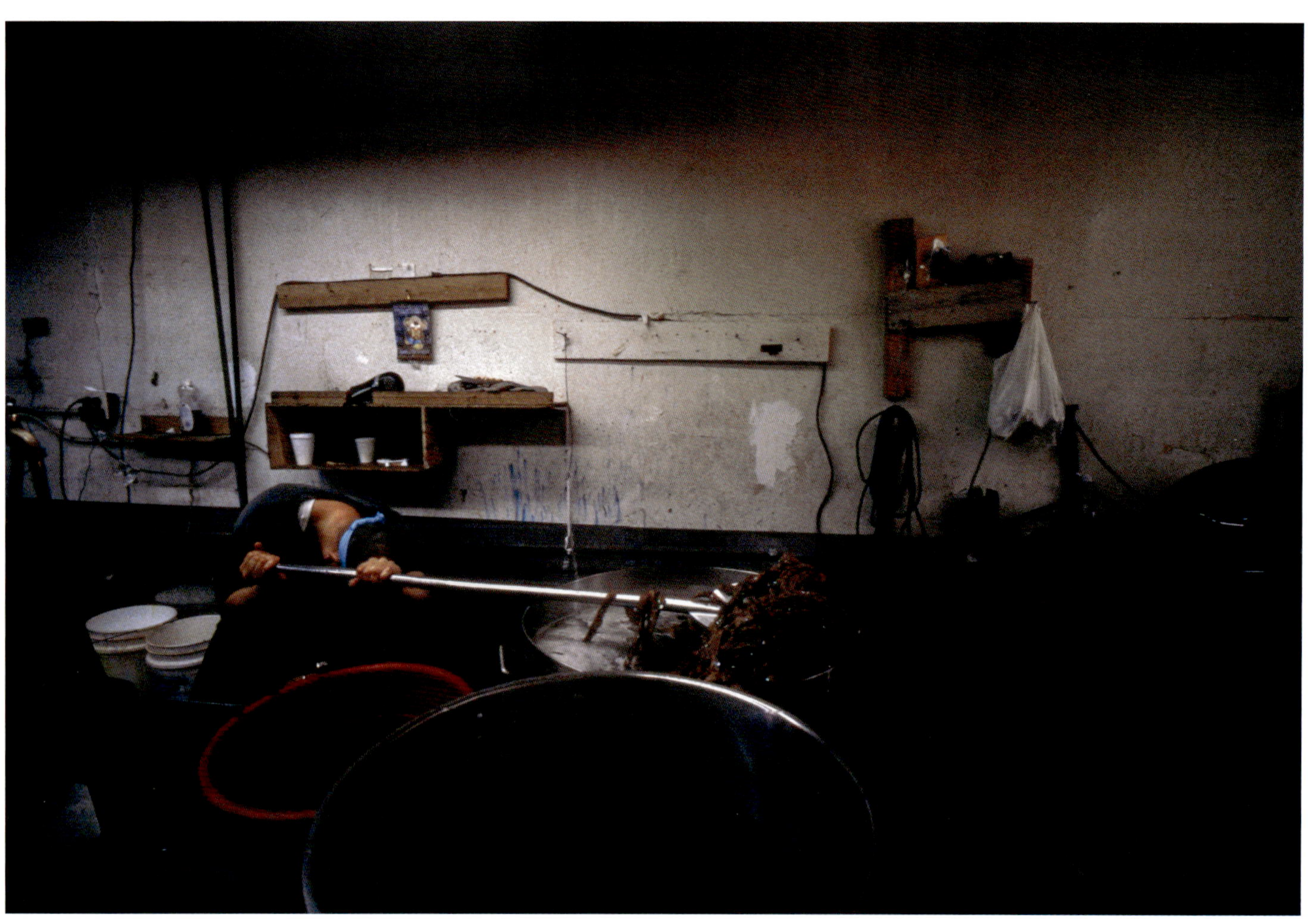

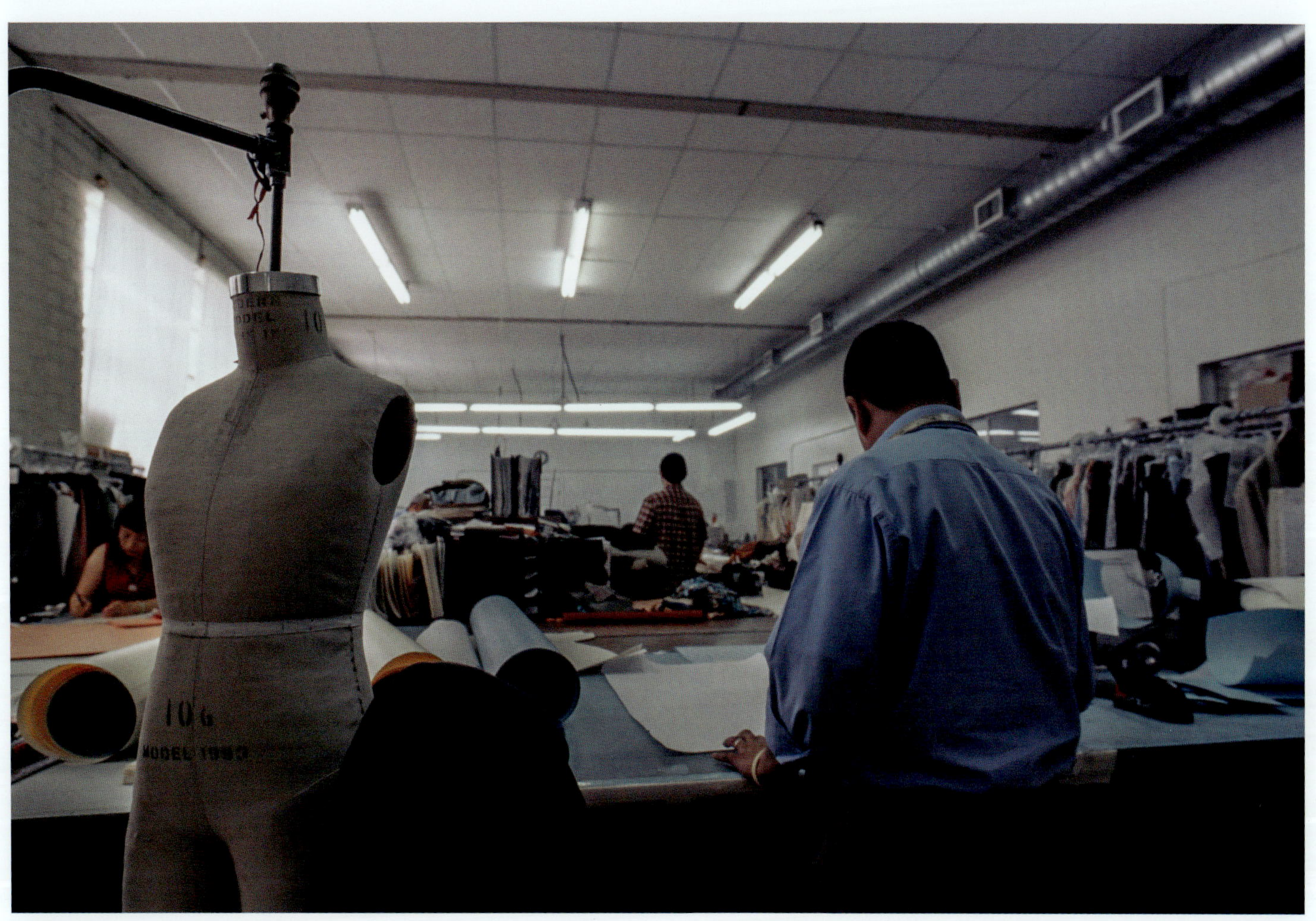

106
MODEL 1963

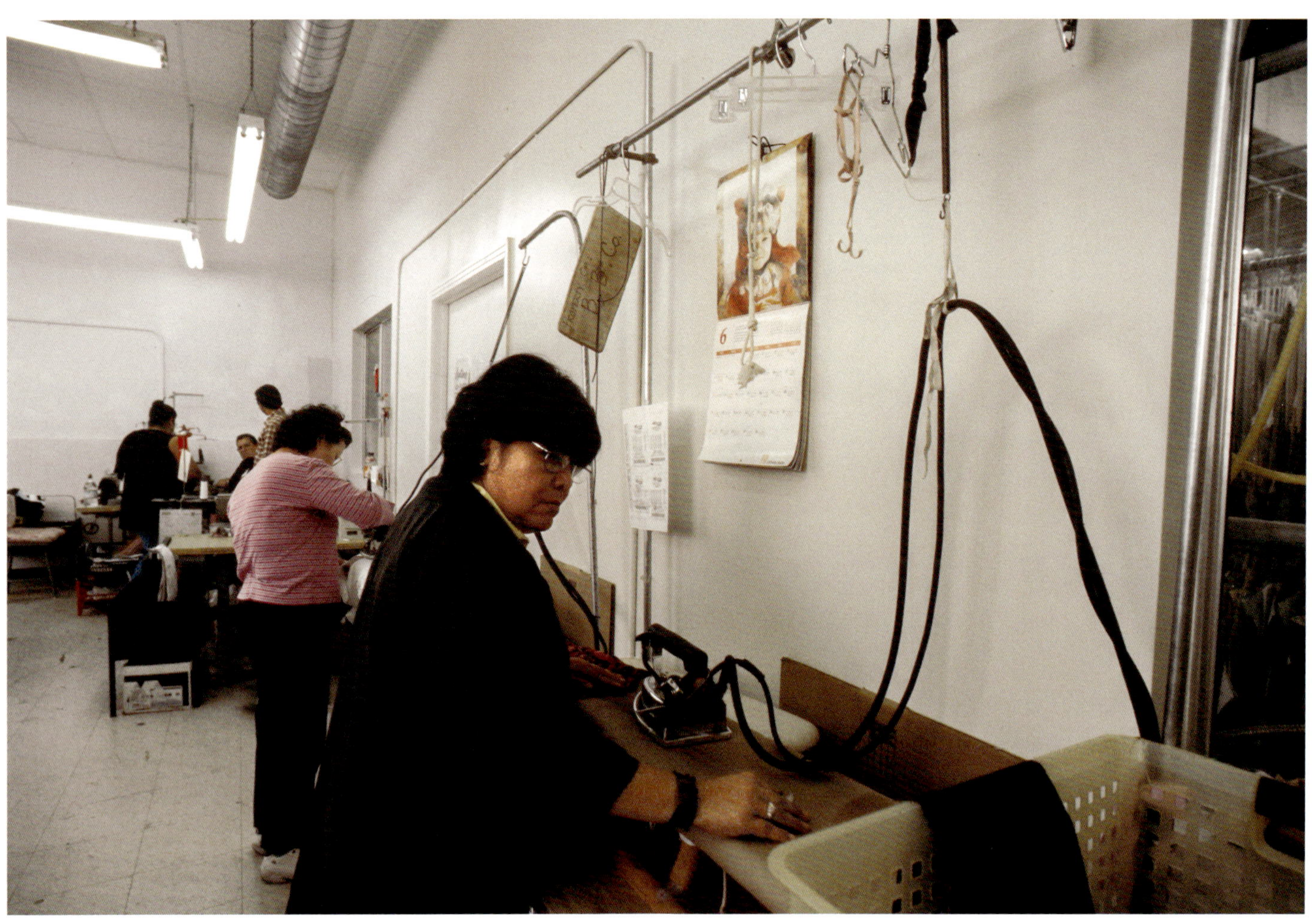

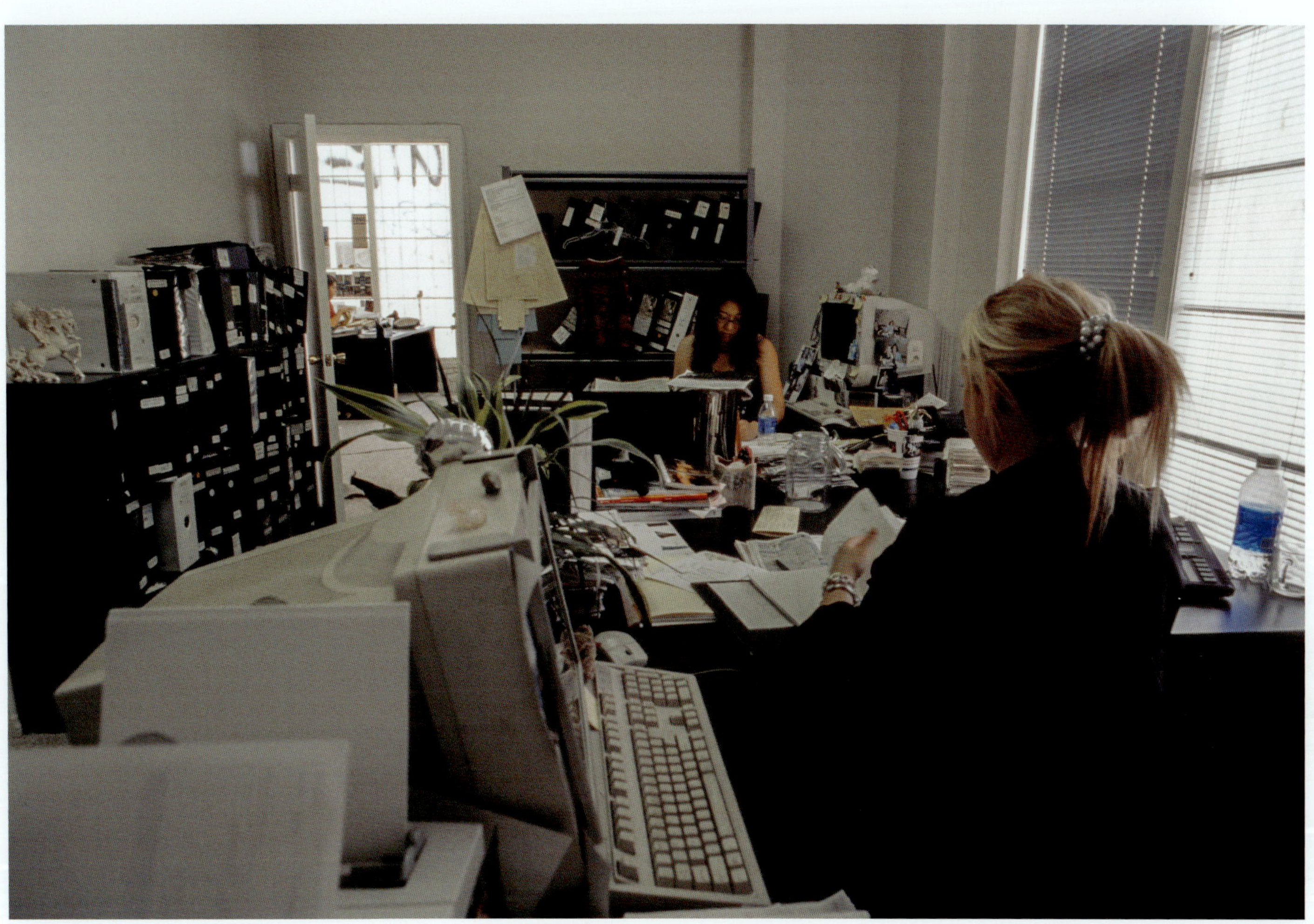

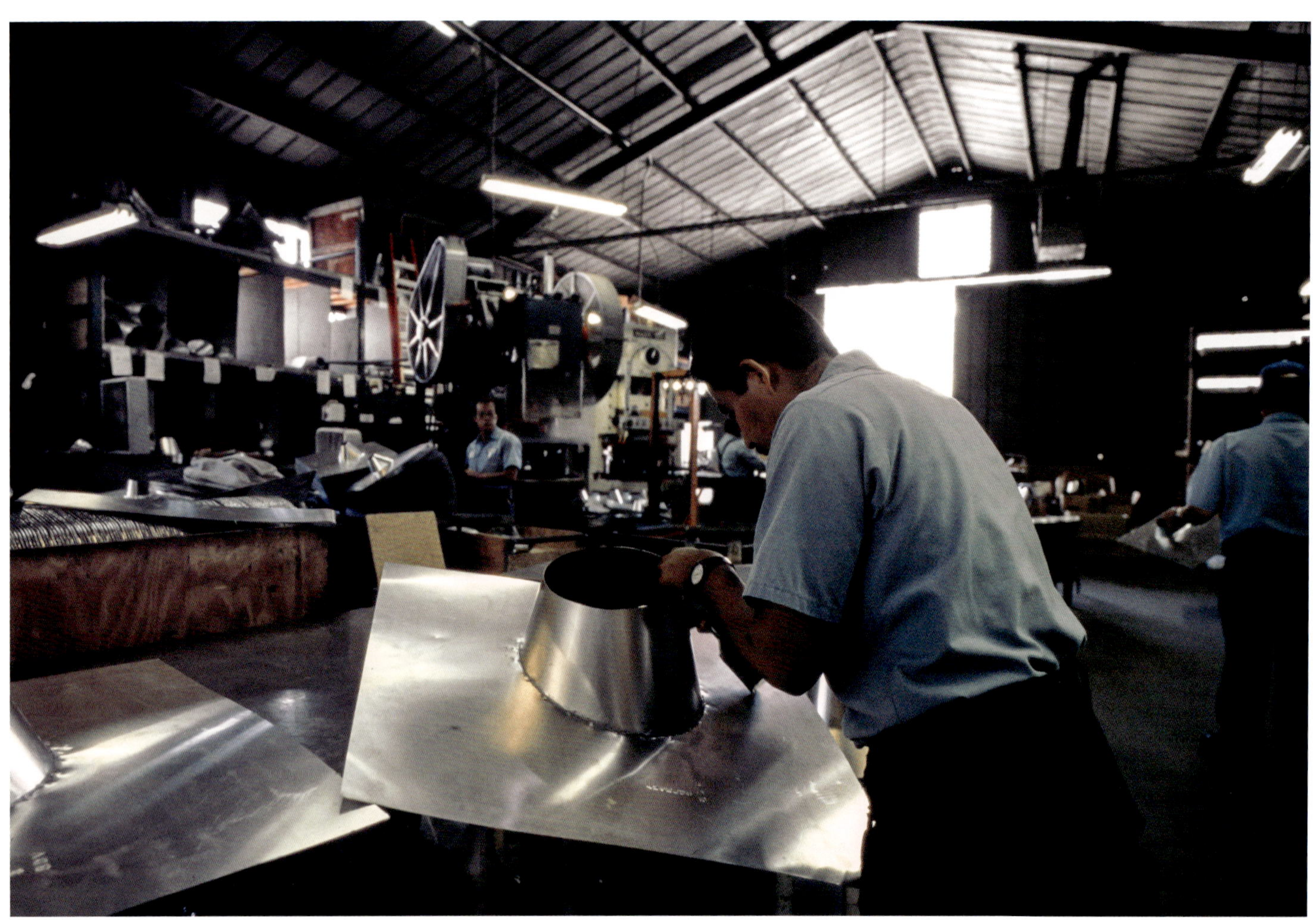

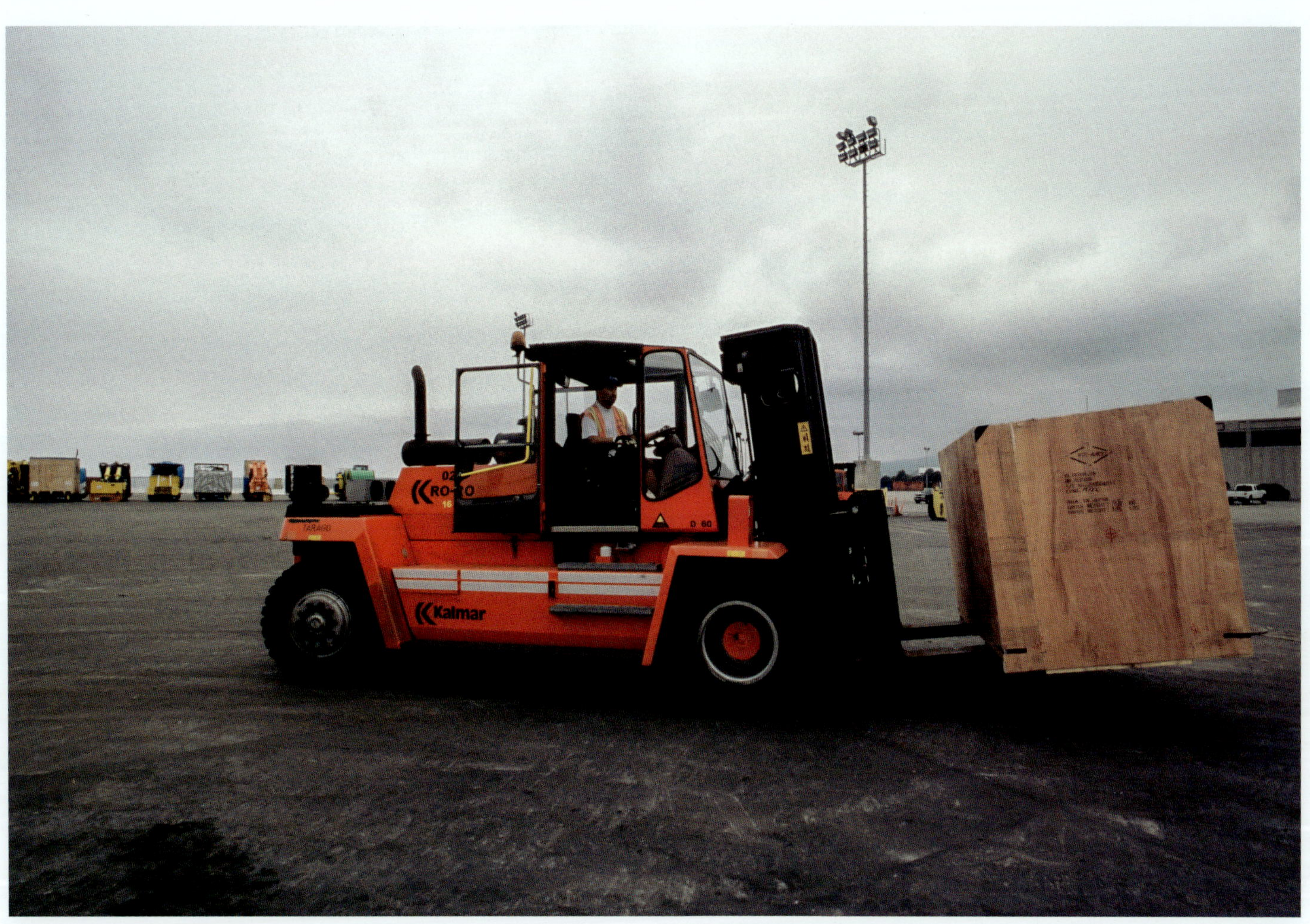

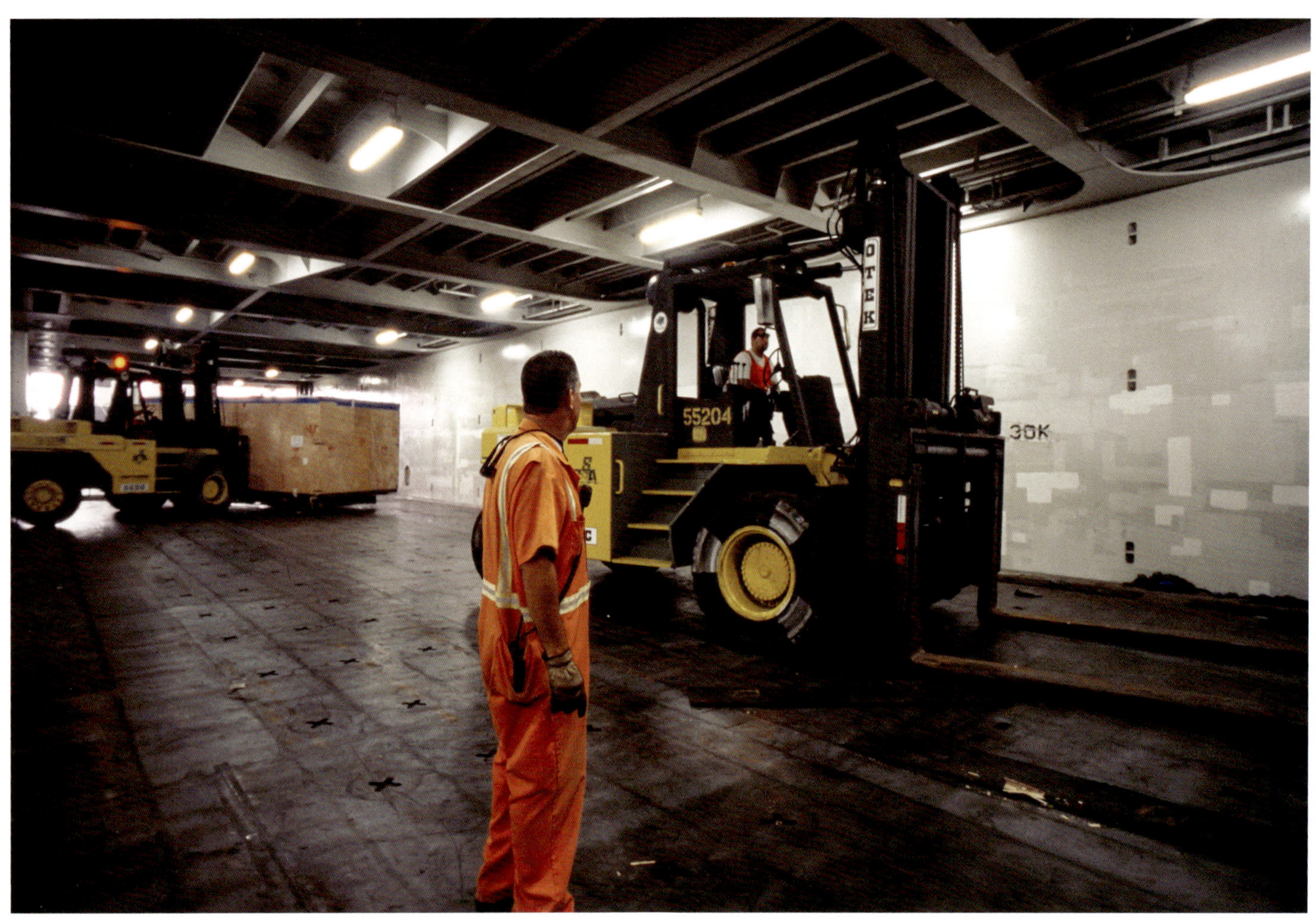

OTEK
55204
30K

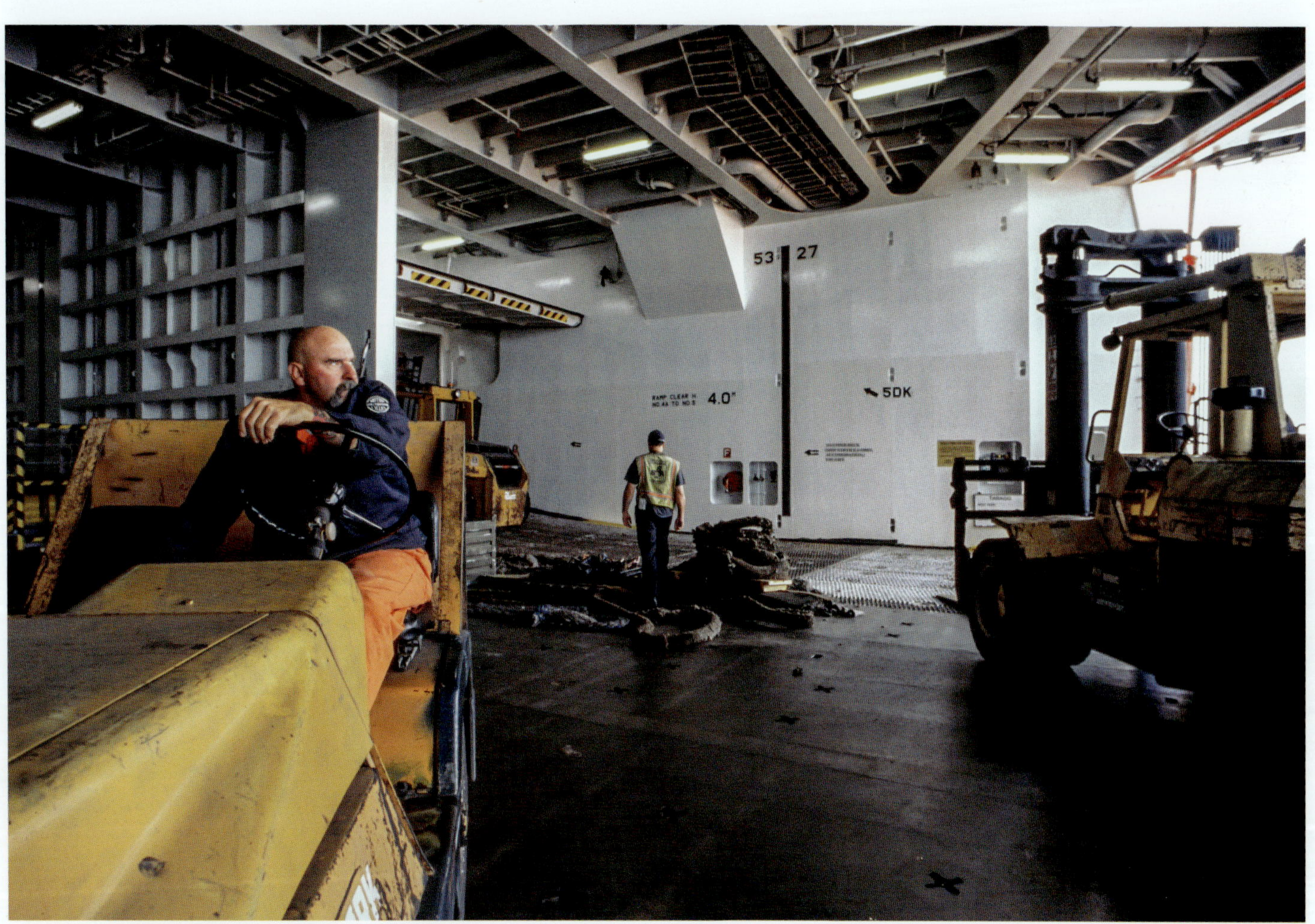

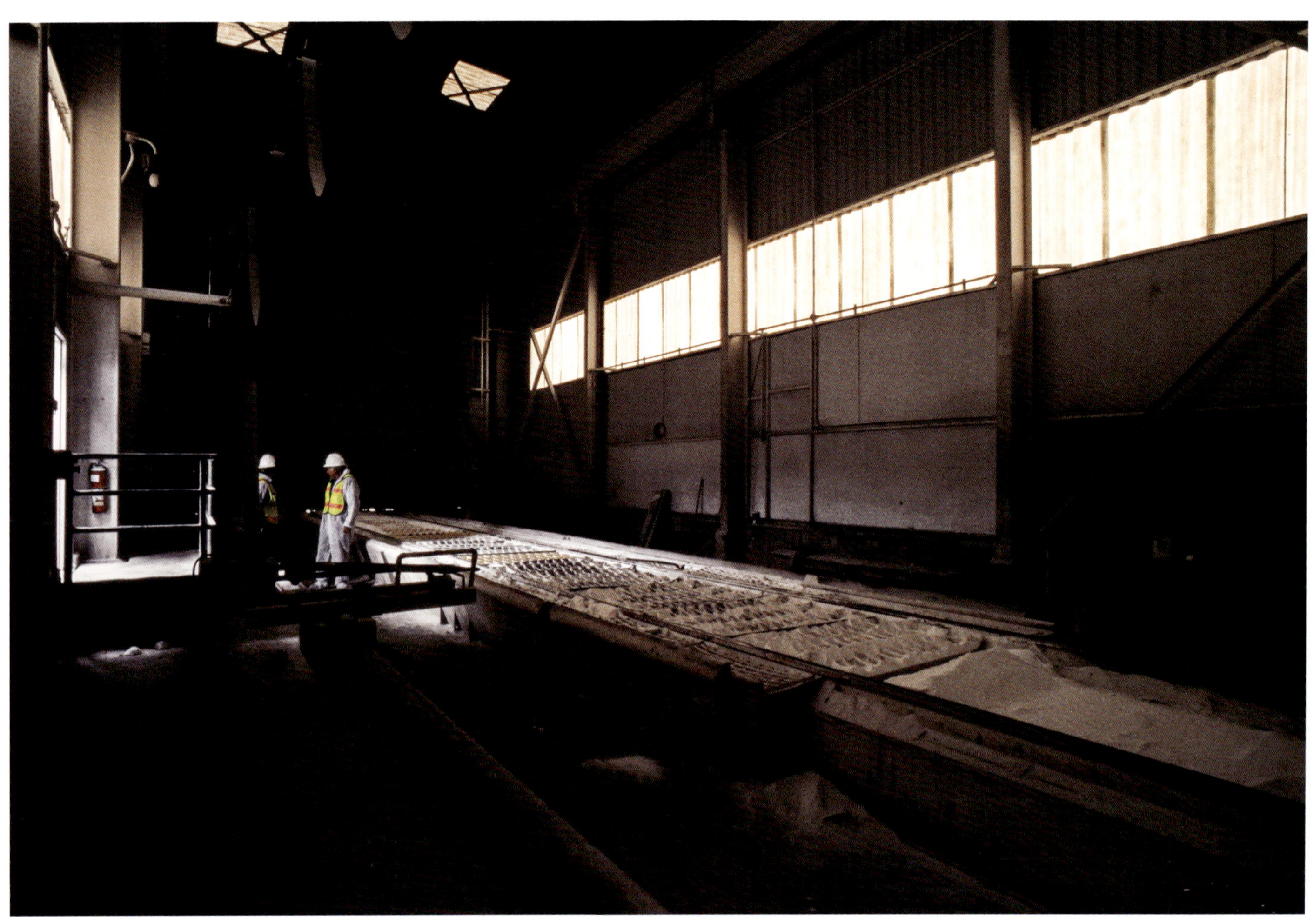

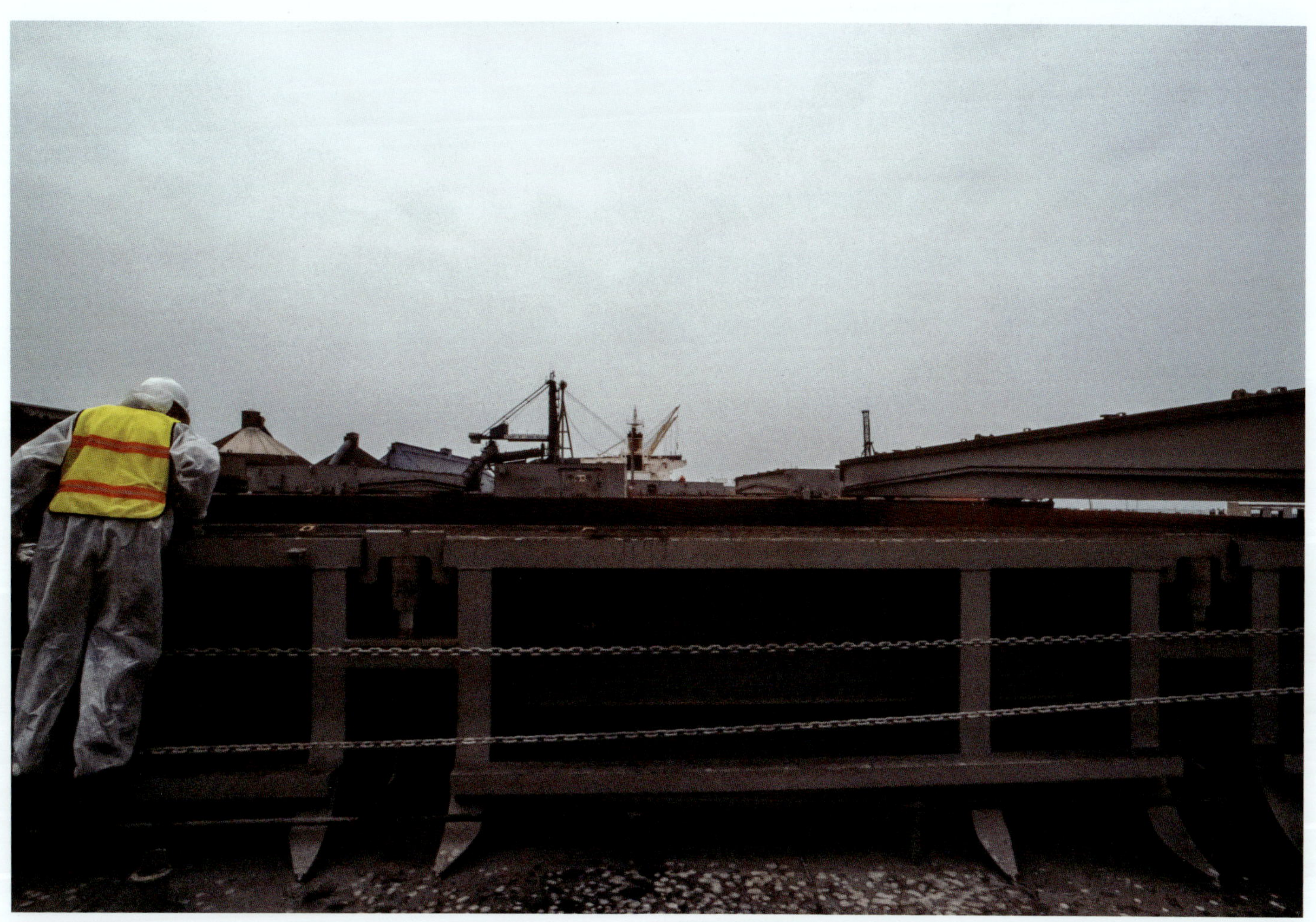

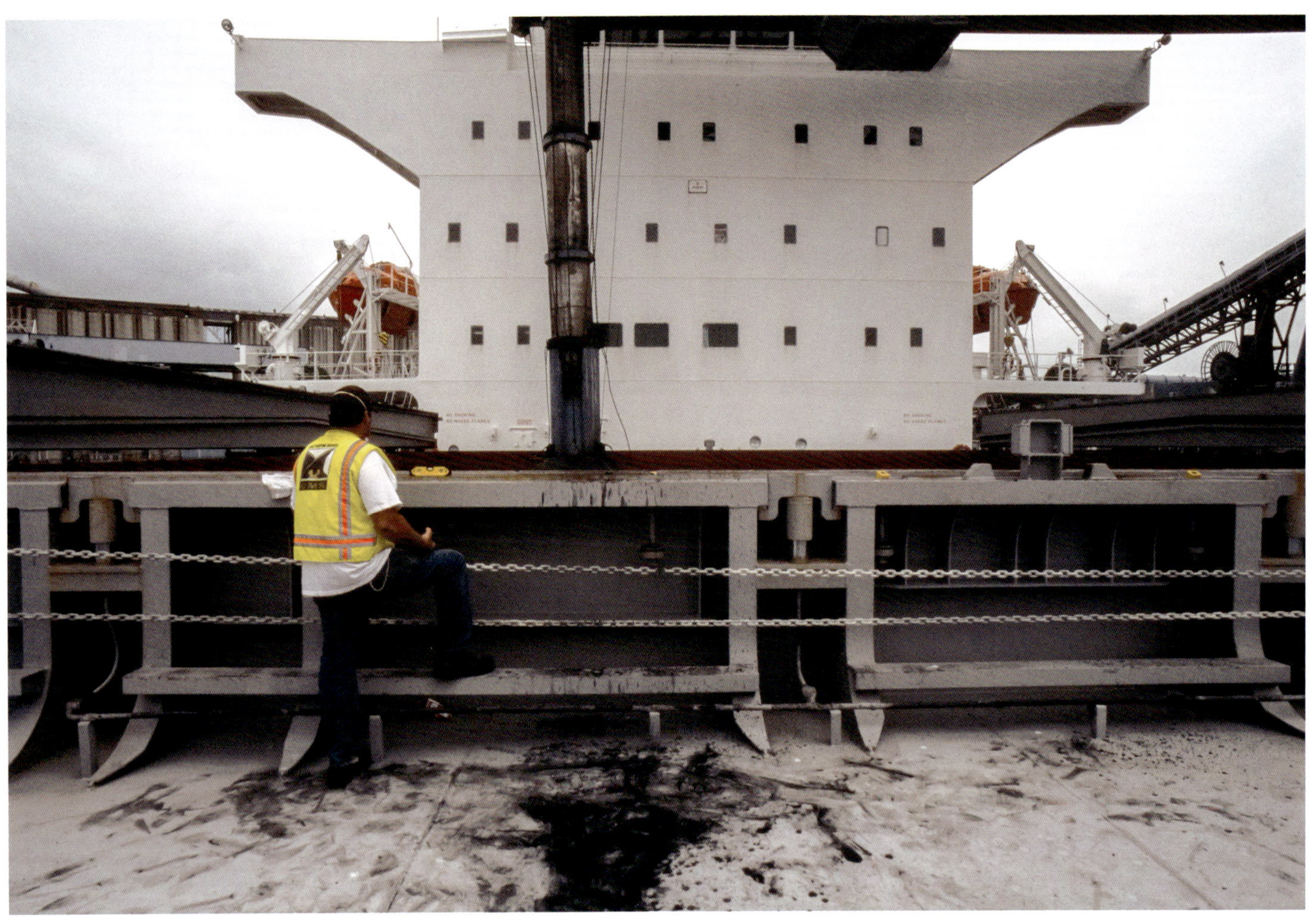

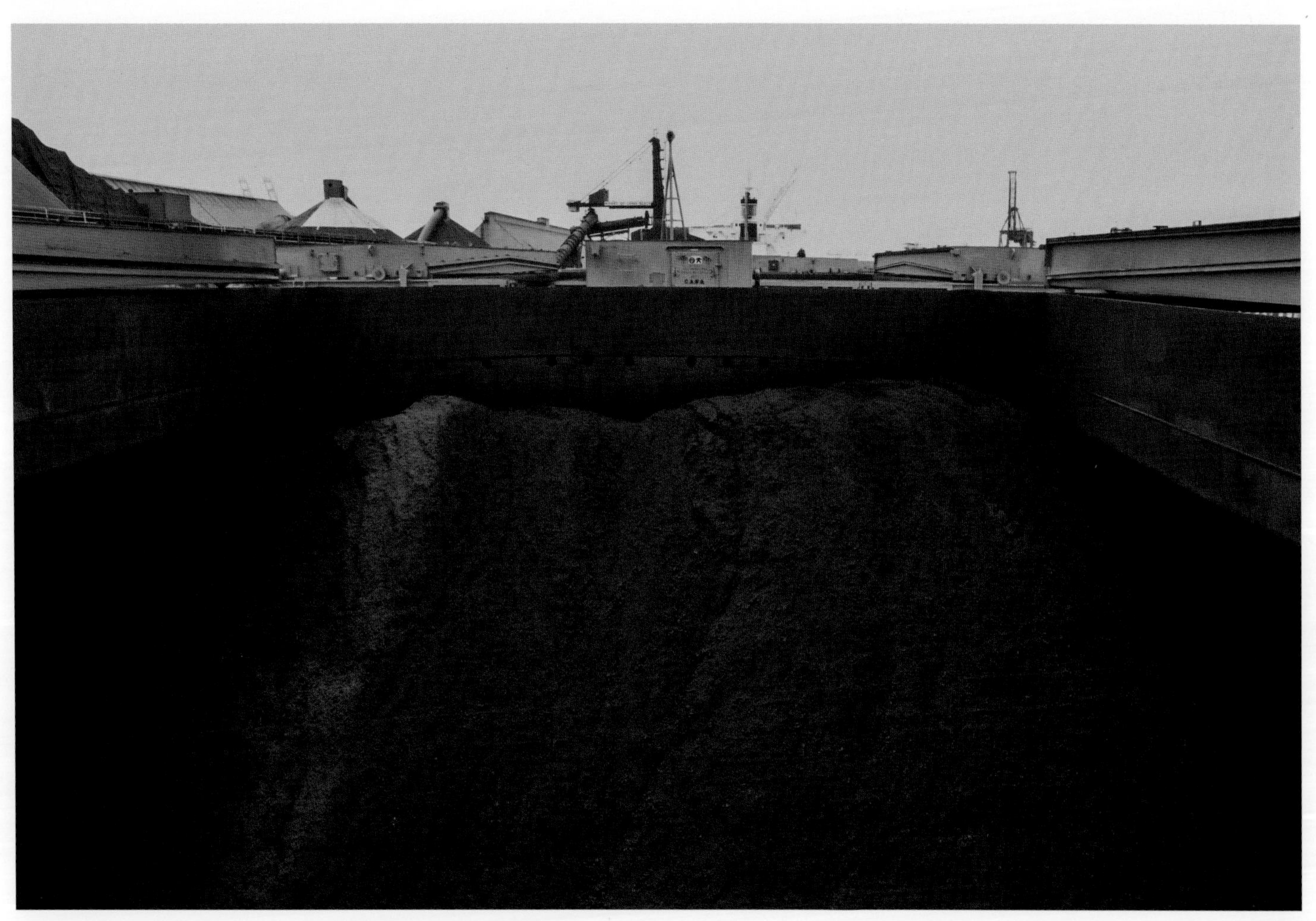

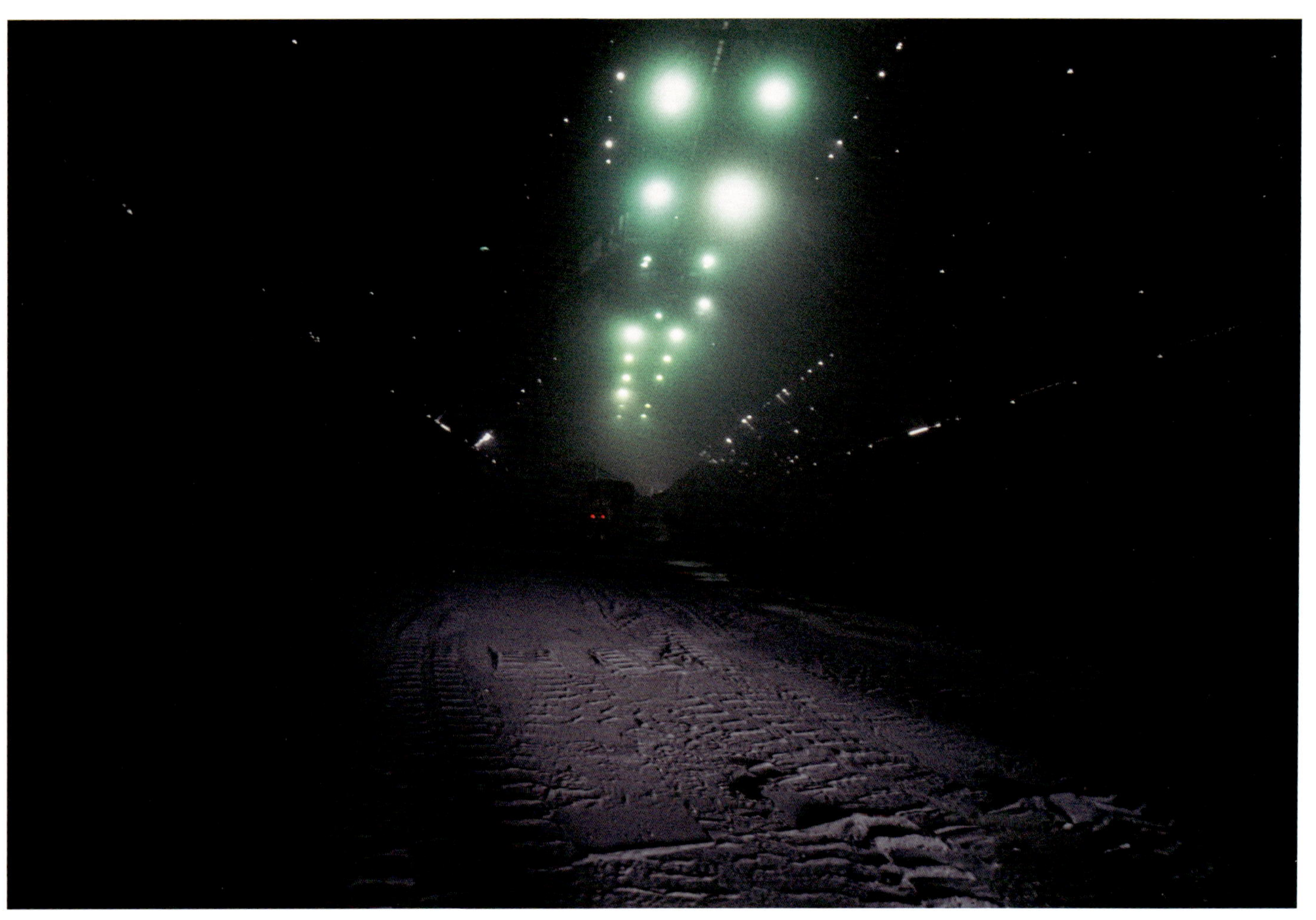

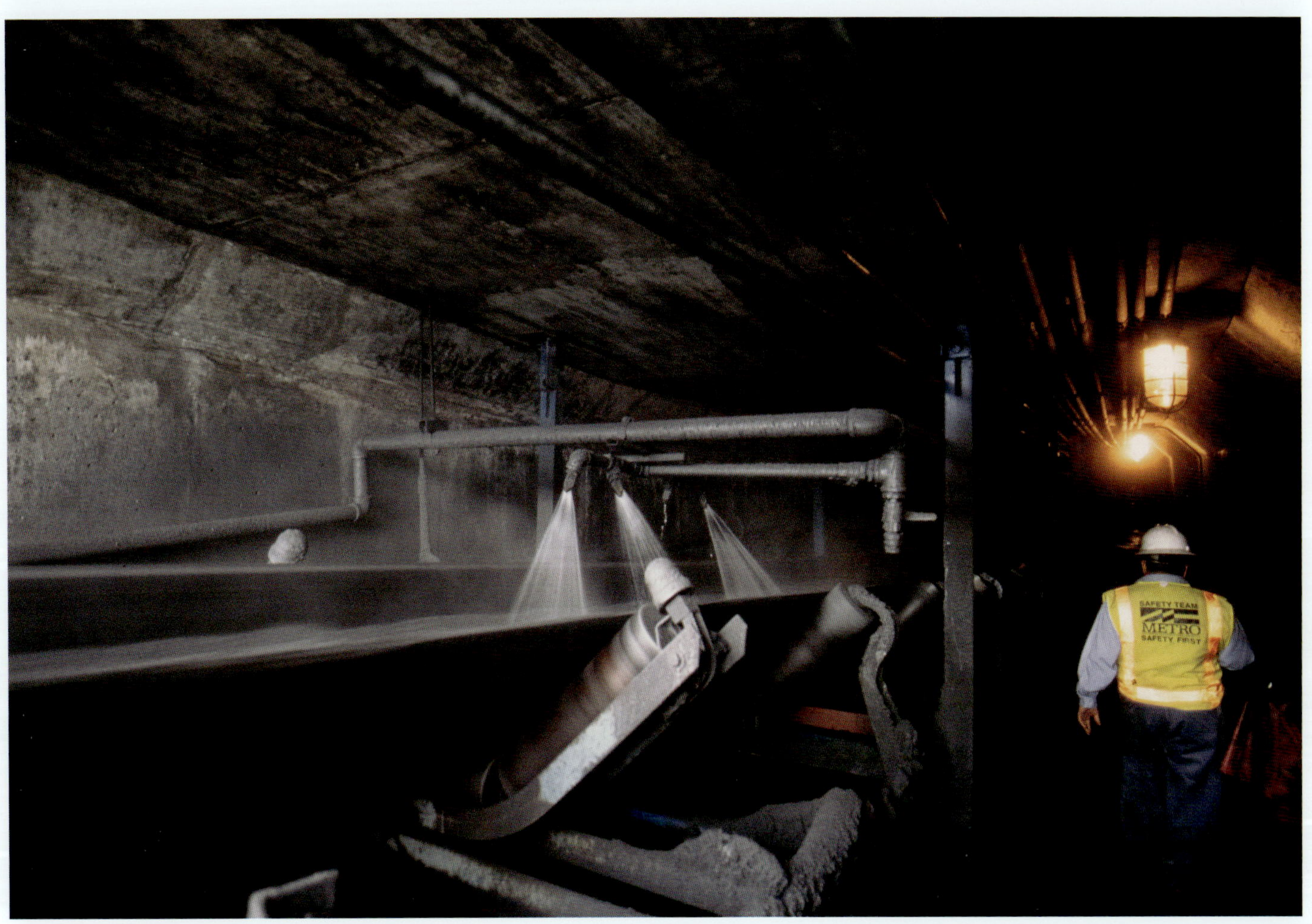

SAFETY TEAM
METRO
SAFETY FIRST

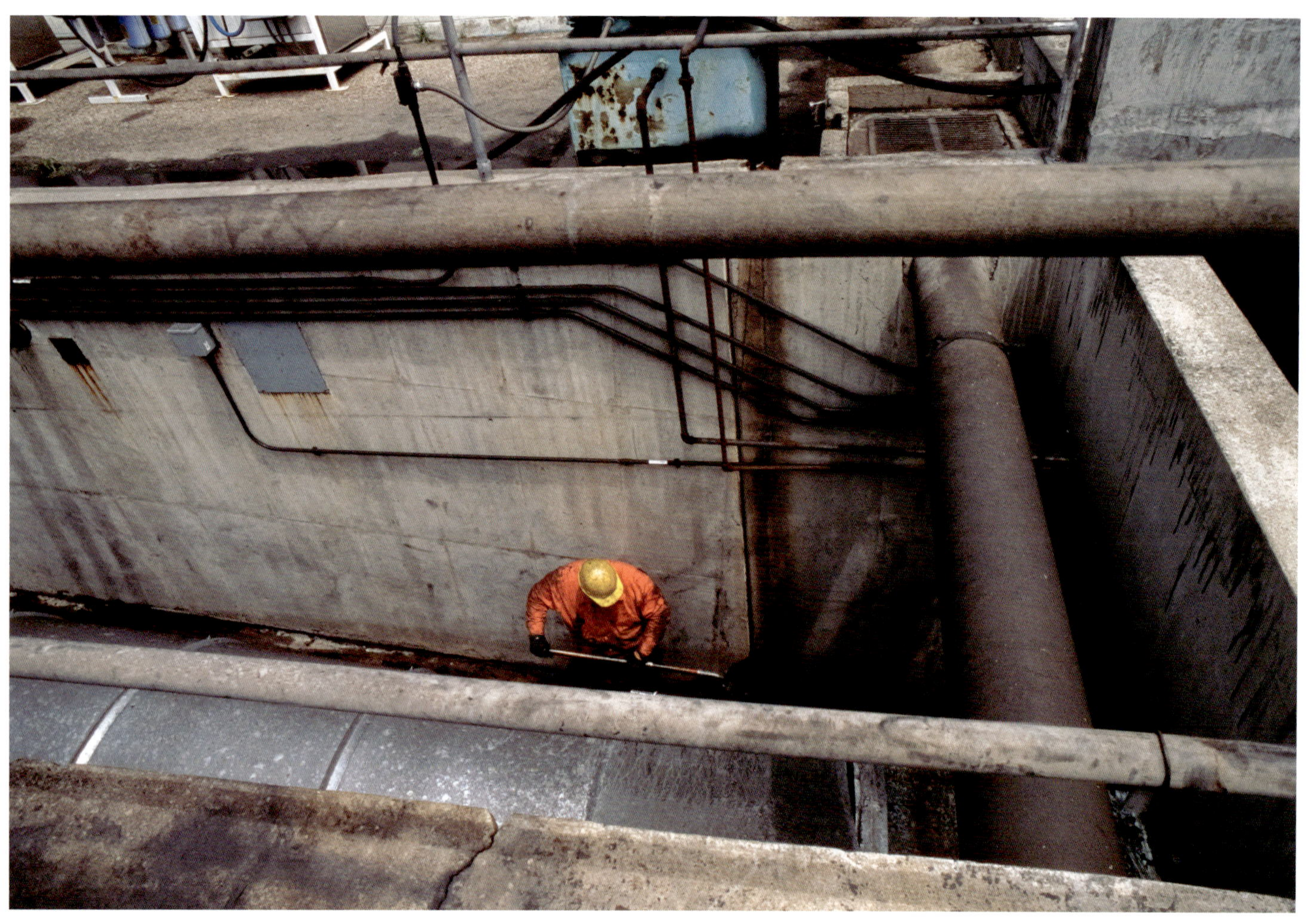

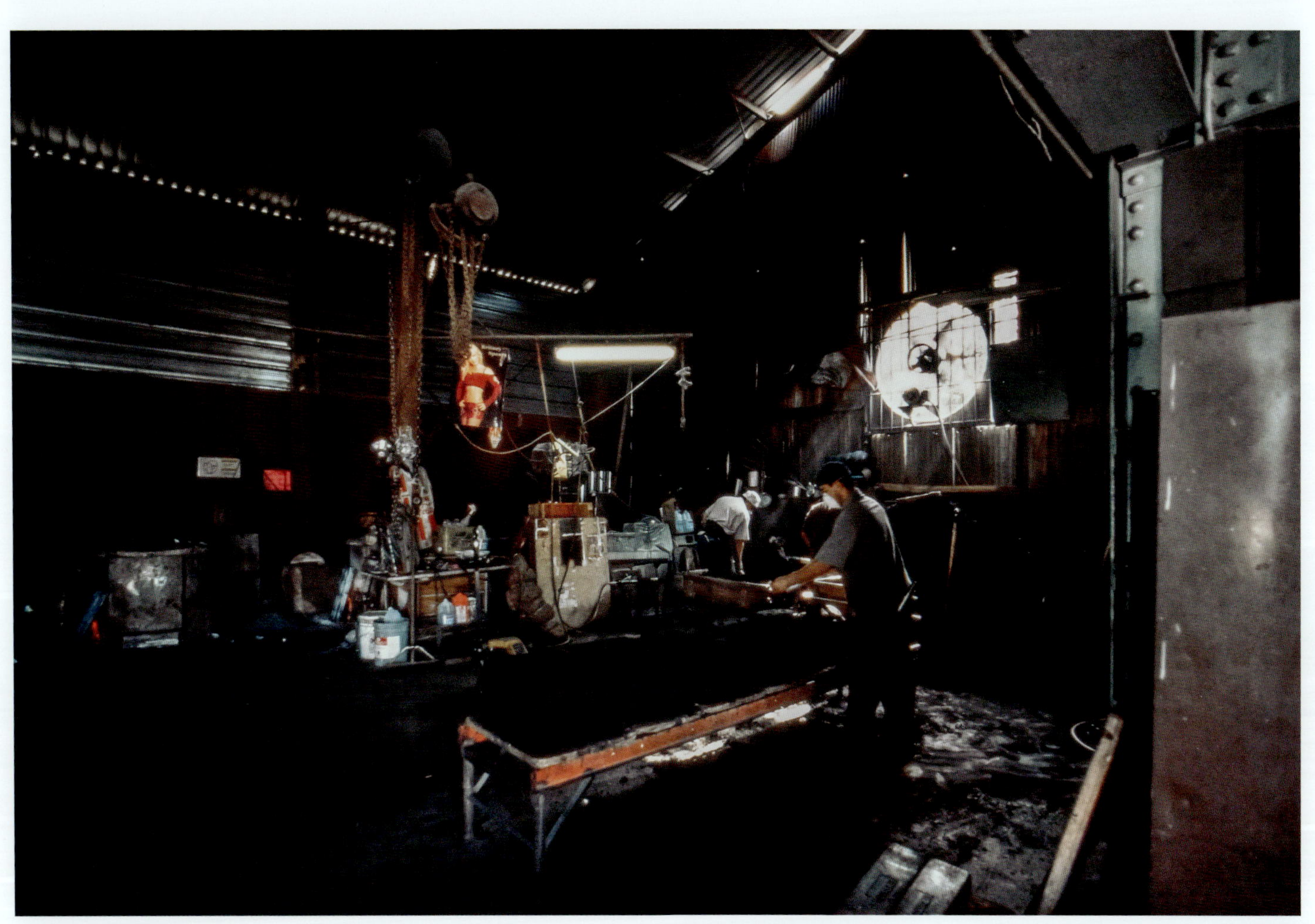

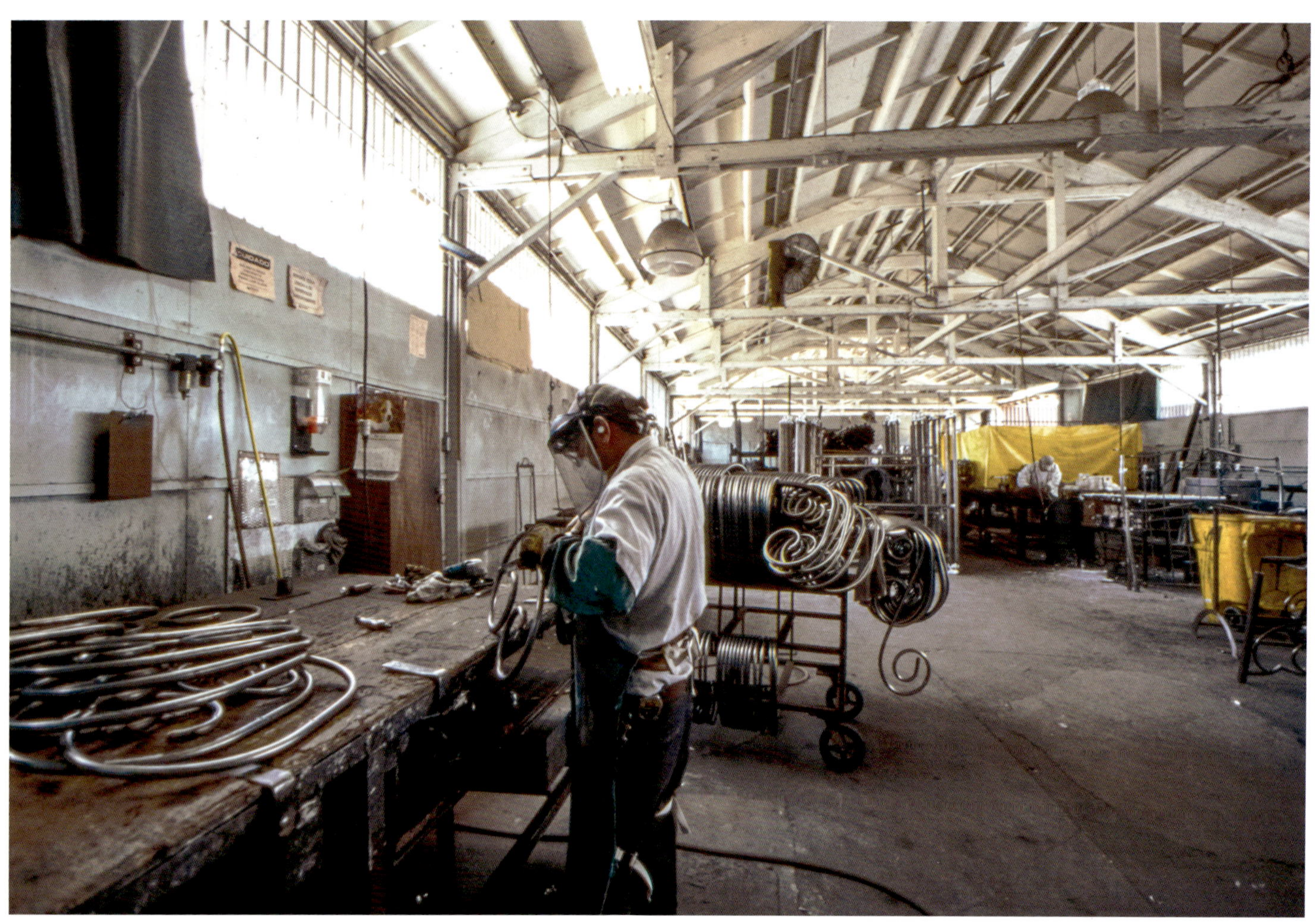

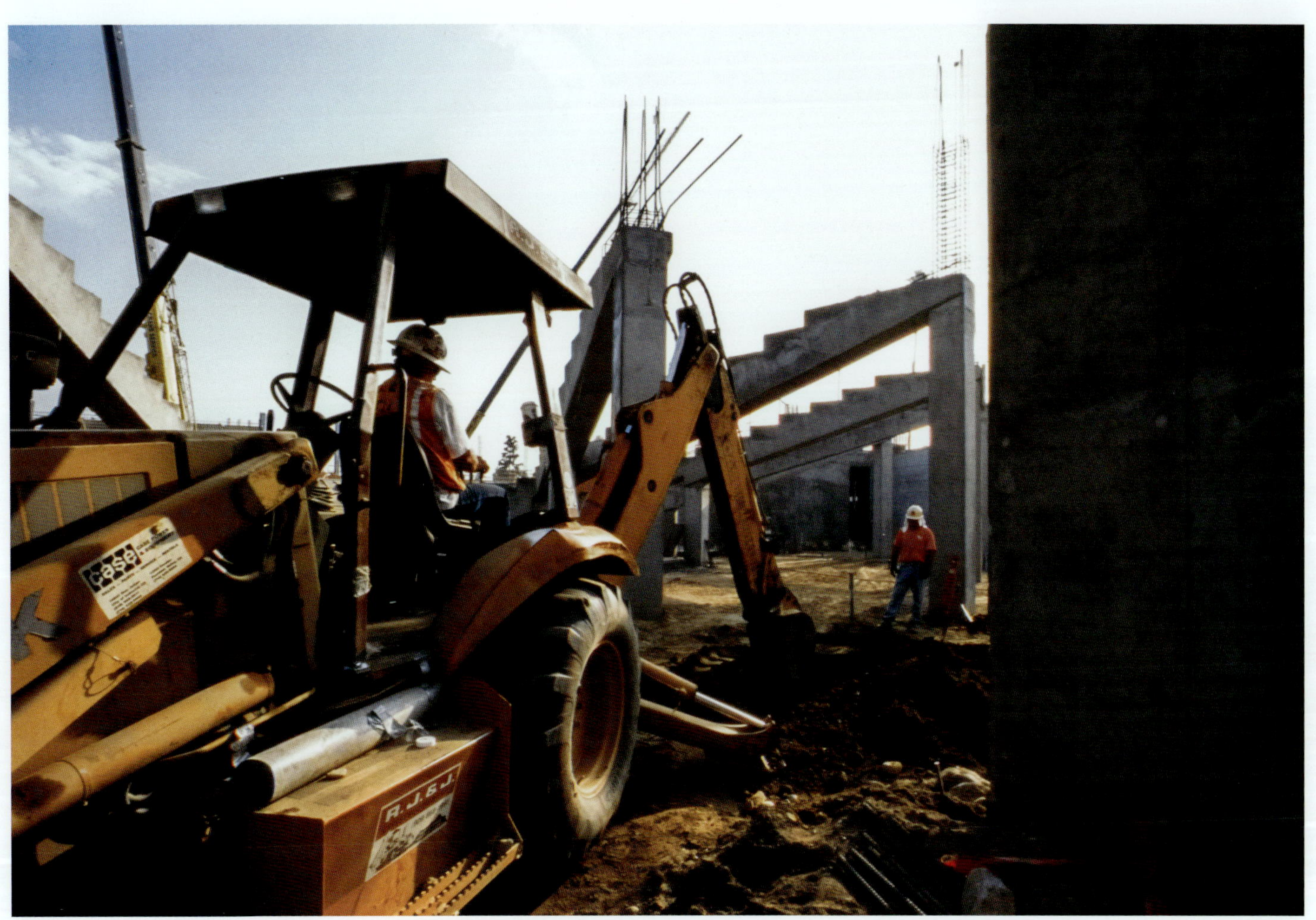

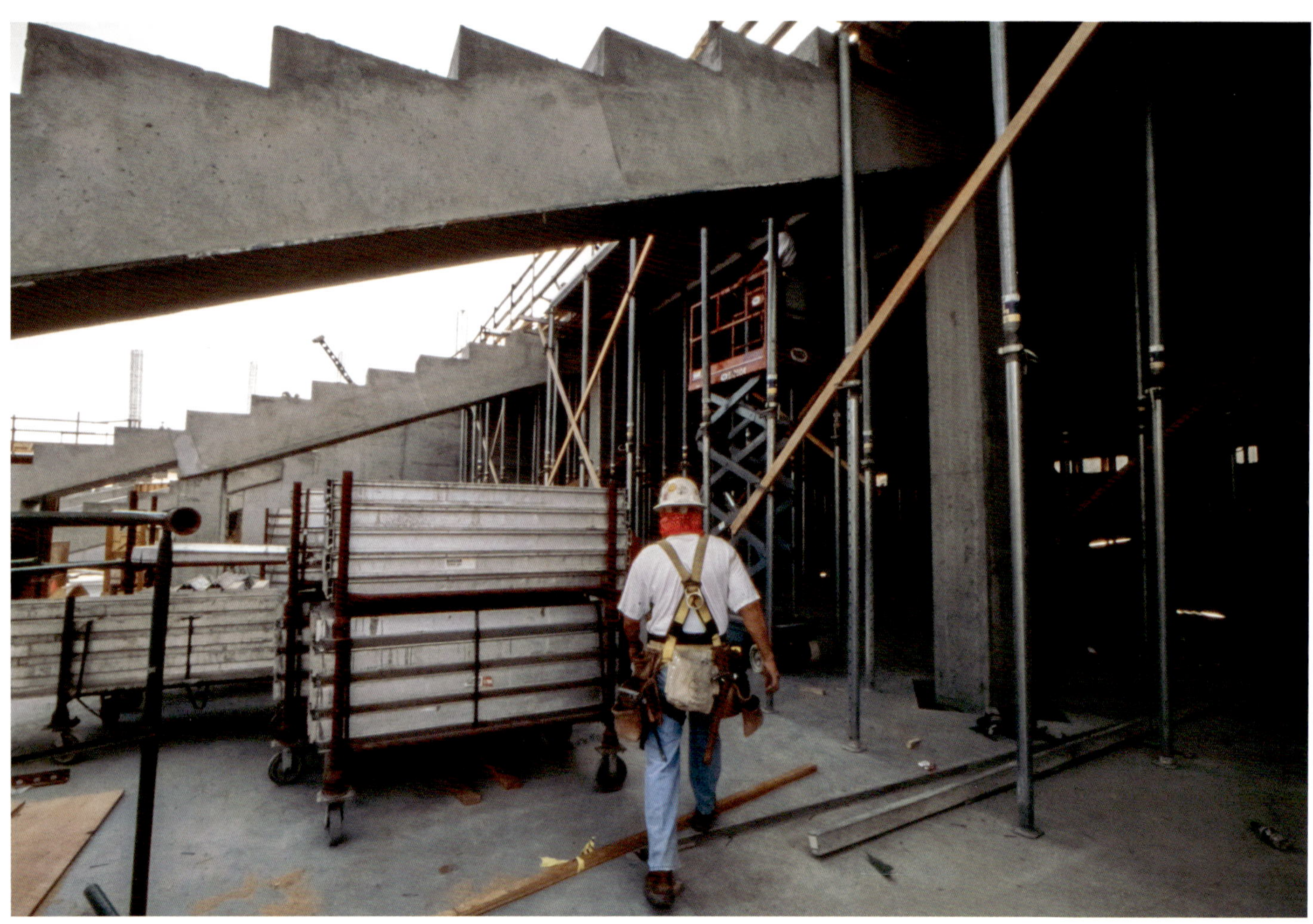

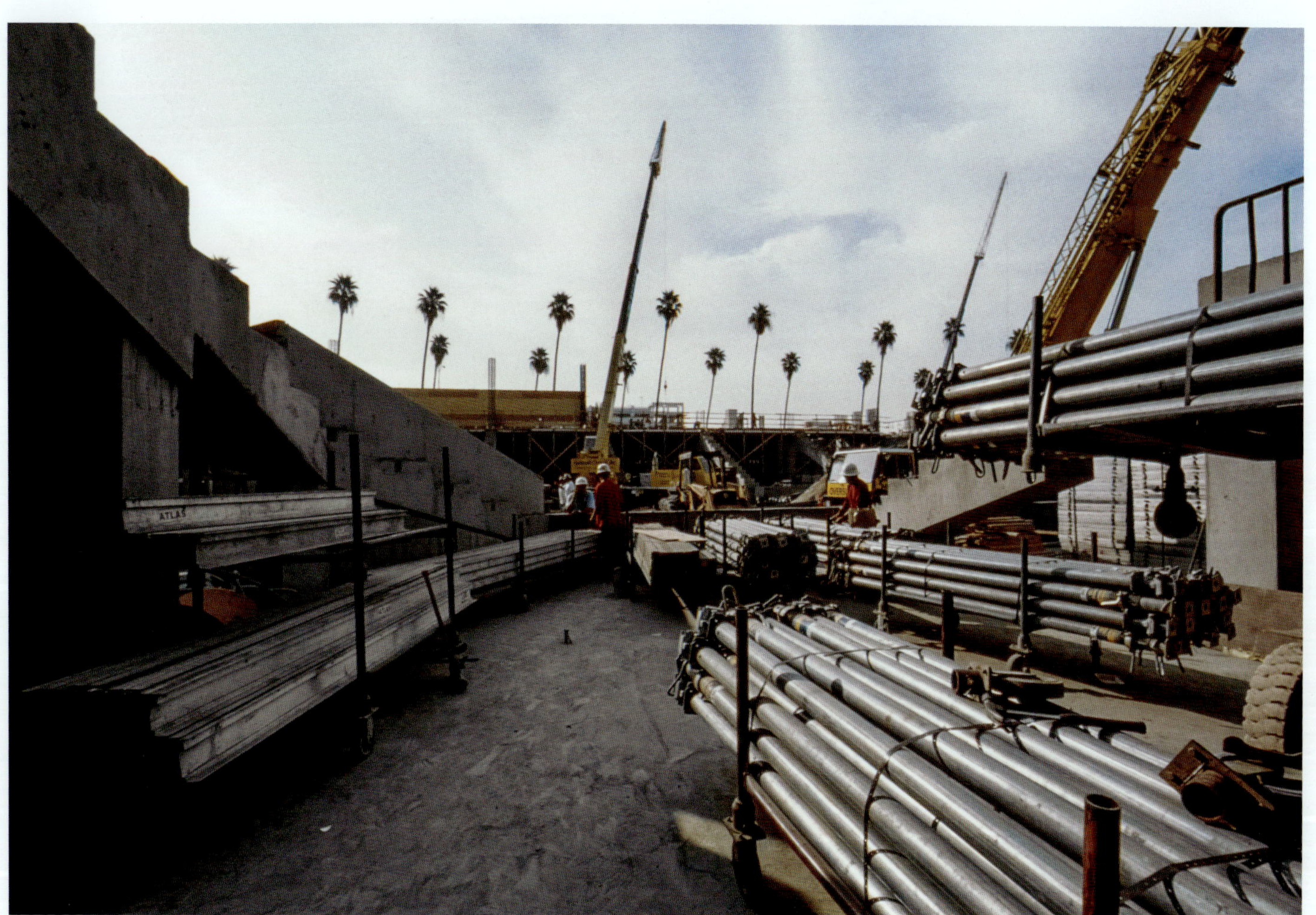

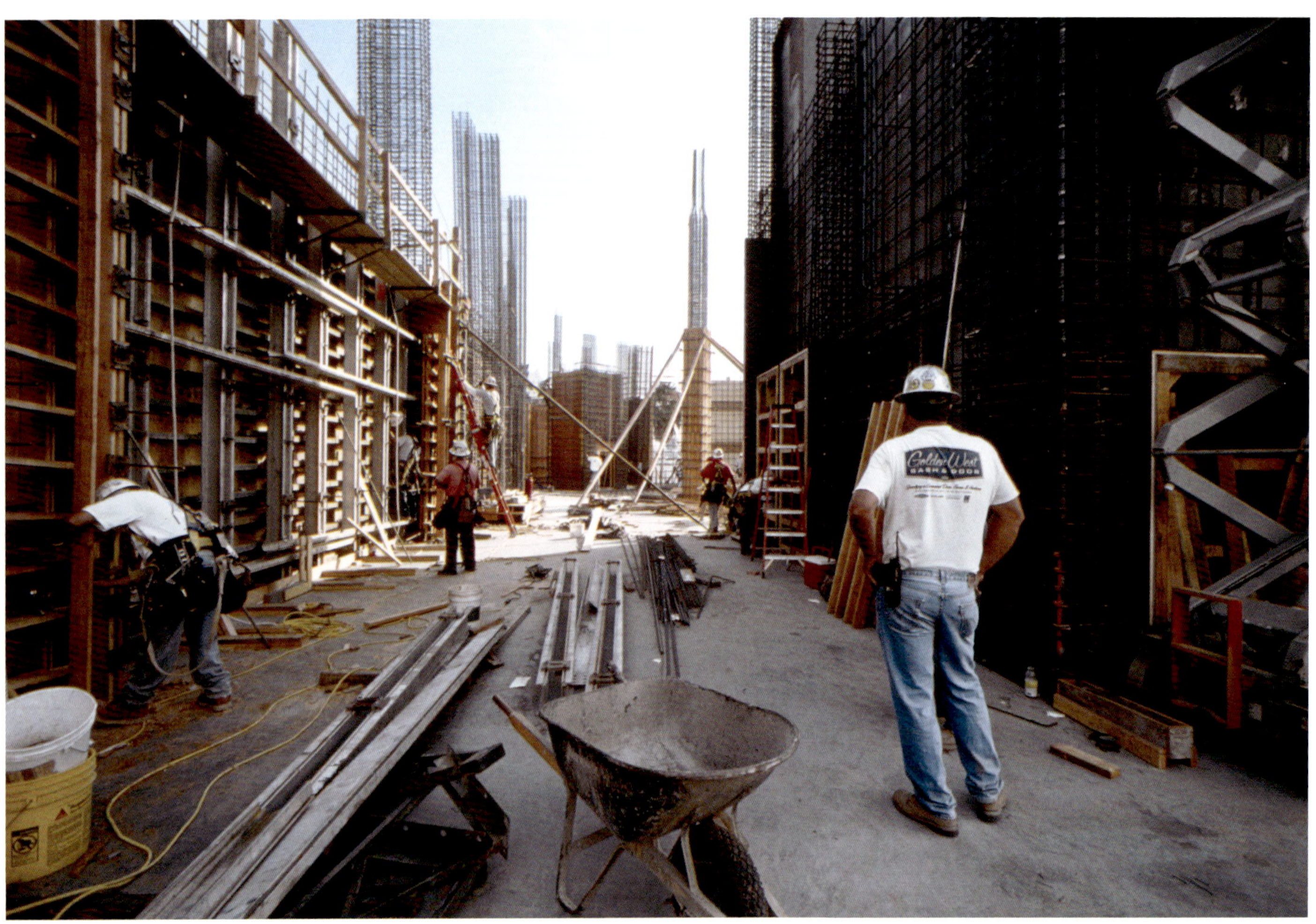

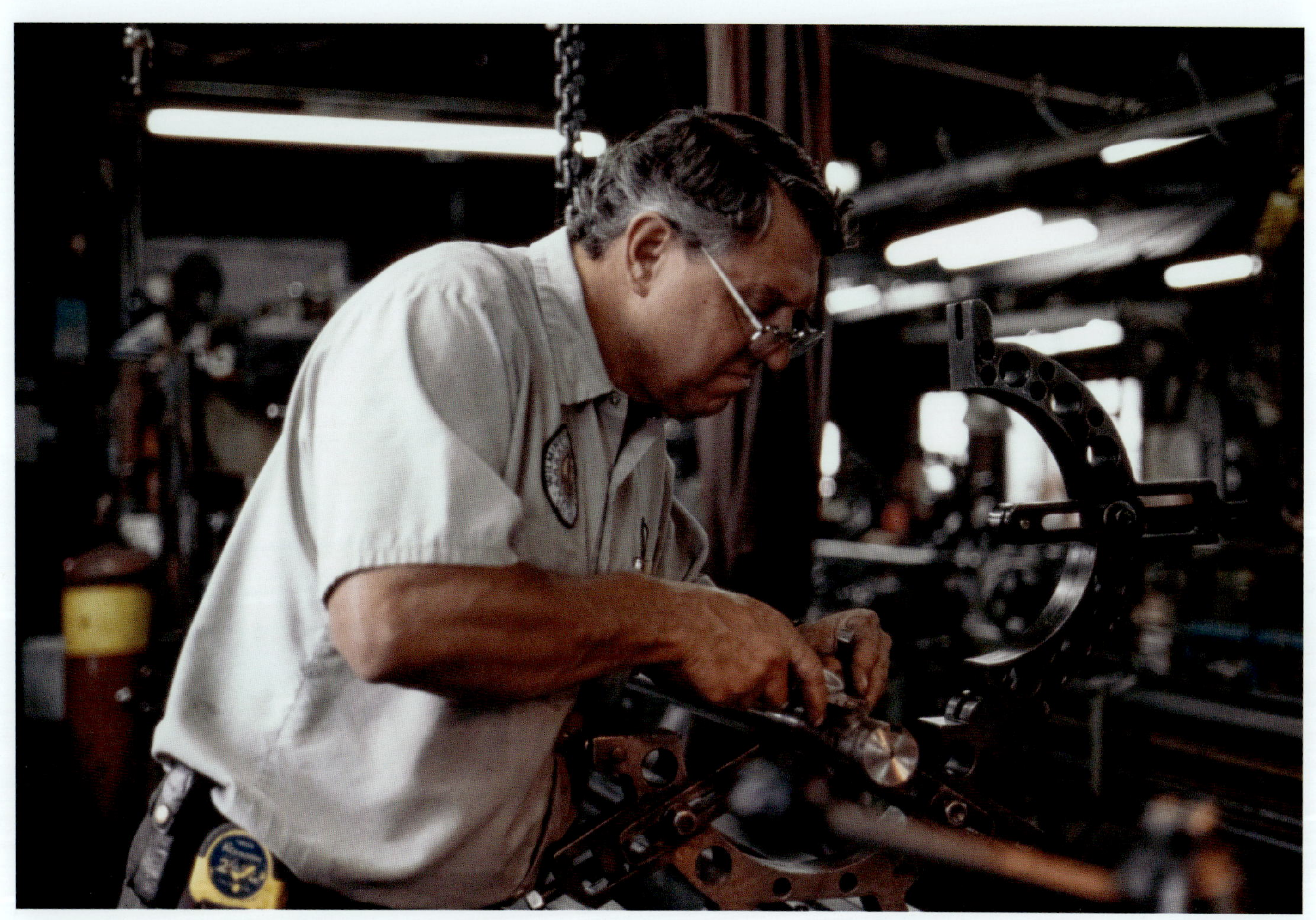

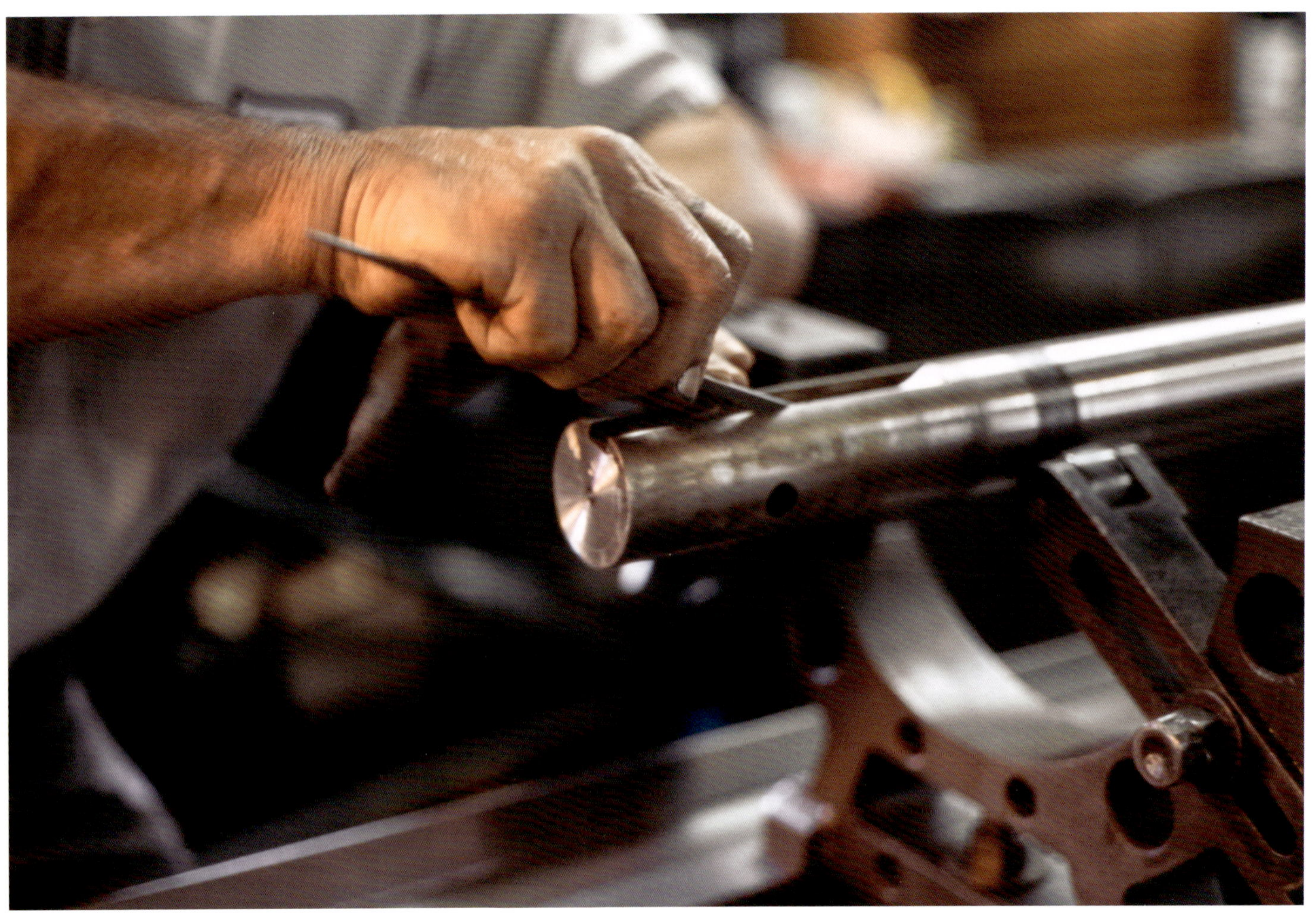

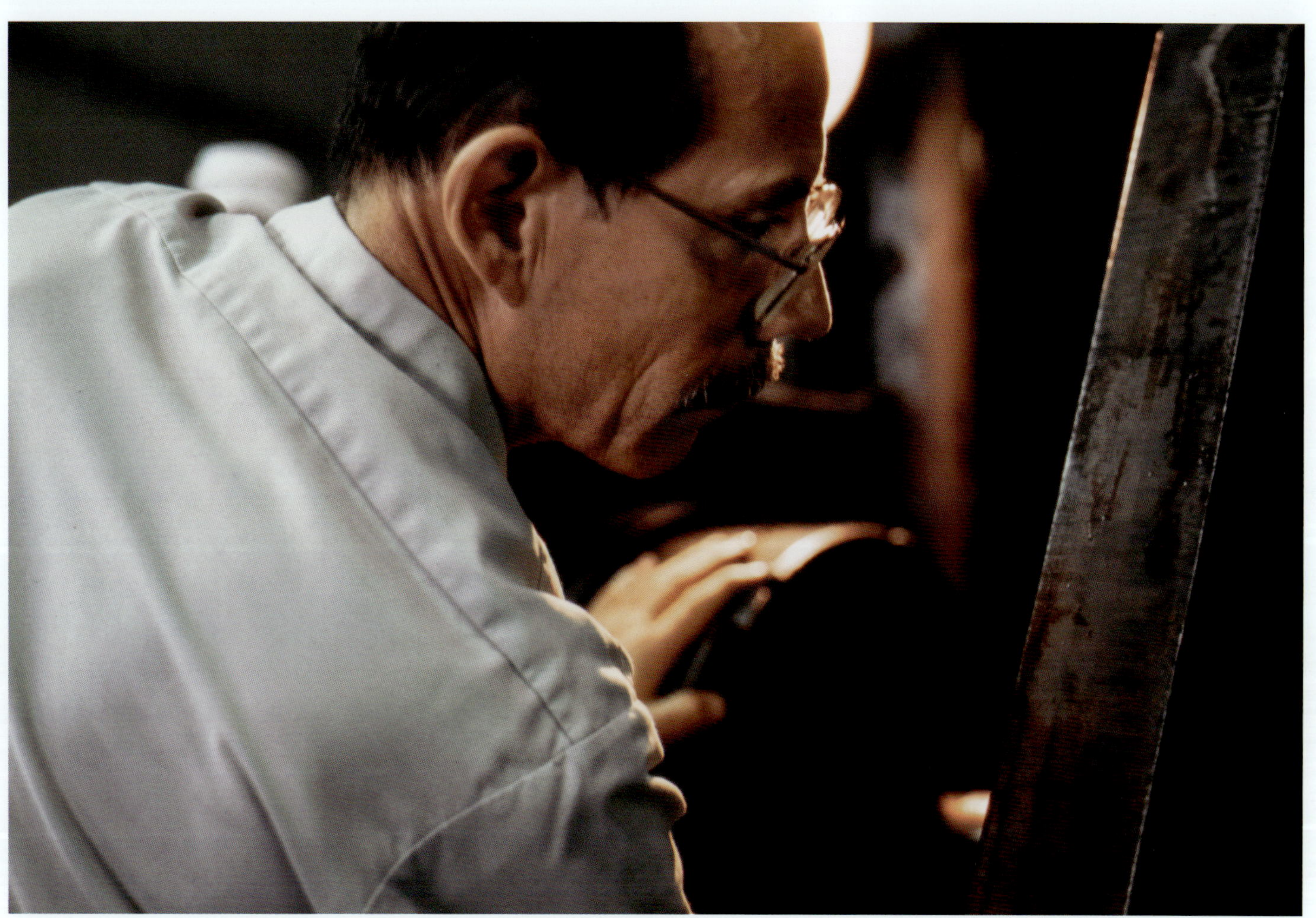

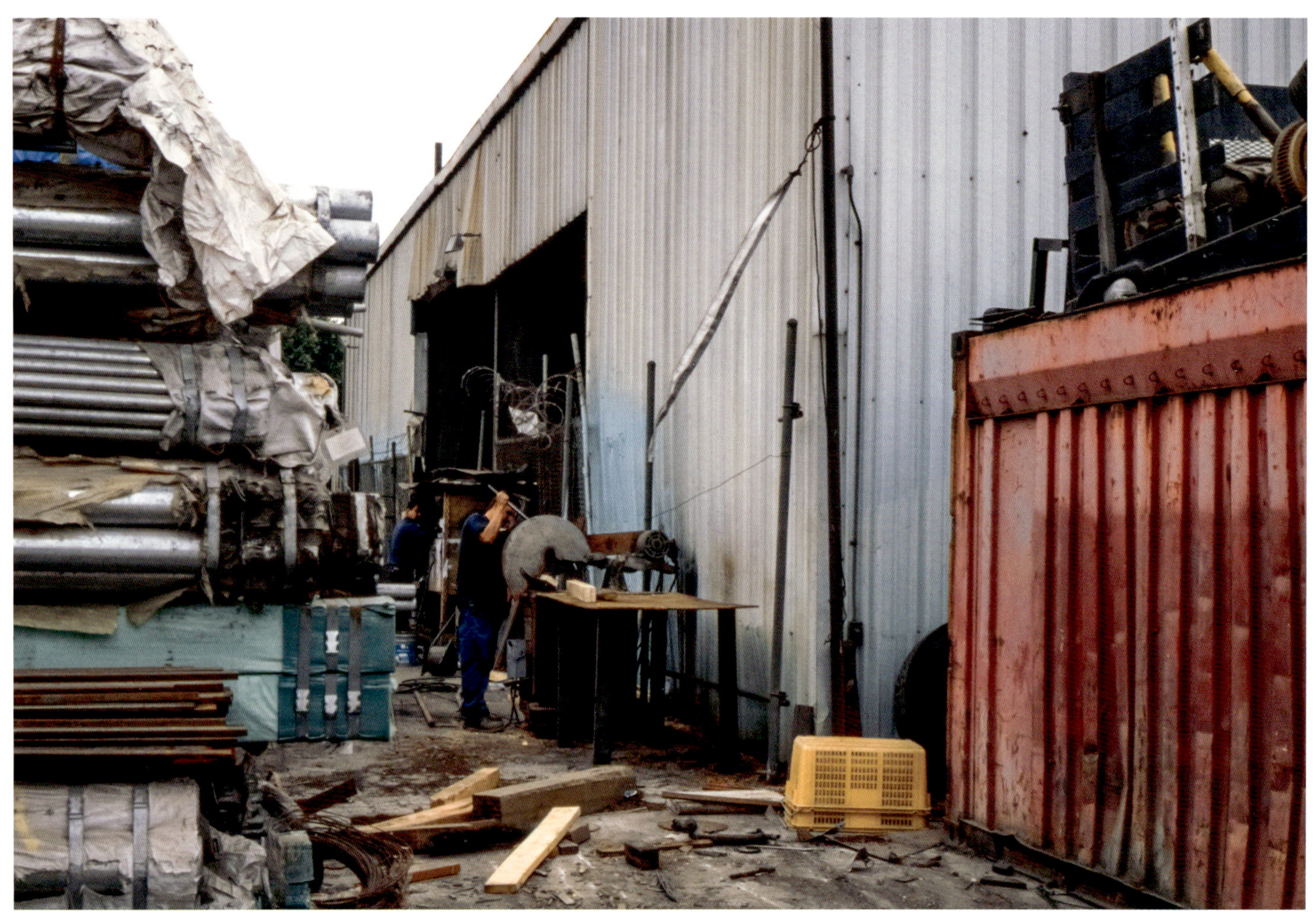

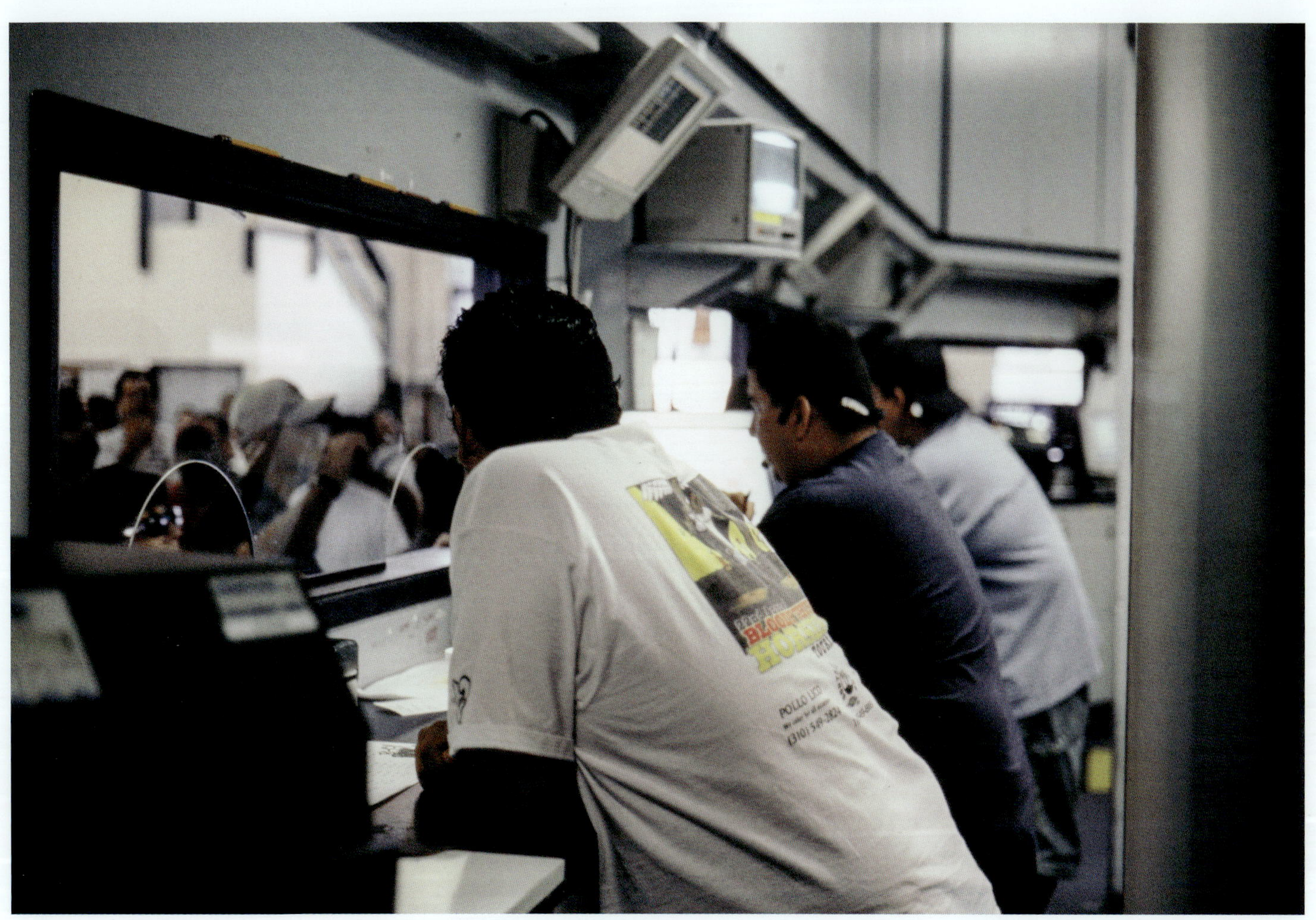

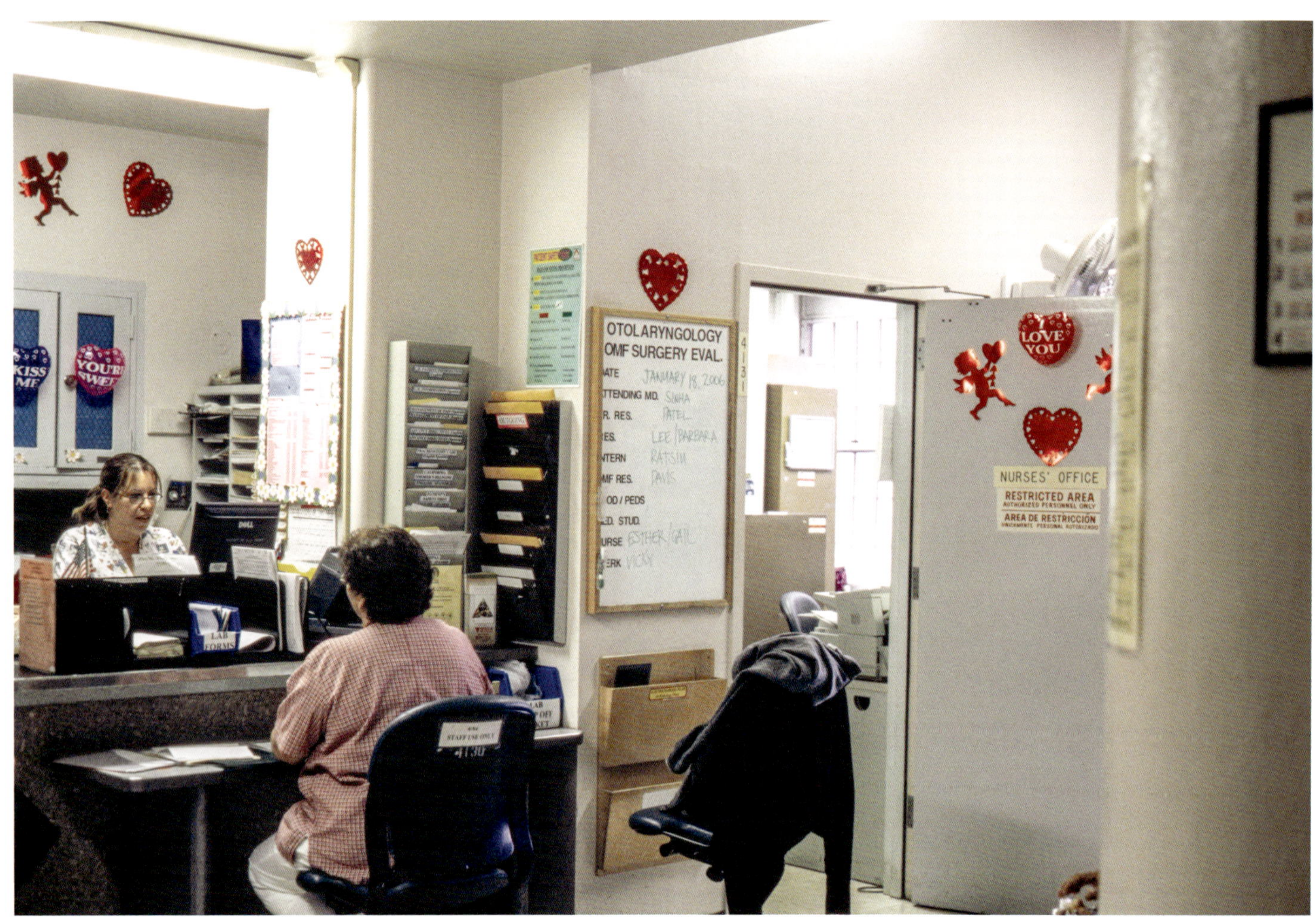
KISS ME
YOU'RE SWEET
I LOVE YOU
OTOLARYNGOLOGY
OMF SURGERY EVAL.
DATE JANUARY 18, 2006
ATTENDING MD. SINHA
R. RES. PATEL
RES. LEE / BARBARA
INTERN RATSIM
OMF RES. DAVIS
OD / PEDS
MED. STUD.
NURSE ESTHER / GAIL
CLERK VICKY
NURSES' OFFICE
RESTRICTED AREA
AUTHORIZED PERSONNEL ONLY
AREA DE RESTRICCIÓN
UNICAMENTE PERSONAL AUTORIZADO
LAB FORMS
STAFF USE ONLY
4130

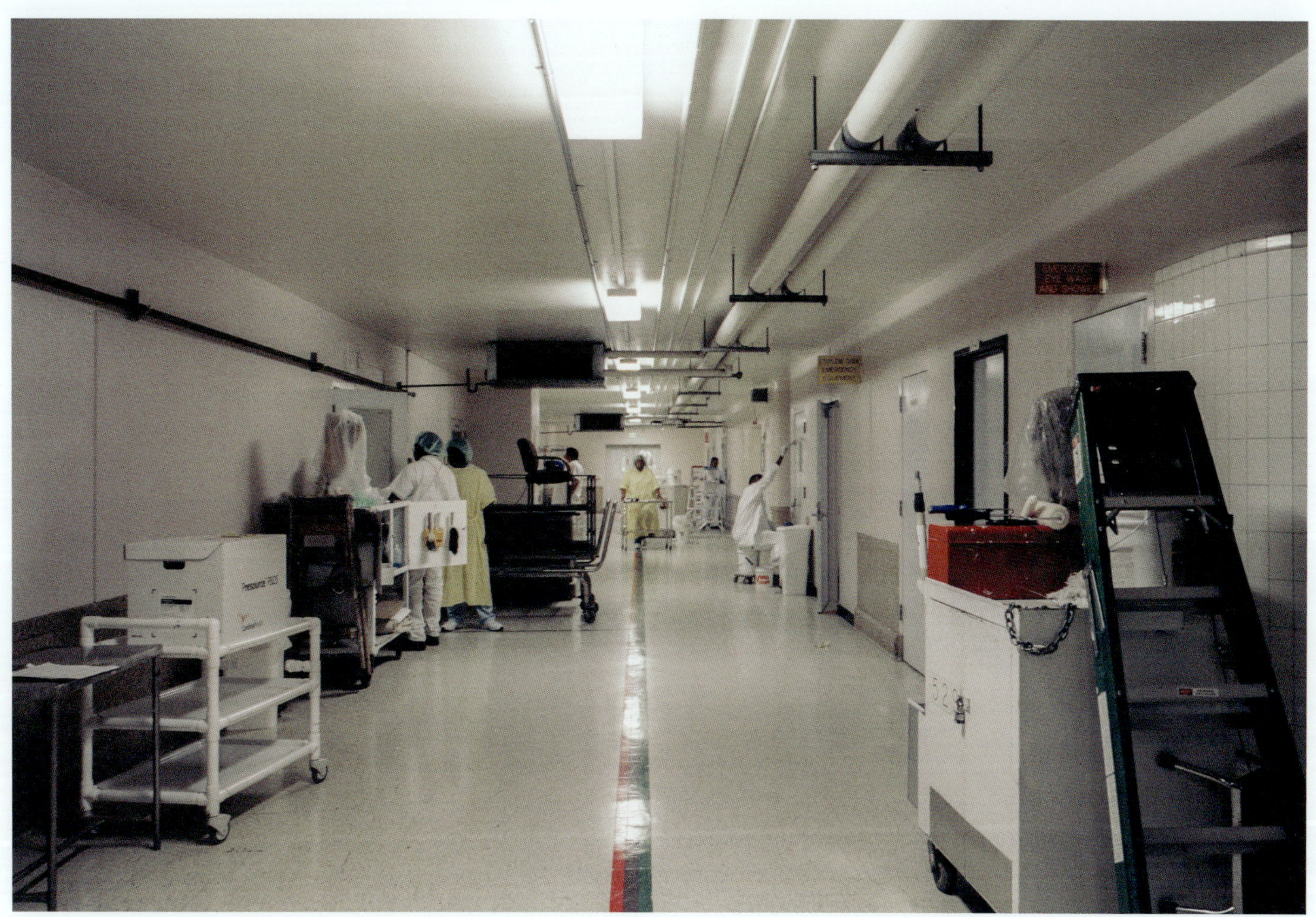

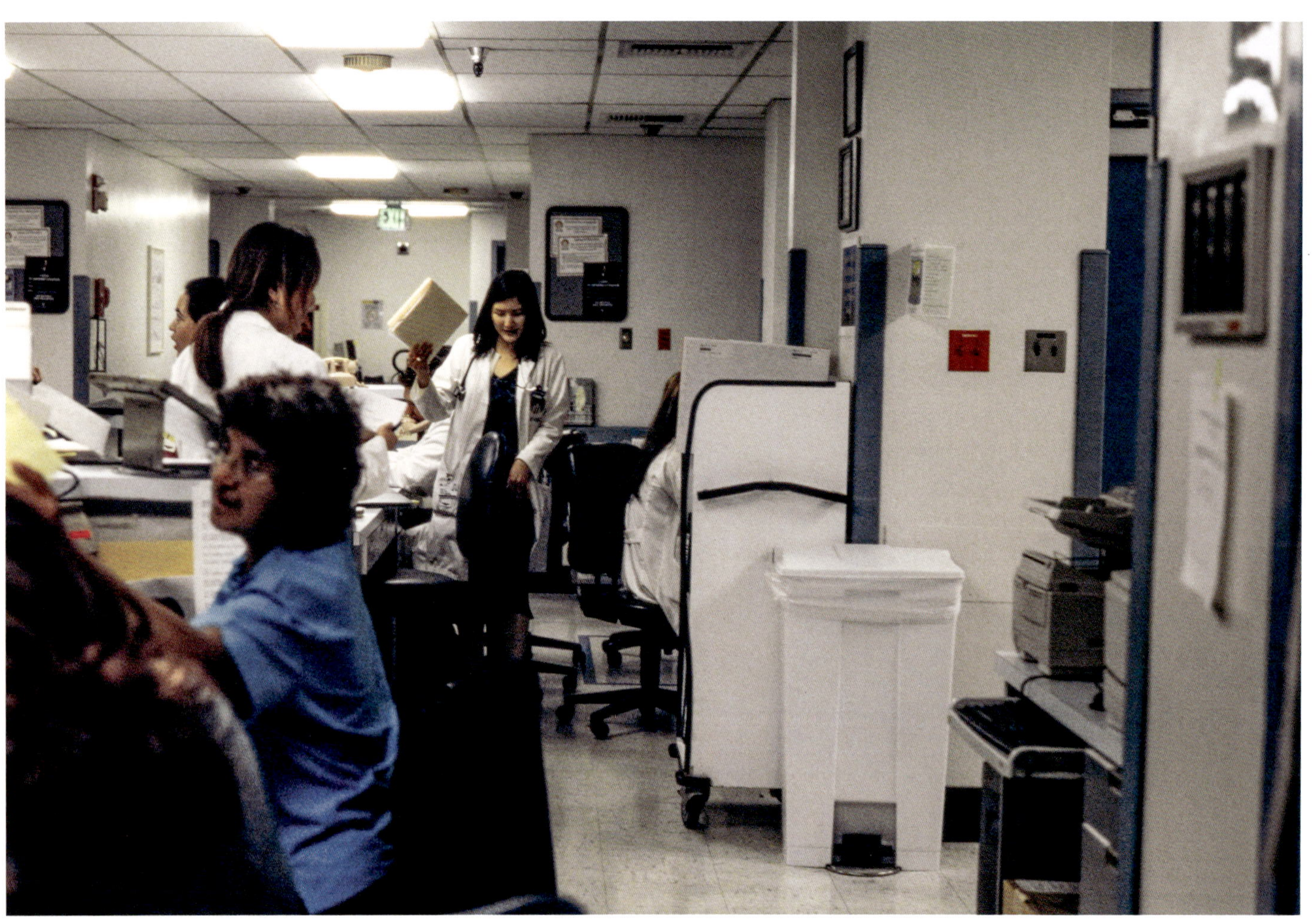

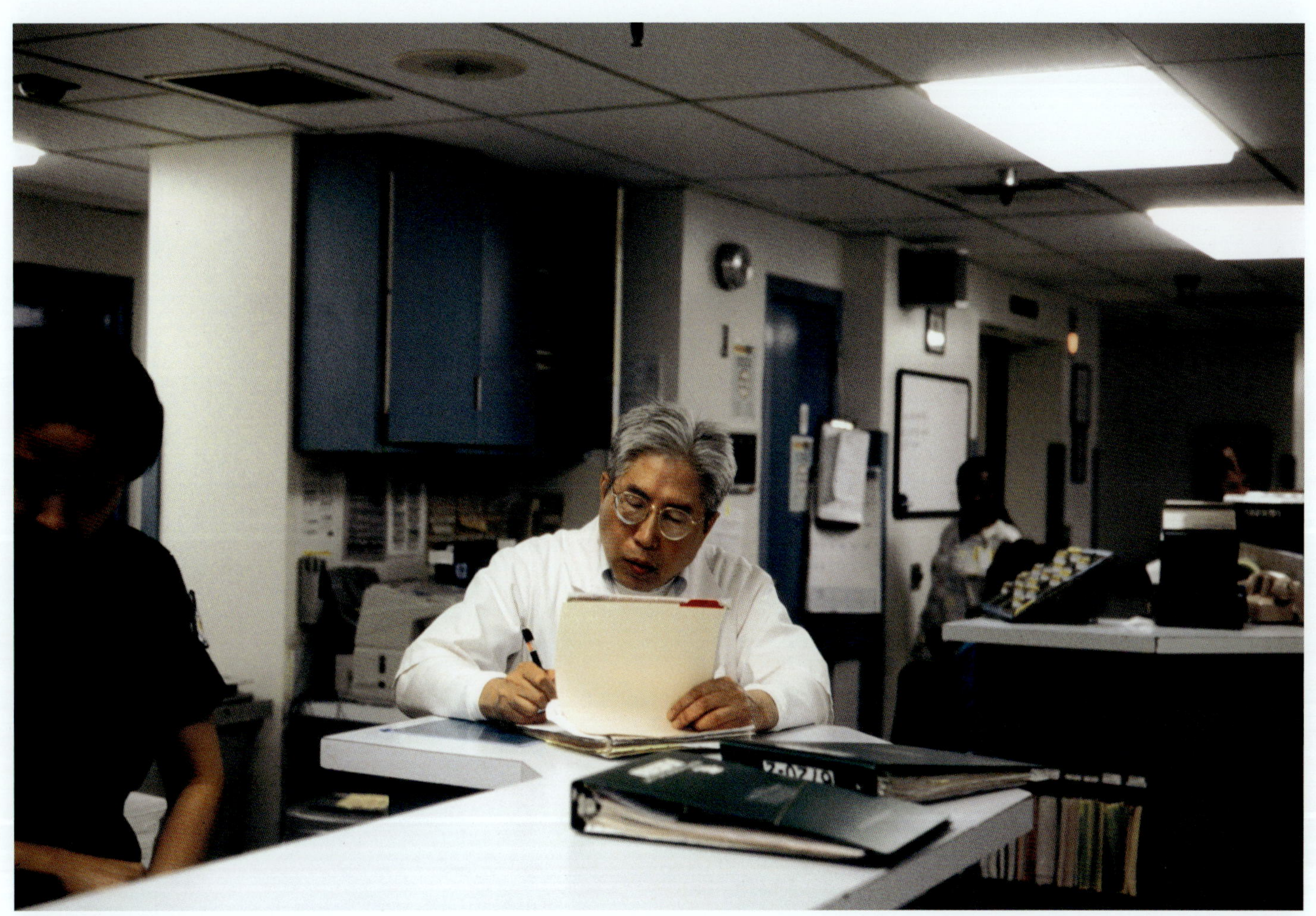

LOCATIONS

1	S. Central Ave. and E. 69 St.
2	(unknown)
3	Avalon Blvd. and ~E. 40 Pl.
4	Upholstery shop, next to 1109 S. Santa Fe Ave.
5	Union Central Cold Storage, 1525 Industrial St.
6	Seville Olive Company, 663 S. Anderson St.
7-8	Block: S. Anderson St./Sunrise St./S. Clarence St./Jesse St. and to E. 6 St.
9-10	Continental Processors, 681 S. Clarence St.
11-12	Furniture manufacturing, W. Washington Blvd. (btw. S. Normandie Ave. and S. Budlong Ave.)
13	Shamrock Die Cutting, 353 S. Clarence St.
14-15	I. M. David Furniture, 1556 W. 130 St., Upholstery shop
16-20	I. M. David Furniture, 1556 W. 130 St.
21	Knitting mills, ~2100 Sacramento St.
22-23	BNSF Intermodal Facility on E. Washington Blvd. off Sheila St.
24	CCC Steel, 25 E. Victoria St. or California Metal Distributors, 222 E. Manville St.
25	LATC for Union Pacific, Mission Rd.
26	Country Eggs, 333 N. Mission Rd.
27-31	Al Larson Boat Shop, 1046 S. Seaside Ave., San Pedro
32	SW Marine, 985 S. Seaside Ave.
33-34	Tri-Marine Fish, 222 Cannery St.
35	McKenna Boiler Works, 1510 N. Spring St.
36	Walker Foods, "El Pato," 237 N. Mission Rd.
37-40	Color Graphics, 150 N. Meyers St.
41	Fashion Connection, 7316 Fulton Ave.
42	BA Marble and Granite, 7311 Fulton Ave.
43	Sign Group/Karman, 9812 Independence Ave.
44	Carey Steel, 10201 Canoga Ave.
45	Dynamic Cabinet Designs, 10215 Canoga Ave.
46	Silkscreening and insignia sewing, near W. Jefferson Blvd. and S. Rimpau Blvd.
47-48	California Tool and Die, 421 S. Irwindale Ave., Azusa
49	Off Line, 2750 S. Maple Ave.
50-52	Fineman-Brown Upholstery, 1062 N. Orange Grove Ave., W. Hollywood
53	ABC Caskets, 1705 N. Indiana St.
54	Sandler Bros., 4101 Whiteside St.
55	RG Die Cutting and Foil Graphics, 3620 Fowler St.
56-58	Hanson Tank, 1600 E. Washington Blvd.
59-63	forge
64-65	Alphacast Foundry, 826 S. Santa Fe Ave.
66	Joanne's Cutting and Fusing, 1705 W. 134 St., Gardena
67-69	Angelus Plating Works, 1713 W. 134 St., Gardena
70	Washington Ornamental Iron Works, 17926 S. Broadway, Gardena
71	Cutie Clothing, 1951 Central Ave., South El Monte
72-73	Metal fabricator, ~6700 Stanford Ave.
74	Pallet Masters, 655 E. Florence Ave.
75-77	Costa Macaroni, 4790 Valley Blvd.
78	Sears building going down, at W. Pico Blvd. and San Vicente Blvd.
79	Tree trimmers on Gale Dr., Beverly Hills
80	Dyeing shop, near S. Western Ave. and W. 39 St.
81-83	Lunachix, 2401 S. Broadway
84	Angelus Sheet Metal, 4800 Valley Blvd.
85	RO-RO ship, SSA Pacific (Marine): Warehouse, getting on ship
86-87	RO-RO ship, SSA Pacific (Marine) mid-decks, and then up to 6 and 7
88	Bulk ship, at Metropolitan Stevedore, Long Beach Pier 212
89-90	Bulk ship, loading at Metropolitan Stevedore, Long Beach Pier 212
91-92	Bulk ship, checking for even-ness of loading of petroleum coke (petcoke)
93-94	Bulk ship, loading of petroleum coke (petcoke)
95	Alphacast Foundry, Santa Fe Ave.
96	Wesley Allen, 1001 E. 60 St., 90001
97-100	Construction of USC Galen Center, W. Jefferson Blvd and S. Figueroa St.
101-103	Wilmington Iron Works, 402 W. C St., Wilmington
104	Ancon Marine, 1022 Eubank Ave., Wilmington
105	ILWU Hiring Hall, Longshoremen's Dispatch Hall, 343 Broad Ave., Wilmington
106-109	LA County-USC Hospital, 1200 State St.

"NATURE'S WORKSHOP": ACKNOWLEDGMENTS AND NOTES

The author thanks Kathy Kolnick and Todd Gish for research assistance. Martin Krieger, Ted Muller, Robert Lewis, and Dick Walker offered incisive comments on drafts.

1. The undiscovered city–to all wonders of Southern California, add another: industrial Los Angeles turns out more dollar product than Pittsburgh, *Fortune* 39 (1949) 76–83, 148, 150, 153–54, 156, 158, 160; quotes pp. 78, 82.

2. The magnitude and nature of change in California during the war years is a topic of scholarly debate. For an introduction see R. Lotchin, World War II and urban California: city planning and the transformation hypothesis, *Pacific Historical Review* 62 (1993) 143–71, a critique of G. Nash, *The American West Transformed: The Impact of the Second World War* (Bloomington, 1985) and M. Johnson, *The Second Gold Rush: Oakland and the East Bay in World War II* (Berkeley, 1993). See also Lotchin, *Fortress California, 1910–1961: From Warfare to Welfare* (New York, 1992).

3. In "Symbolic landscapes: some idealizations of American communities," Donald Meinig fixed southern California as the culture hearth for the third of three symbolic American landscapes: single-family housing on broad, landscaped lots sited along curved streets with direct access to freeways. Meinig overstates the importance of a landscape type that accounts for a small percentage of regional development. Meinig (ed.) *The Interpretation of Ordinary Landscapes* (New York, 1979) 169. For overviews of the literature see M. Marsh, Reconsidering the suburbs: an exploration of suburban historiography, *Pennsylvania Magazine of History and Biography* 112 (1988) 580–605; and J. Phalen, *The Suburbs* (New York, 1995). See also the introduction in G. Hise, *Magnetic Los Angeles: Planning the Twentieth-Century Metropolis* (Baltimore, 1997).

4. Hise, *op cit*, 82.

5. See the essays in a special issue of *American Quarterly* 46 (1994) and the exchange among K. Jackson, R. Fishman, and R. Harris in *Journal of Urban History* 13 (1987) and 15 (1988). For Los Angeles see Hise, *op. cit.*; R. Longstreth, *From City Center to Regional Mall: Architecture, the Automobile, and Retailing in Los Angeles, 1920–1950* (Cambridge, 1997); B. Nicolaides, *In search of the good life: community and politics in working-class Los Angeles* (Ph.D. thesis, Columbia University, 1993) and ibid. *My Blue Heaven: Life and Politics in the Working-class Suburbs of Los Angeles* (Chicago, 2002); N. Quam-Wickam, *"Petroleocrats and proletarians": work, class and politics in the southern California oil industry, 1917–1935* (Ph.D. thesis, University of California, Berkeley, 1993).

6. The Chamber of Commerce used this logotype from at least 1914. See its *Manufacturers Directory and Commodity Index* from that year and subsequent editions. The Chamber's industrial department adopted the slogan for books and pamphlets, see, for example, *Los Angeles–Nature's Workshop, The Home of Efficient Labor* (Los Angeles, 1921) and *Dynamic Los Angeles County* (Los Angeles, 1938).

7. C. McWilliams, *Southern California: An Island on the Land* (Salt Lake City, 1946/1990) chaps. 12, 16; R. Fogelson, *The Fragmented Metropolis: Los Angeles, 1850–1930* (Cambridge, 1967) especially chap. 6; K. Starr, *Material Dreams: Southern California Through the 1920s* (New York, 1990); M. Davis, *City of Quartz: Excavating the Future in Los Angeles* (London, 1990) 118–20; R. Romo, *History of a Barrio: East Los Angeles* (Austin, 1983) chap. 4.

8. For an early critique of this ideology see W. Woehlke, "Smoke-stacks on the Pacific," *Sunset* 31 (1931) 1161–71. For a contemporary assessment that introduces race as a central factor in labour hiring practices, see C. Johnson, Industrial Survey of the Negro Population of Los Angeles, California, Made by the Department of Research and Investigations of the National Urban League (1926). In *The Productivity of Labor in the Rubber Tire Manufacturing Industry* (New York, 1940), J. Gaffey asserts that labour savings were not a critical factor for establishing west coast operations and the selection of southern California for branch plants.

9. The Chamber published a running account of firms establishing plants. See the annual reports produced by the industrial department as well as 19 articles in *Southern California Business* such as "Bringing new industries to town" (1925) 16–17. According to the California State Mining Bureau, approximately 10,000,000 pounds of lead valued at roughly $700,000 were mined in the state during 1923, *California Mineral Production for 1923* cited in W. French, *A study of locational factors for industrial plants in and about Los Angeles, California* (unpublished MBA thesis, University of Southern California, 1926), 95.

10. "City Industrial Tract," Report for A. Arnoll by H. Lafler, Sales Agent, Walter H. Leimert Co, (c. 1923) in Los Angeles Area Chamber of Commerce collection, Department of Special Collections, University of Southern California, box 74 (hereafter LAACC Collection).

11. French, *op. cit.*, chap. 4; quote p. 23.

12. Eberle & Riggleman Economic Service, "The industrial land situation in Los Angeles," *Weekly Letter* (28 December 1925); idem. "Some considerations of the Los Angeles industrial situation," *Weekly Letter* (21 September 1925) (no pagination). This concern was a constant. Fifteen years later, planner Bryant Hall noted a "disturbing" ratio of industrial land relative to population in the county. See the tabulations and annotations in a joint Works Progress Administration/Regional Planning Commission, Land Use Analysis (1940) part of a WPA sponsored survey of land use and population. Binder in the Regional Planning Collection, The Huntington Library, San Marino, California (hereafter The Huntington).

13. City Industrial Tract, 4.

14. M. Davis, Sunshine and the open shop: Ford and Darwin in 1920s Los Angeles, in T. Sitton and W. Deverell (eds.), *Metropolis in the Making: Los Angeles in the 1920s* (Berkeley, 2001).

15. Editorial, special section, Midwinter Edition, *Los Angeles Times*, January 1, 1905.

16. Los Angeles City Directory Co., (Inc.), *Los Angeles City Directory*, 1905.

17. See the material in the California Ephemera Collection, Department of Special Collections, UCLA, box 39, folder Industry–Historical–CA–1 (hereafter UCLA Ephemera). Quote from brochure: The Development of an Idea. WPA researchers collected these documents for The Industrial Section in Workers of the Writers' Program of the Works Projects Administration, *Los Angeles: A Guide to the City and Its Environs* (New York, 1941/1951), 167. See also A. Bynon and Company, *Los Angeles City and County Directory, 1886–1887* (Los Angeles, 1887), 164 and K. Doyle, A factory here since 1860, *Southern California Business* 10 (1931), 14; Soap company plans new five-story building, *Los Angeles Times* (3 September 1922) Part V, 4.

18. "The Wholesale Terminal–Efficiency For: The Wholesaler, Jobber, Shipper, Merchant, Manufacturer, Consumer," (c. 1916); Los Angeles–A Good Place to Manufacture or Warehouse, (nd); Los Angeles Union Terminal Company, Terminal Refrigeration Company, Union Terminal Warehouse, (nd), all in UCLA Ephemera, box 39, folder Industrial–History #1. Bringing the railway and its freight customer together, *Electric Railway Journal* 50 (July 7, 1917), 6–7.

19. Oxnam quote in Los Angeles tenement problem, Municipal League *Bulletin* 3 (1925), 5.

20. French, *op. cit.* See also the tract maps in The Huntington Library ephemera collection, Eph J3–4(5) as well as the land use maps the WPA produced in collaboration with the Los Angeles Regional Planning Commission (Volume 6, Sheet 37) also at The Huntington.

21. CCIH, A community survey made in Los Angeles City, (San Francisco, 1919). Industrial and Business Property, *Los Angeles Times* (19 January 1926) Part 2, 17. In her "Aircrafters" column published in *The War Worker* 1 (Second half, July 1943), 2, Esther Beverly Owens noted that the Lockheed Aircraft Plant 7, located on Seventh Street "across the bridge from Santa Fe Avenue" was "thickly populated with American Negroes, Mexicans, and members of other groups" busy wiring pivot casings and drilling subassemblies. In Industrial Strength, *Los Angeles Times* (3 August 1997) D–1, the author tours readers through a "200-block area east of L.A.'s skyscrapers" with aging buildings, razor-wire, and homeless encampments, "fertile ground for foreign trade and immigrant entrepreneurs" engaged in the garment, printing, produce, and wholesale sectors.

22. For a discussion of pollution in turn-of-the-century Los Angeles see D. Johnson, *A serpent in the garden: institutions, ideology, and class in Los Angeles politics, 1901–1911* (unpublished Ph.D. thesis, UCLA, 1996) especially chap. 3.

23. For a history of zoning in Los Angeles, and the effect of these regulations for zoning in other cities and national guidelines, see K. Kolnick, *Order Before Zoning: Land Use Regulation in Los Angeles* (Ph.D. thesis, University of Southern California, 2008). For a contemporary assessment of the significance of these statutes see L. Veiller, City planning in Los Angeles, *The Survey* 26 (22 July 1911), 599– 600. For the district boundaries see Ordinance N.17135 (new series, 1908), Ordinance N.17136 (new series, 1908), and Ordinance N.19500 (new series, 1909).

24. Industrial Lands, in the LAACC *Members' Annual* (1929), 82. Agenda item in *Stenographer's Notes, 1922* (14 December 1922), 6. Both items in the LAACC Collection, box 18.

25. On labor-management, strikes, and the 1910 bombings see G. Stimson, *Rise of the Labor Movement in Los Angeles* (Berkeley 1955), especially chaps. 19 and 21.

26. A. G. Arnoll. Balanced Prosperity in the Los Angeles Area, a presentation sponsored by the Inter-City and Suburbanization Committee of the Los Angeles Municipal League. Printed in the Municipal League *Bulletin* 6 (March 1924) np. At the time, Arnoll was assistant secretary for the LAACC and director of its industrial department.

27. Torrance, The Model Industrial City, UCLA Ephemera, box 103, folder Torrance.

28. Manufacturing committee–Westinghouse track connections, in Los Angeles Area Chamber of Commerce, *Stenographer's Notes, Board of Directors Meetings, 1922*, 2–5, LAACC Collection, box 18.

29. G. Law quoted in P. Sheehan, *Hollywood as a World Center* (Hollywood, 1924), 20–21.

30. See Fogelson, *Fragmented Metropolis* especially 123–29. *Los Angeles Times* (18 November 1923).

31. Ibid.

32. H. Allen, *The House of Goodyear* (Akron, 1936); Goodyear Tire and Rubber Company of California, "Three Dynamic Decades in the Golden State," 1920–1950 (c. 1950) in Los Angeles Examiner Collection, Regional History Center, USC, photo folder Goodyear; P. Rhode, "California's emergence as the second industrial belt: the Pacific Coast tire and automobile industries," (unpublished paper in author's possession, University of North Carolina 1994); Civic heads, U.P. officials aid ceremony, Los Angeles may outstrip Akron soon, *Los Angeles Examiner* (24 January 1929); Tire Manufacture a Major Industry Here, *Industrial Los Angeles County* 2 (May 1930) 4; Rubber Industry–Los Angeles County, editorial in *Industrial Los Angeles County* 2 (May 1930).

33. F. Kidner and P. Neff, *An Economic Survey of the Los Angeles Area* Haynes Foundation Monograph Series / (Los Angeles, 1945).

34. Here I am applying an interpretation drawn from D. Holdsworth's assessment of Chicago in "The Invisible Skyline," *Antipode* 26 (1994), 141–46.

35. Plates 14–17 bound as an appendix to *Report and Recommendations on a Comprehensive Rapid Transit Plan for the City and County of Los Angeles* (Chicago, 1925).

36. Author interview with William Daum, Jr., 19 June 1996 at the Daum Company office, 123 South Figueroa, Los Angeles and clippings in office scrapbooks.

37. See the materials in the folder Los Angeles Streets in the Henry Z. Osborne Papers, Department of Special Collections, USC. Quote from Program is Outlined, East Side Organization Names Committees and Prepares to Campaign for Improvements, *Los Angeles Times* (18 November 1929) Part V.

38. The Cat's Out of the Bag, six column advertisement in the *Los Angeles Times*

(10 September 1922) Part V, 3. For Belvedere Gardens see "New Residence Tract" (Janss advertisement) in *Los Angeles Times* (6 March 1921) Part V, 6.

39. Central Manufacturing District, Inc., "Central Manufacturing District of Los Angeles: A Book of Descriptive Text, Photographs and Testimonial Letters About the Central Manufacturing District of Los Angeles–'The Great Western Market,'" (August, 1923), LAACC Collection; Great industrial city here being created by the Central Manufacturing District, *Los Angeles Times* (15 July 1923); Cabbage patch to industrial paradise, *Santa Fe Magazine* (November 1929), 21–25; H. Poronto, How Chicago came to Los Angeles told by head of Central Manufacturing Dist., *Southwest Builder and Contractor* 62 (13 July 1923), 34.

40. On the sale see Los Angeles holdings go to rich group (7 March 1928) and Santa Fe buys industrial hub for $15,000,000 (11 April 1929), both in the *Los Angeles Examiner*. For city biographies of Bell and other incorporated communities see Los Angeles Chamber of Commerce, *Industrial Department, Industrial Communities of Los Angeles Metropolitan Area* (Los Angeles, 1925) and *California Real Estate Magazine* 10/9 (June, 1930), a special issue devoted to Growth and Progress of the Golden West.

41. On the plague see W. Deverell, Plague in Los Angeles, 1924: ethnicity and typicality, in V. Matsumoto and B. Allmendinger (eds.), *Over the Edge: Remapping Western Experiences* (Berkeley 1998) and a photographic collection at the Bancroft Library, UC Berkeley (http://sunsite.berkeley.edu:38008/ead/calher/bubonic/5141). This was an ongoing process. For a post-World War II account see Farewell to "Manana": Hicks Camp prepares to abandon old ways, *Los Angeles Times* (13 May 1949) Part 3, 6, which describes how an enclave of approximately 150 farmworker families living in "El Monte's bit of old Mexico" were being forced out by property owner Harvey Youngblood who planned to develop the site as an industrial park for light manufacturing.

42. Subdividing of land in Los Angeles Board of City Planning Commissioners, *Annual Report, 1929–1930* (Los Angeles, 1930), 49.

43. Los Angeles County Regional Planning Commission and the Works Progress Administration, *Land Use Analysis: Final Report* (Los Angeles, 1941).

44. County of Los Angeles, *Proceedings of the First Regional Planning Conference of Los Angeles County* (Los Angeles, 1922), 6.

45. F. Viehe, Black gold suburbs: the influence of the extractive industry on the suburbanization of Los Angeles, 1890–1930, *Journal of Urban History* 8 (1981) 3–26.

46. For firm locations see the LAACC Industrial Bureau publications *Manufacturers' Directory and Commodity Index*, I consulted the second (1915) and fifth (1920) editions. On Harry H. Culver see a biography ("as of Sept. 1, 1929") and the clippings in the Examiner Collection, Department of Special Collections, USC. For a secondary account of the film industry see S. Christopherson and M. Storper, The city as studio; the world as back lot: The impact of vertical disintegration on the location of the motion picture industry, *Environment and Planning D: Society and Space* 4 (1986) 305–20 and Stephanie Frank, *Building Hollywood: Industry and Urban Development in Metropolitan Los Angeles 1920-1975* (unpublished PhD thesis, University of Southern California, 2008)

47. Department of Public Safety, *Second Annual Police Benefit Book* (Culver City, 1927).

48. This section is drawn from Hise, *op. cit.* chap. 4.

49. D. Hansen (McDonnell Douglas, Long Beach) letter to author, (3 June 23 1994). See also F. Cunningham, *Skymaster: The Story of Donald Douglas* (Philadelphia, 1943) and C. Maynard, *Flight Plan for Tomorrow: The Douglas Story, A Condensed History* (Santa Monica, 1962).

50. "Finest community development in 20 years" and "Typical homes in Westchester district," *Los Angeles Evening Herald and Express* (28 March 1942). See also "City planners flock to study Westchester," *Los Angeles Daily News* (8 May 1942), 27 and the low-altitude oblique aerials of this development in the Spence and Fairchild Aerial Photo Collections in the Department of Geography, UCLA.

51. Industrial Background, chap. 5 in G. Robbins and L. Tilton, *Los Angeles: Preface to a Master Plan* (Los Angeles, 1941), quote from page 61 by John Parke Young.

THE AUTHORS

Martin H. Krieger is a professor emeritus at University of Southern California's Sol Price School of Public Policy. Trained as an experimental physicist at Columbia University, he has taught in planning and public policy at Berkeley, Minnesota, MIT, USC, and Michigan. Professor Krieger has worked in the fields of planning and design theory, ethics and entrepreneurship, mathematical models of urban spatial processes, defense and military policy, uncertainty and ambiguity, and the role of the humanities in planning. His social-science-informed aural and photographic documentation of Los Angeles is archived at USC. Krieger has won three consecutive Mellon Mentoring Awards for mentoring undergraduates, faculty, and graduate students to focus and formulate their research projects. His ten published books describe how planning, design, and science are actually done.

Jonah Greenstein is a gender-nonconforming artist. His two features, *Dedalus* (2020) and *6655 Mount Vernon Road* (2022) are available in the United States and other territories, respectively. Their editing style has been called "balletic" by *The New Yorker*.

Greg Hise is a professor of history, emeritus, at the University of Nevada, Las Vegas. Earlier, he taught at the University of Southern California. Trained as an architectural historian at the University of California, Berkeley, he wrote *Magnetic Los Angeles: Planning the Twentieth-Century Metropolis* (1997), which was awarded the Spiro Kostof Book Prize (Society of Architectural Historians) and the Pflueger Award (Historical Society of Southern California). He co-authored *Eden by Design: The 1930 Olmsted-Bartholomew Plan for the Los Angeles Region* (2000) with William Deverell with whom he co-edited *Land of Sunshine: An Environmental History of Los Angeles* (2005), and *A Companion to Los Angeles* (2010).

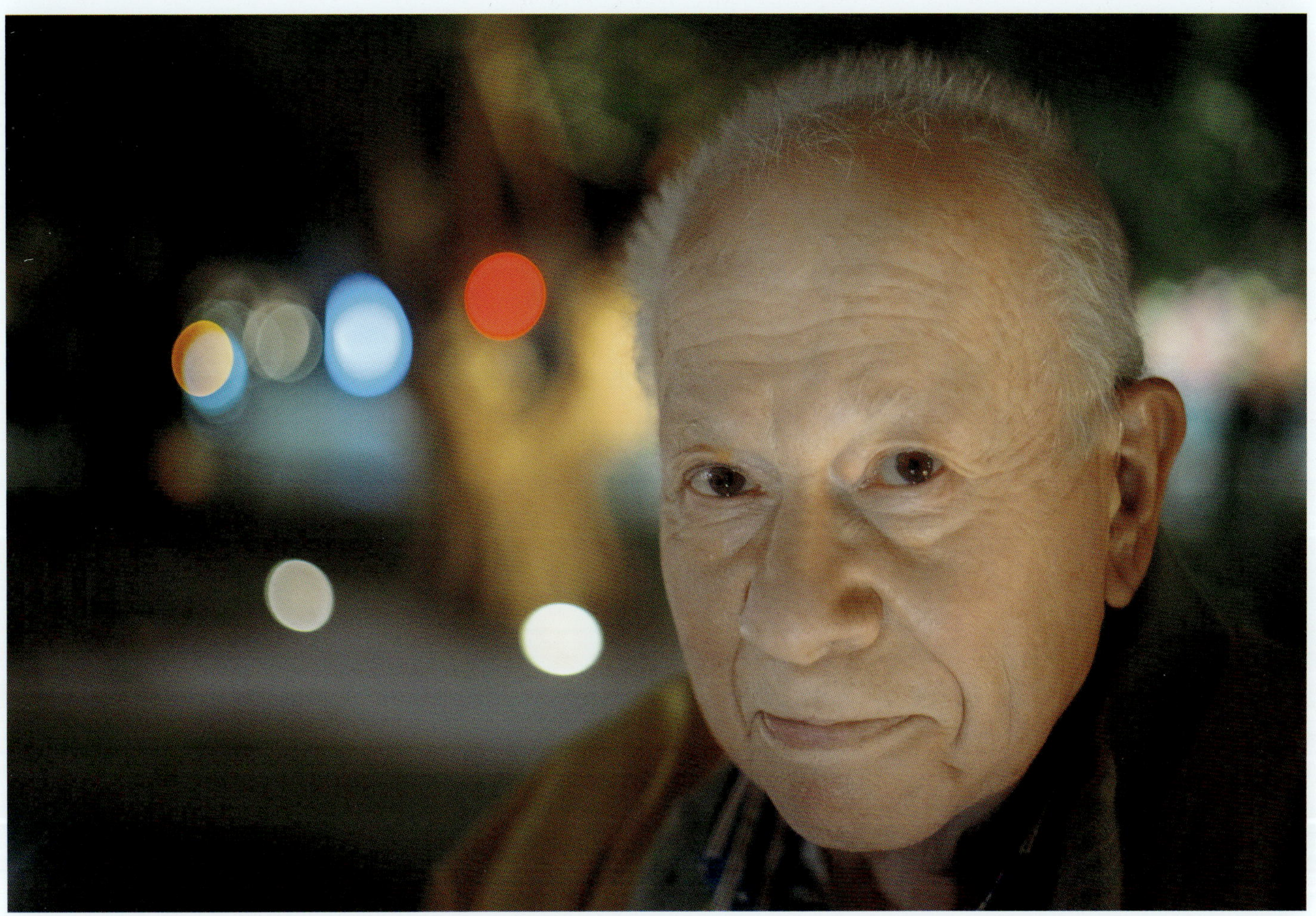

Martin H. Krieger's urban tomography photographs and sound recordings are archived in the Special Collections Library of the University of Southern California, and in the Krieger Collection in the USC Digital Library.

His fieldwork and this book were supported by the John Randolph Haynes and Dora Haynes Foundation.

Goff Books
Published by Goff Books. An Imprint of ORO Editions
Gordon Goff: Publisher

www.goffbooks.com
info@goffbooks.com

Authors: Martin H. Krieger, Greg Hise, Jonah Greenstein
All photographs by Martin H. Krieger
Foreword by Martin H. Krieger
Book design by Jonah Greenstein
Managing Editor: Jake Anderson

10 9 8 7 6 5 4 3 2 1 First Edition

ISBN: 978-1-957183-90-9

Color Separations and Printing: ORO Group Inc.
Printed in China.

Goff Books makes a continuous effort to minimize the
overall carbon footprint of its publications. As part of
this goal, Goff Books, in association with Global ReLeaf,
arranges to plant trees to replace those used in the
manufacturing of the paper produced for its books. Global
ReLeaf is an international campaign run by American
Forests, one of the world's oldest nonprofit conservation
organizations. Global ReLeaf is American Forests'
education and action program that helps individuals,
organizations, agencies, and corporations improve the
local and global environment by planting and caring for
trees.